Fierce Appetites

Fierce Appetites

Loving, Losing and Living to Excess in My Present and in the Writings of the Past

Elizabeth Boyle

SANDYCOVE

an imprint of

PENGUIN BOOKS

SANDYCOVE

UK | USA | Canada | Ireland | Australia
India | New Zealand | South Africa

Sandycove is part of the Penguin Random House group of companies
whose addresses can be found at global.penguinrandomhouse.com.

Penguin
Random House
UK

First published 2022
001

Copyright © Elizabeth Boyle, 2022

The moral right of the author has been asserted

Set in 13.5/17.75pt Perpetua Std
Typeset by Jouve (UK), Milton Keynes
Printed and bound in Great Britain by Clays Ltd, Elcograf S.p.A.

The authorized representative in the EEA is Penguin Random House Ireland,
Morrison Chambers, 32 Nassau Street, Dublin DO2 YH68

A CIP catalogue record for this book is available from the British Library

ISBN: 978–1–844–88544–2

For Nora – here, at last,
are 'the thoughts of my mind'

Contents

JANUARY

Grief

The last words my father said to me were 'Happy New Year'. By the evening of New Year's Day he was back in hospital, drowning in his own fluids. The doctors recommended ceasing all treatment and he was moved into a side room to begin dying. His only surviving brother came to say goodbye, baffled by the injustice of the situation – that he, the eldest child, should be the last one standing, his four younger siblings all gone before him. An Indian priest came to administer the Last Rites. My youngest brother-by-the-same-father, unbaptized, the son of my Scottish Protestant stepmother, stood silently, uncomprehending, while I mouthed the responses to the Catholic sacrament with no belief other than that this is what our father would have wanted.

We went home to sleep. My stepmother took the night shift, whispering memories to her unresponsive husband, playing songs to him on her phone. Around 6 a.m. we got the call: the time was near. My brother and I got into the car and he drove the journey along dark roads to the hospital. I tried to think of some profound life advice that I might have received from my father. He had once suggested that I spice up a stale relationship by having an affair, but that didn't seem like a suitably solemn lesson, although I had indeed followed the advice at the time. (It didn't help.) Nothing else came to mind.

My brother and I arrived at the hospital and kissed our father's forehead. At 8 a.m. we realized the coffee shop had opened and we slipped out to buy oversized Americanos.

My brother poured seventeen sachets of sugar into his black coffee. I muttered to him, 'If Dad dies while you're adding all these fucking sugars I will never speak to you again.'

We walked back to the ward. Dad had died, with my stepmum at his side, while we were adding endless sugar to coffee, and that somehow seemed right, and we hugged and cried and I left the room to tell a nurse that Dad was gone.

One medieval Irish poet, speaking of grief, wrote 'my heart is a clot of blood'. My heart was a clot of blood as I sat in the hospital coffee shop sending messages, receiving condolences, waiting for my eldest brother-by-the-same-father-and-mother and his daughter to arrive at the hospital, and for my father's body to be prepared in the mortuary.

Sometime in the middle of the eighth century, the poet Blathmac, son of Cú Brettan, wrote of the Crucifixion that:

> The whole world grew dark,
> the land shook under gloom.
> At the death of noble Jesus
> great rocks broke asunder . . .
>
> A stream of blood gushed forth – too severe –
> so that the skin of every tree became red.
> There was gore on the surfaces of the world,
> in the treetops of every great forest.
>
> It was fitting for God's elements,
> beautiful sea, beautiful sky, this earth,
> that they should change their aspect
> when keening their hero.

I stepped outside for a while and saw that the January sky was very blue. But nothing changed, the world did not grow dark, there was no gore in the treetops, the elements did not shake. The world kept turning, but my heart was a clot of blood.

A friend sent me a collection of poetry, *A Scattering*, by Christopher Reid, and I devoured it. The crystalline poems told the story of his wife's illness and death, and his own grief. I saw myself and my father reflected in one particular poem, 'The Unfinished (I)', where Reid wrote of the 'rigmarole / of unheard farewell'. There was agony in something so simple, so gentle: 'Sparse breaths, then none – / and it was done.' I would leave the book beside my father's coffin at his wake.

Although he had lived in England for thirty-five years, my father had requested a traditional Irish wake. This was to be followed the next morning by a private committal at the crematorium. Our English friends and neighbours were unfamiliar with the idea of a wake: some were uncomfortable with the coffin in the house; even more were confused by the sight of folk musicians setting up in the living room. By the end of the night, after more than a hundred people had passed through our door and we were drunk, singing and dancing in the kitchen to a Dubliners album, almost everyone had been converted to our rituals of death. Blathmac, son of Cú Brettan, had written about keening for Christ, his whole poem an address to Mary, asking to join with her in lamenting the death of her son. Our public mourning had been bacchanalian and we had run through the entire emotional spectrum, fuelled by copious amounts of alcohol.

In the morning, we followed the hearse to the crematorium, where a priest spoke the words of committal and we howled and keened and drowned in our private grief. And then it was done. We drove home, and opened up a box of Filipino cigars which my father had mysteriously acquired at least fifty years previously and had saved, waiting for some special occasion which never came. My youngest brother had been preparing them carefully for days, with thin slices of apple and orange to moisten the old, dry tobacco. We shared one of them, passing it round like a joint, while drinking cans of Guinness in the back garden. My brother's efforts had paid off: our throats were filled with rich smoke.

I became obsessed with reading autobiographies and memoirs, as though the very act of individuals saying 'this is me; I have lived' could mitigate the experience of death. I read Lenny Henry, *Who Am I, Again?*, in which he recounted the beginnings of his stellar career in comedy, and the racism — both overt and covert, structural and internalized — that he faced. I read Deborah Levy, *The Cost of Living*, in which she outlined her struggle to live a radical, intellectual life in the face of motherhood and the demands of domesticity. I read Dorothea Tanning, *Birthday*, in which she strove to carve out her own identity as an artist and writer in the shadow of her more famous husband, Max Ernst. I read B. L. Coombes, *These Poor Hands*, in which he gave a powerful account of his life as a miner in South Wales in the early twentieth century – the danger, the poverty, the dirty tactics of the mine owners and their fight against their own workers. I read Rob Doyle, *Threshold*, and I wasn't sure whether it was memoir or fiction or something occupying the broad territory between the two. I have become conditioned over decades to see all things with my historian's eyes, and so, to me, Doyle's account of wanking, drug-taking, hang-overs and casual sex was the most medieval of all of the books I read during that time because with his words it was the hardest to distinguish between the authentic and the invented self.

There are a lot of first-person voices in medieval litera-ture but they do not necessarily tell us much about the writer. Writers adopted poetic voices. As in Doyle's *Thresh-old*, the medieval 'I' has the potential to be someone else entirely. When a medieval Irish poet says *Mé Éba* 'I am Eve', or 'I am Líadain', or 'I am the Buí, the veiled woman of Beare', we can't know who exactly is claiming Eve or Lía-dain or Buí as their identity for the length of a poem. One brilliant medieval Welsh poet writing in the ninth or tenth century claimed to be a seventh-century royal woman, named Heledd, the sister of Cynddylan, ruler of the king-dom of Powys. This anonymous poet, who adopts the voice of a woman living nearly three centuries earlier, imagines Heledd's grief over the death of her brother at the hands of an English army. The poem *Stafell Gynddylan* 'Cynddylan's Hall' describes the empty royal hall, ruined and desolate, a symbol of Heledd's grief. The poet writes:

Cynddylan's hall is dark tonight
without a fire, without a bed.
I will weep for a while, then I will be silent.

Cynddylan's hall is dark tonight
without a fire, without a candle.
Who will give me sanity but God?

Cynddylan's hall is dark tonight
without a fire, without a light.
Grief for you comes over me.

The person who became 'Heledd', for the purpose of poetic creation, laments the ruined hall, without a roof, without a fire, without a war band feasting and women tending them, and her grief seems limitless, leaving her teetering on the edge of sanity. The poet may have been making a universal statement about grief, but perhaps they saw resonances of a historic loss in some particular circumstances of their own time.

There is a popular misconception that people in the Middle Ages didn't grieve as much or as deeply as we do today. Perhaps because of the extremely high rates of infant mortality, and images in modern culture of the Middle Ages as a time of endemic warfare, people tend to think that societies became numbed to death. But the medieval literature of grief disproves that claim. People suffered from the loss of their loved ones then just as much as we do now: that gave Blathmac the words to keen Christ, it gave a medieval Welsh poet the empathy to become 'Heledd'.

The image of the ruined hall as a symbol of loss was a common one in medieval literature. The fragmentary Old English poem 'The Ruin' centres similarly on a deserted and abandoned hall, after the calamitous death of its men.

> Slaughter spread wide, pestilence arose,
> and death took all those brave men away.
> Their bulwarks were broken, their halls laid waste,
> the cities crumbled, those who would repair it
> laid in the earth. And so these halls are empty,
> and the curved arch sheds its tiles,
> torn from the roof. Decay has brought it down,
> broken it to rubble . . .

This destruction spread out from the single hall to entire cities, the ruined buildings an inescapable reminder of loss and abandonment. These big spaces, Cynddylan's hall, the English ruin, are deprived of their men, their feasting, their war bands.

A van arrived at our house to take away the NHS medical equipment provided to my father during his long years of illness: a hospital bed and the hoist that his Romanian carers used to lift him when they visited first thing in the morning and last thing at night. We were left with his armchair, a hideous beige-brown velour chair – the kind that you plug in, with a push-button control to raise and lower you into a standing or seated position. My father used to sit in it all day, watching police procedurals on TV. The empty space left behind for those Welsh and Old English poets was vast – a fireless hall with crumbling roof, an entire kingdom. My ruined space, my grief, was exactly the size of an empty armchair.

My parents separated when I was a baby – perhaps even a little before that; the chronology of my early life is fuzzy – and I lived with my father from when I was three years old. He was drunk for most of my teenage years and ill for most of my adulthood. But he was warm and charismatic, and keen for me to have opportunities denied to him. He had left school at the age of fourteen and never had the chance of any further education. In the first few days of 2008, he had lain in intensive care after suffering a major haemorrhage caused by gastric varices (which in turn were caused by cirrhosis of the liver), as I sat beside him making the final edits to my PhD thesis, waiting for him to regain consciousness. As I checked footnotes and corrected typos, he detoxed: thrashing and moaning, lashing out at nurses and shitting himself. He recovered, never drank again, and lived another twelve years, his body slowly crumbling from alcoholic liver disease, diabetes and Parkinson's.

I submitted the PhD thesis, graduated from Cambridge, and went on to a career very different from the various jobs he had lost, pulling pints and drinking the bar owners' profits. He always missed Dublin, but there had been few jobs there in the early 1980s and he'd had no choice but to emigrate. He was proud of me and I was proud of him, this man who had reared me, at a time when it was unusual for fathers to have sole custody of a child. He was my favourite person in the world. It would have been fitting for God's elements that they should change their aspect when I was keening my hero.

At the mortuary, we had been handed a NHS leaflet on dealing with grief. One of its sensible pieces of advice is not to make any major life changes in the first year of losing someone close to you. In medieval literature, characters are not given self-help pamphlets. When they suffer grief, they destroy mountains, raze kingdoms, tear their hair out and scorch the earth. I just sat numbly at the kitchen table, drinking gin and sending unwise WhatsApp messages to ex-lovers.

A lot of Irish people know, or think they know, the story of *Longes mac nUislenn* 'The Exile of the Sons of Uisliu', popularly called the 'Deirdre story'. Sometimes known as 'Deirdre of the Sorrows', she was an object of fascination for Irish romantic-nationalist writers like Æ Russell, W. B. Yeats and J. M. Synge. Retold in modern literature as the story of a tragic heroine, who commits suicide after being torn from her lover, the original Old Irish story is far more complex and ambivalent. In the oldest extant version of the tale, Derdriu is the child of a royal storyteller and his wife. While her mother is serving Conchobar, the King of Ulster, and his assembled warriors, the unborn Derdriu cries out from her womb. The sound unsettles the men who were gathered there and Conchobar's wizard is called to decipher the meaning of the ominous cry. In two poems, rich with the imagery of colour – blue eyes, black brows, white teeth and red bloodshed – the wizard prophesies that Derdriu will grow up to be very beautiful, but also the cause of great slaughter; that – like Helen of Troy – her beauty will be blamed for terrible deeds and many deaths. The response of the Ulster warriors is that the unborn child should be killed, in order to prevent the prophecy from coming true. But Conchobar, King of the Ulstermen, has already been seized by lust at the description of the adult Derdriu: he goes against the will of his people, and he earmarks Derdriu to be reared as his sex-slave.

The girl is reared away from society, by foster-parents, and the only other adult who has access to her is a female satirist. Her upbringing, away from the norms of 'civilized' culture, leaves her unable to act in a manner deemed appropriate for a young woman within the community. Her existence is outside the bounds of the social order, in part because her very reason for being – to satisfy Conchobar's lust – is itself outside the moral order of society. In one of the most famous images of early Irish literature, one day she sees her foster-father flaying a calf in the snow, and a raven drinking the blood which has spattered on the ground. In spite (or because) of the innate violence of the scene, Derdriu announces that she would love a man who possessed those three colours: lips as red as blood, skin as white as snow, hair as black as a raven. Her satirist companion, Leborcham, replies that, as luck would have it, there is a man nearby who meets her requirements: Noisiu. Derdriu experiences lust of her own, and falls in love with him from that physical description alone.

Not long after, she sees Noisiu in the flesh and engineers a situation whereby she walks past him, pretending – like a teenager in a nightclub – that she hasn't seen him. He greets her as a 'fine heifer' and she comments on the lack of 'bulls' in the vicinity. He realizes who she is and, remembering the wizard's prophecy, notes that she has the 'bull' of the territory, that is, King Conchobar. Derdriu responds that a young bull would be more to her taste, and – having clearly learned some lessons from Leborcham – she uses the techniques of satire, threatening Noisiu with mockery and public shame, if he does not take her. Her sexual forthrightness and agency would have seemed shocking (though perhaps also thrilling) to a medieval audience.

Conchobar is enraged at the loss of his sexual plaything and Derdriu, accompanied by Noisiu and his brothers, along with their retinues, all flee to a neighbouring kingdom. Conchobar's army pursues them throughout the island of Ireland and they are forced to take refuge in Britain, where a local king allows Noisiu and his brothers, the eponymous 'sons of Uisliu', to join his army as mercenary soldiers.

My father, too, had been a mercenary in the service of a British monarch. After leaving school at fourteen, he had a succession of factory jobs, and he knew that opportunities for him in Dublin were limited. He followed in the footsteps of his brothers and enlisted in the Royal Air Force. He worked as a storeman throughout his time as an RAF serviceman and, in a singularly undistinguished career, left the forces sixteen years later at exactly the same rank he had entered. But advancement had not mattered to him, and neither had any questions of ethics or national loyalty in joining the British armed forces, although of course the RAF and the Royal Navy were the preferred options for Irishmen who didn't want to face the possibility of having to serve on Irish soil. (Since British troops withdrew from Northern Ireland in 2007, increasing numbers of Irish men and women, mostly from disadvantaged backgrounds, have joined the British Army, in addition to the Air Force and Navy, although it is rarely spoken about in either country.) What mattered to my father was a regular income and the chance to see the world, and that is what he got, with postings at various times in Kenya, Germany and what is now the United Arab Emirates. Although he returned to Ireland after his period of service, he never lost his 'grateful immigrant' mentality and was quite happy to return to England in the 1980s. That the sons of Uisliu sought temporary refuge in the service of a British king is an early literary reflection of the long-standing relationship between the islands of Britain and Ireland, a relationship that is fraught and complex and full of bloody violence.

For Noisiu and his brothers, their respite is short-lived because the British king also comes to desire Derdriu: he does not want to kill Noisiu outright but (with echoes of the biblical story of King David and his betrayal of Uriah the Hittite over David's lust for Uriah's wife, Bathsheba) he sends the sons of Uisliu into the most dangerous battle situations in the hope that they will 'accidentally' be killed. When this fails, he decides to act decisively to take Derdriu for himself, so she, and the brothers, and their retinues, escape once again, this time to one of the islands between Britain and Ireland.

Back in Ulster, the people are angry at what has happened and encourage Conchobar to bring the sons of Uisliu back to Ireland safely. In accordance with medieval Irish law — betraying the early medieval context in which the author was writing, rather than the Iron Age society in which the action is set — Conchobar sends guarantors of their protection, one of whom is the warrior Fergus mac Róich. However, Conchobar is acting duplicitously and has arranged for Fergus to be distracted from his responsibilities with feasts and carousing, and thus Fergus leaves Derdriu, Noisiu and the rest of their entourage to make their way back to Ulster in the care of his son, Fíachu. Conchobar has made a pact with one of his former enemies, Éogan mac Durthacht, King of Fernmag (Farney in modern-day Co. Monaghan), who is waiting at Emain Macha, Conchobar's royal stronghold, to do Conchobar's dirty work. He 'greets Noisiu with the point of his spear', as the author puts it, in response to which, Fíachu 'put his arms around Noisiu and pulled him down and covered him', so that the spear goes through the body of Fíachu, Fergus's son, and kills him along with Noisiu. Noisiu's brothers are 'hunted' and killed, and Derdriu is captured and brought to Conchobar, her hands bound.

We are faced with two grieving characters: Derdriu, who has lost Noisiu, her lover, and Fergus, who has lost Fíachu, his son. Their reactions could not be more different. Fergus's grief is externalized: he torches Emain Macha, and he and his comrade, Dubthach, engage in a battle, against their own king and community, which leaves three hundred dead. Dubthach slaughters the young women of Ulster and, in the aftermath of the massacre – all of which had, of course, been prophesied from the outset – Fergus, Dubthach and their retinues leave Ulster and go into exile in Connacht, and 'there was weeping and trembling in Ulster every night for sixteen years'.

Derdriu's grief, by contrast, is internalized. For a year after Noisiu's death she hardly eats or sleeps, and she never smiles. Her head bowed, she recites poems, remembering Noisiu's beauty and lamenting his death. The second of the poems the author gives Derdriu is shot through with colour and despair.

> Conchobar, hush!
> You have brought me grief compounded by sorrow.
> As long as I live, surely,
> your love will be of no interest to me.
>
> You have taken from me – great crime –
> the one I thought most beautiful on earth,
> the one I loved most.
> I will not see him again until I die.
>
> His absence is my despair,
> the absence of the son of Uisliu.
> A black gravestone over his white body
> once so well known among men.
>
> Brighter than a meadow his glistening cheeks
> red his lips, his brows beetle-black,
> his shining, pearly teeth
> the noble colour of snow.

Well known his bright clothes
among the warriors of Britain;
fair and brilliant his cloak — a noble union —
with its fringe of red-gold.

His satin tunic a true treasure
with its hundred gems — a gentle number —
and as decoration, clear and shining,
fifty ounces of white gold.

A gold-hilted sword in his hand,
two spears with javelin points,
a shield with a rim of yellow gold,
and a boss of silver.

Fair Fergus betrayed us
after bringing us across the great sea;
he sold his honour for beer,
his great deeds are no more.

Although the Ulstermen might gather
around Conchobar upon the plain,
I would forsake them all openly,
for the company of Noisiu son of Uisliu.

Break no more my heart today.
I will reach my grave soon enough.
Sorrow is stronger than the sea
if you are wise, o Conchobar.

Sorrow is stronger than the sea but there can be colour in
grief. Derdriu recalls Noisiu's red lips, his white body, his

rich clothing, his black gravestone. I think of that bright blue sky the morning of my father's death.

As the prophecy that began the tale looked forward with horror, Derdriu's lament at the end of the story looks back with grief. Conchobar, however, is not done with her, and he asks Derdriu what she hates most in the world. She says she hates two men: first, Conchobar, and second Éogan, the king who killed Noisiu. So, Conchobar decides to send Derdriu to Éogan for a year, to be used by the man who killed the man she loved. In a perverse echo of the language of 'heifers' and 'bulls' that filled her first conversation with Noisiu, Conchobar remarks that Derdriu, standing between him and Éogan, is 'a ewe between two rams'. In the face of such unendurable treatment, and in fulfilment of the prophecy, Derdriu takes her own life, smashing her head against a rock.

There are so many rich seams of meaning in that story: judgement on Conchobar's lust and deceitfulness, and on powerful men generally, with Conchobar's actions echoed in those of the British king and Éogan mac Durthacht. There's meditation, through the use of prophecy, on free will and whether we are all victims of fate. There's commentary on the acceptable bounds of female agency. And there's a portrait of two opposing responses to death – Fergus's raging, savage destruction (drawing, no doubt, on his guilt as much as his grief), in contrast with Derdriu's eloquent, internal suffering which was eventually too great to bear.

Sometimes when I give lectures to my students about this tale, I can barely read Derdriu's lament aloud without my voice cracking, as the words seem to bear the weight of my every loss. We bring ourselves to the study of the past, whether we wish to or not, and, for a brief moment, before the students run headlong into discussions about whether or not Derdriu is a feminist icon, or whether the tale is a sub-version of the supposed 'heroic ethos', a silence hangs in the air and I wonder whether they too know that feeling: that we are all both Fergus and Derdriu. We have let down our loved ones in some vague way and now it is too late to fix anything. We have all sold our honour for beer at some time or other. The sadness is too great to go on, and all that is left is the desire to burn it all down, strike out with our sword, and lose ourselves in blood and pain and slaughter. Instead, I sit at the kitchen table with another drink, dashing my head against invisible rocks.

All expressions of grief which survive from the Middle Ages are, by definition, public expressions of grief, because they were written down. It is difficult enough to know what is in the private depths of a person's heart when they are right in front of us, let alone when they've been dead for a thousand years. The best we have is public or communal statements, preserved for posterity. Literacy in medieval Ireland was a deeply Christian phenomenon and many – perhaps most – medieval Irish authors lived in religious communities following a monastic rule. Monastic thought could be suspi-cious of unregulated emotion. Excessive laughter was to be avoided just as much as excessive anger; apathy was to be avoided as much as lust. The goal was to move away from base and transient human experiences and to focus the mind on the eternal, the unchanging, the transcendent. Thus Fergus's immoderate rage was seen as a negative thing – 'hostility destroyed the world', as the author of the earliest surviving version of the *Táin* (a medieval saga narrative) wrote – as was Derdriu's depression. Neither was supposed to be viewed as noble or heroic or admirable, even if they may seem so to you now. Fergus's exile and Derdriu's death were the tragic consequences of too much emotion, although in both cases Conchobar's lust was the excessive and uncontrolled emotion that was ultimately to blame.

Perhaps the most extreme example of the negative consequences of unchecked emotion was the story concerning the origins of idol-worship. The narrative has its origins in the Bible, in the Greek Jewish book known as Wisdom. There we are told that a young man died and his father was so consumed by grief that he commissioned the building of a statue of his son.

> For a father being afflicted with bitter grief made to himself the image of his son who was quickly taken away: and him who then had died as a man, he began now to worship as a god, and appointed him rites and sacrifices among his servants. (Wisdom 14: 15)

The biblical account goes on to say how the skill and ability of the artist, who sought to create the best representation of the son in order to satisfy his patron, was in part to blame for the people being 'carried away by the beauty of the work'. Thereafter, men 'serving either their affections, or their kings, gave incommunicable names to stones'

(Wisdom 14: 21) and this – the beginnings of idolatry – gave rise to awful consequences, such as bloodshed, theft and perjury, which spread across the world as a direct result of the grief of one father for his son.

Some medieval monastic thinkers read this story as a cautionary tale: excess grief unleashing a great evil. One eleventh-century Irish poet composed a poetic version of the Wisdom story, embellishing it with some details from apocryphal literature. The father was given a name: Sarofanes. And Sarofanes' grief was the world's undoing.

> It closed in, in the space of a moment,
> it was boundless after its closing,
> grief for him in his heart;
> the man became a devil . . .
>
> A human image of him was made,
> solidly, out of every ingot
> of the silver and the gold of Arabia.
> The clear beauty of the boy was glorious.
>
> An evil-doing devil went
> into the image after it was made.
> It destroyed the succession of kings,
> through swearing oaths on it, through gazing at it.

Our modern sensibilities condition us to feel sympathy for the father's 'boundless' grief. And perhaps the average medieval reader might have felt the same. But monastic ideology sought to contain earthly emotions by highlighting the disastrous events which resulted from them. For this Irish poet, the global phenomenon of idol-worship and its attendant sinfulness was something which could only be remedied by the global spread of Christianity, and he ended his poem by tracing the journeys of Christ's apostles across the world, bringing with them what the poet saw as the light of truth – the only thing with the power to defeat the darkness of idolatry.

As a modern atheist, it can sometimes be easier for me to relate to sagas like those of Fergus and Derdriu because God is not on the surface of those tales. But the more you read of them, the more you understand about the world in which they were composed, and the more you realize that He lurks beneath every word. The medieval poets who wrote about dead princes and lost lovers, desolate halls and guilt-fuelled rage were no less Christian than those who wrote about keening for Christ or who reworked biblical stories about how paternal grief could unleash evil on the world.

At my father's committal, the priest spoke his powerful words about death and resurrection and life everlasting. He was kind and gentle and knew full well that the only believer in the room was the dead man in the coffin. But we played out the Catholic rituals of death because what else were we supposed to do? Rosemary and five red roses on my father's coffin – one rose for his wife, one for each of his four children. An ode to Dublin, sung by The Fureys, played softly as we walked away from him. In a few weeks, I will collect his ashes and bring them home to his city.

I decide to visit one of my best and oldest friends and so, less than forty-eight hours after my father's committal, I am on a plane to Biarritz and from there a bus to San Sebastián.

He meets me at the bus station and doesn't hesitate to point out that I look terrible: tired, bloated and grey. We have been friends for twenty years, our friendship played out across the UK, Germany, Ireland and the Basque Country. He is a Chilean heavy metal musician and I am an Irish academic: we make an unlikely pair, and yet somehow we have never ceased our conversation. It is the feast day of St Sebastian, and we run down a side street to escape enthusiastic Basque nationalists, marching in Napoleonic dress. We take shelter in a cinema and watch Robert Eggers' *The Lighthouse*, with Spanish subtitles, and the floor of the cinema vibrates under our feet from the booming soundscape and I forget my grief and I continue to forget it as we dissect the film in a bar afterwards.

The next day is my friend's birthday and we eat a fabulous dinner with his ex-wife and his daughter, and then the two of us hit the heavy metal bars and drink shots until the early hours. At some point in the night he has to step outside to do a live interview on Chilean radio, and then we carry on drinking and talking and I realize that there will be life after grief. I am not going to destroy the world and the grief will not destroy me. It is safe for me to enter the depths of sorrow as long as I have friends and family to guide me back to the path towards life. Derdriu had been reared outside of society: she had no friends or community to help her. At least Fergus did not go into exile alone: he took three thousand of his people with him. It is time for me to go back to Dublin, go back to work, mark my students' January exams and prepare for the new semester, which begins at the start of February.

FEBRUARY

Mothers

I had phoned my mother that January morning to tell her that my father was dead. I called again a week later to ask if she would be attending his wake or funeral. She said no. She would have a Mass said for his soul at her local church, but she would not be coming to pay her respects. I didn't hear from her again for a full month: not a call or a text or an email or a message of any kind. Although the silence was, of course, a message of sorts.

Part of the enigma of the first years of my life is the very different accounts given by those who lived through them. I, being too young to remember, have no narrative of my own. I can only sift through the conflicting testimonies, weigh them in my hands, and consider which has the feel of truth. This is what I do now on a grander scale in my job as a historian, but my training started young. One of my mother's sisters attended my father's wake. She brought one of her daughters, my cousin, several years older than me, who recalled changing my nappies when I was an infant; more precious crumbs of memory that I could add to my store.

A mother's love is not guaranteed. When I was nineteen years old, my mother told me to my face that she didn't feel any maternal instinct towards me. For whatever reason, she simply hadn't bonded with me. Shortly after my third birthday I was sent to live with my father and stepmother, and at that point my mother's obligation to me ended. My stepuncle once told me that he would never forget the sight of her handing me over, without complaint or visible emotion.

A few years later, she would apply for custody of my older brother, but not me.

Giving birth to a baby created from your own egg, fertilized by the sperm of another human, is the narrowest form of motherhood – motherhood as a product of reproduction. More importantly, there is motherhood as an emotional bond, which is a construct, and that construct comes in many shapes and sizes. The world has always been full of stepmothers, foster-mothers, fathers who do the 'mothering', aunts and cousins and grandparents who take on primary caring responsibilities, adoptive mothers, institutions that rear children (for better or worse), and innumerable kinds of almost-mothers, surrogate mothers, 'they-were-like-a-mother-to-me's. I was reared by a stepmother who mothered me as best she could, even when I sometimes believed that she was like the mythic wicked stepmother from a fairy tale, and treated her accordingly.

There are probably quite a lot of medieval Irish poems that were written for female ears, but the ninth-century Irish poem *Ísucán* is one of the few that is explicitly so: 'Sing a rightful harmony, maidens,' the poet exhorts. It may well have been written by a woman too, possibly for an audience of nuns and other women living in religious communities. Understanding the poem fully requires a tiny language lesson: you need to know that *-án* is a diminutive ending in Irish, that is, it is added to the end of a word to convey the sense of 'little', so that Colm, 'dove', becomes Colmán, 'little dove'. There is an affectionate or intimate tone to this diminution, in the same way that Robert might become Robbie to his friends, just as I, Elizabeth, am Lizzie to those who love me.

In this poem, Jesus, *Ísu* becomes *Ísucán*. How to render that in English? Those who have attempted to translate the poem have gone for things like 'Jesu-kin', but that sounds more like a Beatrix Potter character than a declaration of intimate affection for Christ. 'Baby Jesus'? Too primary school nativity play. Perhaps it's better to stick with *Ísucán*, now that you know what it means. To add to the difficulty, the poet uses the *-án* ending with all sorts of unexpected words throughout the poem, building a sustained atmosphere of affectionate intimacy.

> *Ísucán,*
> nursed by me in my little hermitage,
> everything is false – even a cleric with great wealth –
> except *Ísucán*.
>
> The fosterling nursed by me in my house,
> is not the fosterling of an unfree peasant;
> Jesus with the men of heaven,
> at my heart every night . . .
>
> Noble Jesus of the angels,
> no ordinary cleric,
> nursed by me in my little hermitage,
> Jesus son of the Hebrews . . .

In the Middle Ages, levels of infant mortality were high. Mothers could expect to lose half their children before they reached the age of five. Death in childbirth was also a huge factor in female life expectancy. Babies lost their mothers and other women raised them. It has been suggested that perhaps *Ísucán* was written for nuns whose responsibilities included fostering orphaned, abandoned and unwanted children, left to be reared by the Church, and that the poet sought to remind them that in caring for these vulnerable little ones they were doing God's work. Sure, didn't Jesus say that whenever you did good things for the least amongst us you did those good things for Him? The poet imagines nursing Ísucán, comforting this baby who is also God, and thereby encourages the women in their work by allowing them to see the baby in their arms as Christ.

But there's more to women than babies, and there's more to the Ísucán poem than nursing them. The scholar Eleanor Knott (1886–1975), a brilliant woman herself, observed that the poem is also full of sophisticated legalistic vocabulary which had particular resonances in medieval Irish society. The relationship between the woman and Christ is not only a breast that nurtures and a mouth that suckles, but also a complex one of mutual obligation. Jesus is, simultaneously, a vulnerable baby and like a high-king who requires tribute in return for the legal protections He offers. If Ísucán makes grants like an earthly lord – offering the safety and security of the monastery in this life and the promise of heaven thereafter – He demands prayer as His payment. The women who lived in female monastic communities in medieval Ireland knew their legal status, their rights and responsibilities.

I cannot help thinking of the children reared in Church institutions in Ireland in more recent times: how many felt the warmth and affection articulated in the Ísucán poem? And if there was love to be had, how often was it underpinned by obligation rather than compassion? If I couldn't force my mother to love me and rear me, how could a baby, torn from its mother and placed in an institution, hope for love from strangers? One thing is certain: too many people did not see that these children born of 'sin' were themselves innumerable Christs, Ísucáns, high-kings who deserved tribute, and what they did to the least of them they did to Him.

As with so many of the women of medieval Ireland, the poet who wrote Ísucán is anonymous. They composed their poem in the ninth century and their identity is lost to us, but about a century or so later, someone else came along and claimed that the poem had been written by St Íte. Íte lived in the sixth century, so she can't be the author of the ninth-century poem (even saints aren't *that* miraculous), but people hate not knowing things and would rather invent connections than admit uncertainty, and so Íte's name has been attached to the poem ever since.

The historical Íte is thought to have founded an important female monastic community at Killeedy, modern-day Co. Limerick. We have no written sources about her from the time she was living, so we can say little more than that, but a later account of her life (unreliable because it draws on all sorts of literary tropes and saintly clichés) tells us that the community also had a school where children were educated. You can see why someone would want to connect her with the Ísucán poem, no matter how anachronistically. But the fact of the matter is that there were numerous women in ninth-century Ireland who would have lived in monastic communities, received an education sufficient to compose poetry, understood their own legal status, have seen nuns fulfilling a need to act *in loco parentis*, and whose names have disappeared into the great chasm of the past. Any one of them could have written *Ísucán*.

It is unbelievably difficult to rear someone else's child. My stepmum raised three children who were not biologically her own, plus two who were. She did her best to treat us all equally, but as a typically sensitive teenager, I couldn't help but perceive every small, unintended slight as evidence that I didn't quite belong. In February, though, as I trawled the depths of my grief for my father, my stepmum was the one who comforted me, and I hope I comforted her in return, and I came to appreciate that my chosen family, one constructed from all sorts of parts that don't quite fit perfectly, can form bonds stronger than blood.

Ties of blood can be pretty shitty, really, when you think about it. A lot of people who are interested in medieval Irish literature focus their attention on *Táin Bó Cúailnge*, 'The Cattle-Raid of Cooley', usually just referred to as the *Táin*. It's available in modern English poetic 'translations' ('adaptations', really, or 'versions') by such heavyweight poets as Thomas Kinsella and Ciaran Carson, neither of whom sought to accurately repre-sent any surviving manuscript copy of the text but who rather assembled idealized versions by the standards of twentieth- and twenty-first-century narrative expectations. There are two main versions of the *Táin*, quite different in many aspects of plot, characterization, tone and purpose, one created in the eleventh century from sources that were a few centuries older, the other written in the twelfth century.

Kinsella and Carson both kind of smooshed the two versions together to create great works of English literature, but they don't really tell us much about the originals. In both original versions, Ailill and Medb, the King and Queen of Connacht, lead an army of combined forces against the kingdom of Ulster, in an attempt to capture a bull. In both versions, Medb is an infuriatingly idiotic bitch, but she's even more of an idiotic bitch in the second version than the first. For some reason – perhaps because they've never actually read either version of the *Táin*, or perhaps because they can only read them with modern eyes – some commentators think that Medb is some sort of feminist icon, rebelling against the patriarchy and leading her troops into battle like a triumphant heroine in a fantasy novel. But she's not. She's deliberately constructed as a horrible character. She ignores tactical advice, she makes stupid decisions, she has her period at the worst possible moment on the battlefield, creating great lakes of her menstrual blood, and devising all those other strategies that the (probably, though not certainly) male authors of both versions of the *Táin* came up with to convey their fundamental point that women are not capable of leading armies.

On top of all that, she is portrayed as a bad mother. So single-minded is she in her misguided pursuit of the damn bull, that she is willing to give her daughter, Finnabair, to any man who can kill the one warrior stopping her from taking it: Cú Chulainn. She doesn't give a toss about Finnabair's consent or desire or autonomy, but will offer up her daughter just as she offers land and wealth to anyone who can kill Cú Chulainn; Finnabair is simply another treasure to be awarded to a victorious man. One way that critics excuse her behaviour is to say that it's sexual liberation. OK, sure, it's great to be sexually liberated, but don't hand your daughter over to men like meat on a plate. And don't mistake eleventh-century Ireland for 1960s California, all bra-burning and free love. You can't redeem Medb's character that way. The authors wanted the audience to think that Medb was bad, faithless, impulsive and selfish.

Another thing modern critics do is assume that there is some other version of the *Táin*, a lost, earlier version, that would have been a feminist, unrepressed story with a triumphant and successful Medb, until those dastardly monks got their hands on it and rewrote it with their misogynistic Christian ideology and turned Medb into a villain. But there is no earlier version. There is no triumphant Medb. There is no pre-Christian Medb. Medb only exists in medieval Irish literature as a bad would-be leader, fated to be killed (in another medieval Irish tale) by a block of cheese. What a way to go. She's not a goddess, not a pagan survivor: she's a fictional character, in literature that is a product of its time — a time in which women were expected to guard the virtue of their daughters, not whore them out as incentives for war. Why would you want a blood mother who thinks you're nothing more than a deal-sweetener, when you could have a foster-mother who thinks you're Christ?

That being said, there are good biological mothers in medieval Irish literature, of course. I think my favourite is the slightly overbearing mother of Donn Bó in the story of the Battle of Allen (*Cath Almaine*). Donn Bó has never spent a night away from his mother before he's called up to battle, heading down south from Uí Néill territories to the province of Leinster in order to fight for his king, who's trying to exact an unjust tax from the Leinstermen. Donn Bó can sing, he has lovely hair, he's a mammy's boy, and the mammy won't let him leave until she exacts a promise, sworn in the name of St Columba, that Donn Bó will return to her safely from battle. You can imagine her anguish at the thought of her precious boy going away to war, and her tough-as-boots demand for an oath guaranteeing his safe return. This was good thinking on her part, because when Donn Bó is killed in battle, decapitated, the power of the saint ensures that his body is miraculously healed and Donn Bó is taken back to his mother. Many a mother throughout history will have done the same, but for most the oath will not have guaranteed their sons' safety.

Many soldiers don't ever return from conflict, alive or otherwise: they're condemned to remain forever missing in action. The overall message of the Battle of Allen (as indeed of the *Táin*) is about pointless cycles of pointless violence. The men of Leinster defeat their northern enemy, after a great slaughter which leaves other mothers – less fortunate than Donn Bó's – wailing and lamenting the corpses of their sons on the battlefield, but the victory is short-lived because soon afterwards Leinster is at war again, this time with Munster. And it all begins again, with new mothers and new children to make fresh corpses.

I once tried to create a family of my own. When I was a PhD student, I became pregnant after attending a booze-laden book launch at the Irish Embassy in London. The man who impregnated me, possible candidate for the title of nicest guy on earth, was a PhD student too, a scientist from Donegal, and, although we hadn't been together very long, he took the pregnancy in his stride. A few months along, he rolled over in bed one morning and suggested that we should get married and that seemed like a good idea at the time, so I waddled along to the registry office, heavy-bellied with new life, and just like that: we were a family. I went into labour a few months later: after forty-seven hours of pain, a doctor cut open my belly, put his hands inside me and extracted a life. He handed the baby to her father, who held her as I haemorrhaged two litres of my own blood. A few hours later, as someone else's blood was being transfused into my body, I watched TV and saw Israeli tanks rolling into Lebanon, artillery fire, missile strikes, and I was seized with terror at having brought a human into a dangerous world. Six weeks later, I was diagnosed with postnatal depression.

And a few years after that, just as easily as our family had been created, I took out my metaphorical baseball bat and smashed it to smithereens. And my daughter stayed with her father, and the cycle of failed motherhood continued into another generation. Thirty years after my father had, unusually, taken custody of me, I left my six-year-old daughter in the custody of her father.

One of the strategies we deploy in order to be able to live with ourselves is to seek justification for our actions, both at the moment that we are screwing up and afterwards. That justification may change over time: I have variously ascribed my actions to the postnatal depression, to the effects of traumatic childhood events, to whatever vaguely reasonable excuse presented itself. And those things probably did play their role. But I was also just a selfish arsehole, no bones about it. I am deeply sorry and will carry that regret with me for as long as I live.

In February I begin teaching my undergraduate course on visions of, and voyages to, supernatural places in medieval Irish literature. I give a couple of lectures on the Middle Irish story 'The Voyage of Máel Dúin', which is about the search for justification, the desire for vengeance, the need for forgiveness. It is also about the way families can be configured. The main character is a child born of rape: Máel Dúin's biological mother was a prioress, his father a violent warrior who, in the course of raiding in another kingdom, attacked a community of nuns, grabbing the prioress's hand as she went to strike the bell, forcing her to the ground, and violating her.

Nine months later, the prioress gives birth to a son, Máel Dúin. She gives the baby boy secretly to her friend, the queen, who raises Máel Dúin as her own child and tries to convince people that she is his biological mother. He is reared as a royal son and he flourishes and excels in all things. He is beautiful and skilled and talented. Too much so. In a fit of jealousy at Máel Dúin's superior skills, another boy reveals to him that his parentage is unknown. The author writes that, 'Máel Dúin fell silent, because until then he had thought he was the son of the king and queen.'

Máel Dúin confronts his adoptive mother and demands to know the identity of his biological parents, and the queen replies telling him not to listen to the wounding words of other boys. She says to him *Messe do máthair*, 'I am your mother,' and she tells him that no one has a greater love for their child than she does for him. I think that Máel Dúin's silence as he realizes that the king and queen are not his biological parents, and his adoptive mother's simple declaration – '*I am* your mother' – are among the most powerful moments in medieval Irish literature. You can feel his world crumble, as his family life is shown to be built on a shameful secret, and you can feel her world fall apart, as he rejects her love in that moment and insists on knowing his biological parentage. In a timeless act of selflessness, his adoptive mother personally takes him to meet his biological mother. The author's sensitivity to the complexities of identity and parenthood – the drive to know one's biological origins, the deep love an adoptive mother has for her child – is remarkable.

Máel Dúin talks with his biological mother and, although his biological father has died some years previously, he travels to his father's territory and meets his paternal kin — who all seem to be much nicer than the douchebag, rapist dad. Máel Dúin becomes convinced that he needs to find the man who killed his father and avenge his father's death — which is precisely the crazy sort of thing people do when they have difficult and complicated relationships with their birth parents — so he sets off on the voyage from which the story gets its title. He encounters all sorts of wondrous islands and marvellous (super-)natural phenomena during his voyage, escapes from various tricky situations, and comes across a lot of strange, religious people.

Máel Dúin's voyage is one of self-discovery too, the journey as a kind of working out of one's issues, a search for redemption. At the end, he learns that he would be better off forgiving the man who killed his biological father than perpetuating the cycle of violence. An ancient hermit, clothed only in his own long, grey hair, tells Máel Dúin that forgiveness is better than vengeance, because we are all flawed in our own ways, all of us in need of absolution for something or other.

Máel Dúin returns home, to tell everyone about the things he has experienced and learned. The author doesn't tell us whether his adoptive parents were there to welcome him home. We do not know whether his journey of redemption also led him to understand how fortunate he was to have been so loved by the king and queen, whether he came to realize that a chosen family can be stronger, more loving and more secure than a biological one. The author of the tale ends by citing the famous line from Virgil's *Aeneid*: *haec olim meminisse iuvabit* – one day, we'll look back on this and smile.

Maybe, one day, I'll look back on all this and smile.

Women who give their children away, or abandon them, in medieval Irish literature, do so for various different reasons. Often it is their only option. In some cases, they leave their babies somewhere to die; luckily – for the sake of the baby, for the sake of the plot, for the sake of the moral of the story – someone usually passes by and finds the baby and rears them.

In the eleventh century, when the fortunes of the dominant royal dynasty in Ireland, the Uí Néill, were threatened by the up-and-coming Munster dynasty of Brian Boru, an author sat down to write a story, drawing on some earlier sources, about the Uí Néill's eponymous ancestor, Níall Noígíallach, 'Níall of the nine hostages'. The tale begins with a king, who has a wife, with whom he has numerous sons. But the king also has slaves, as kings usually did at that time. One of his slaves was – anachronistically, given that the story is set in the late Roman period – a daughter of the 'king of the Saxons', who has been taken from Britain during a slave-raiding expedition. This fictional slave-raid, then, is roughly contemporary with the real slave-raid that brought St Patrick to Ireland for the first time. The king rapes his slave, as so many enslaved women have been raped before and since, and she becomes pregnant. The king's wife is jealous and angry, as so many wives of slave-owning rapists have been before and since, and she torments this dark-haired woman from Britain, forcing her to engage in heavy work through-out her pregnancy in the hope that she will miscarry. The girl goes into labour 'but did not cease from her service'. She gives birth to a boy, on the green at Tara, 'but dared not pick him up from the ground, and left him there exposed to the birds'. And no one came to rescue the boy because of their fear of the king's wife.

Happily, though, a poet named Torna passes by some time later and sees the baby being attacked by the birds. He picks him up and holds him to his breast and in that moment Torna sees what will become of the child: he will grow up to cause great bloodshed, leading armies victoriously into battle, and will rule Ireland for twenty-seven years as Níall 'of the nine hostages', and his descendants will be king after him. So Torna fosters Níall and brings him up in secret until he is old enough to return to Tara.

Níall comes upon his biological mother as she is carrying water in the service of the queen. He tells her to put the water down and she replies that she dares not because of her fear of the queen.

Níall says: *'Ni bia mo máthair'*, ol se, *'oc fognum, ⁊ me mac rígh Herenn'* – 'No mother of mine shall serve when I am the son of the King of Ireland.'

Their first meeting is struck through with a similar mixture of indignant emotion and fierce pride and primal longing for biological connections as in the story of Máel Dúin. And yet it is hardly more affecting than the first tender encounter between Níall and the parent who chose him, Torna the poet.

Níall frees his mother from her bondage, much to the wrath of the king's wife. The queen demands of her husband that he choose a successor from amongst his sons, but now that his mother has been freed, Níall too is a potential candidate for kingship. The old king is unable to choose and leaves it to a wizard to determine the outcome of the succession dispute. This wizard comes up with various feats of strength and ability at which, needless to say, Níall excels, and he is awarded the kingship, and the vision that Torna had seen as he held the vulnerable baby to his chest is made real. This baby will go on to become a king and the supposed founder of the dynasty – the Uí Néill – whose claims to political primacy over the island of Ireland would endure for centuries.

Of course, these great works of literature take the tropes of the impregnated enslaved woman, the child born of rape, the baby exposed to the elements, and make happy endings out of them. Even the Ísucán poem hints at babies being taken in, loved and reared in constructed families of different shapes and sizes. We do not have the stories of those whom no one rescued. This month, the Russian government repatriates twenty-six children, aged between two and fifteen, from the al-Hawl refugee camp in northeastern Syria. News reports say that Russia estimates that there are more than two hundred Russian children still in Syrian refugee camps, their lives at risk from violence, malnutrition or exposure, the sons and daughters of Russian women either married to Syrian men or to Russian men who joined Daesh and travelled to Syria to fight. Babies exposed to the birds.

The Russian government evacuates the children, but says that it has no plans to repatriate the adults. Like Medb in single-minded pursuit of the bull, these mothers have endangered their daughters and sons, and to what end? What happens to these children who are now parentless? Will a poet clutch them to his chest and dream great futures for them?

Seven years before, I had left my daughter in the UK with her father and taken up my dream job in Ireland. I too went single-mindedly in pursuit of something I believed in utterly. I was off to do great things: educate people, discover new knowledge, live a life of learning, devoted to books and history and scholarship. I was no better than Medb, no better than a Russian woman trapped in a Syrian refugee camp, no better than the prioress giving Máel Dúin to her friend to raise, no better than Níall's mother abandoning her baby to be food for crows, and worst of all I was no better than my own mother, and I hated myself for that.

After I moved to Ireland, I travelled back to the UK every other weekend to spend time with my daughter, and she spent her holidays with me; she had a wide and deep network of family, friends, school and social life in the UK that she would have had to rebuild from scratch if I had brought her to Ireland with me. And yet nothing could – or can – shift the pervasive sense that I have abandoned her, that I have failed in my fundamental duty as a mother, even if she grows up to become a king, or a saint, or a voyager.

Although inheritance laws in medieval Ireland favoured the nuclear family, with wealth and property going from a father

43

to his sons by his legal wife, other legal and social structures created other sorts of familial bonds, especially the practice of fosterage. Fosterage was a widespread institution in early medieval Ireland, regulated by law, and financed by fosterage fees that were calculated according to the social status of the biological parents of the child being fostered. Children were fostered with families of the same rank, and the fees were paid to cover their living costs and education.

The purpose of fosterage was a bit like a live-in apprenticeship, but the highest status children were being trained in aristocratic life – warfare and leadership for boys, embroidery for girls. Other foster-parents slightly lower down the social scale might train girls in domestic skills like grinding cereals to make flour and boys in farming, craftsmanship or a trade. According to the law texts of the time, fosterage would usually begin at the age of seven and children could remain with their foster-families until adulthood.

The emotional consequences of this are plastered all over medieval Irish literature, because the inevitable result of this practice seems to have been close emotional bonds between foster-parents, foster-children, foster-siblings, often far closer than between those related by blood. This could be a positive thing, of course, right up to the moment when foster-brothers had to face each other on the battlefield.

One of the men that Medb offers her daughter to in the *Táin* is named Fer Diad. Fer Diad refuses to fight Cú Chulainn because they are foster-brothers, but Medb plies Fer Diad with drink and flattery, and offers of land and wealth and her daughter's body, and finally she shames him into combat with Cú Chulainn. When Cú Chulainn defeats his foster-brother, Fer Diad says that his ribs are broken 'like spoils', his heart is gore. 'I fought well, but I have fallen.'

Cú Chulainn's distraught lament for the foster-brother he has just killed is a poignant evocation of the love that can form in childhood between those who are raised together as siblings, regardless of their biological connection or lack thereof.

> All was play and pleasure,
> until I met Fer Diad at the ford.
> Alas for the noble champion,
> laid low there at the ford.
> All was play and pleasure,
> until I met Fer Diad at the ford.
> I thought that beloved Fer Diad
> would live after me forever.

My own ties of siblinghood – technically, I have one full biological brother, two half-brothers and one stepsister, although I do not regard them in terms of 'halves' and 'steps' – seem to me as constructed and contingent as those of fosterage. Amongst the family that I love the most, I have a niece who was raised by her grandmother, another niece who is adopted by my half-brother and not technically tied to me by blood. My stepsister was raised by her half-brother, who is no relation to me at all. The cousins to whom I am closest were adopted by my uncle and are not my blood relations.

None of these accidents of biology matter. We create our

own family through emotional bonds that are forged in the fires of experience and circumstance, companionship and loyalty. Fer Diad's unwillingness to fight Cú Chulainn was not grounded in fear of his adversary's military superiority, but in the fact that the loyalty formed from the love of foster-brothers trumped the loyalty of province or political allegiance in the mind of the author of the earliest version of the *Táin*. He crafted the *Táin* to be a story about how pernicious loyalties based on kingdoms and politics can be, and how fundamental are the ties of love created amongst those who grow up together, who nurture the children of others.

Do you remember Fergus, who sold his honour for beer when he was supposed to be guaranteeing the safety of Derdriu and the sons of Uisliu? He had taken his people into exile in Connacht, and there he still is at the beginning of the story of the *Táin*. He owes an obligation to Medb and Ailill, who have given him and his people sanctuary in their kingdom, and he fights on their side as their army creeps through Ulster in pursuit of the bull that Medb so desires. And yet he is conflicted by ties of love and loyalty, and he actively undermines the progress of the Connacht army, avoiding conflict with Cú Chulainn, preventing a slaughter of the Ulstermen, because his bonds of love and affection tie him to them.

The things we fight for, and the reasons we fight for them, can be so elusive, so futile, and yet so deeply felt. Every year, I try to explain the emotional complexities of the *Táin* to a new generation of students: Fer Diad and Cú Chulainn, fighting on opposite sides of a conflict and yet deeply bound by love for each other; Fergus's divided loyalties; Medb's myopic willingness to sacrifice her daughter for the sake of a bull. And yet every year I receive essays telling me that Medb is a goddess and Cú Chulainn a hero. Simple. Black and white. The skill and psychological depth of a talented author erased into myth; the emotional complexities of fosterage ties subsumed into fables of good versus evil. Like newspaper reports of mothers in Syrian refugee camps, like them and us, like right and wrong, there can be no nuance, no multiple identities, no emotional conflict, no pull of loyalties. This woman is a good mother and that woman is a bad mother. This is a family and that is not a family.

I had a spare bedroom in my apartment in Dublin, and in November 2018 I had given it to a Syrian refugee who was stuck in the Direct Provision accommodation centre in Mosney in Co. Meath, with no access to job opportunities or independent accommodation. He had been a student, studying Maths and Computer Science, when the civil war had broken out in Syria, and he found himself increasingly hemmed in: Assad's forces on one side, Islamist forces on the other, and his family stuck in the middle of it. He came via Greece to Ireland and was abandoned by an inhumane system to face whatever fate might come.

A campaign by the Irish Red Cross drew my attention to his plight, we met, I handed over a set of keys to him, and he moved in a few weeks later. He too became part of my family. An adopted nephew, perhaps, or another little brother. Or a foster-son. He lost a year and a half of his young life in Mosney after already losing years in a Syrian war zone and a

Greek refugee camp. If you can get out of Mosney by car, and drive half an hour down the R150, you'll get to the hill of Tara, where the foreign-born mother of Níall Noígíallach had to abandon the baby who would become King of Ireland.

Between lectures to my students about Máel Dúin and his mothers, I think about the silence of my own mother.

My stepmum and I send messages back and forth to each other as we try to navigate our grief together.

I think about my dad and how never again will he pick me up and hold me to his chest and dream a great future for me and take me away to nurture me.

I think about my daughter in Britain, being reared by her father and stepmother, and I think about the Syrian boy that I gave shelter to.

I think about mothers whose children are taken from them against their will; mothers who give up their children in the hope that they will have a better life; mothers who sacrifice their children for the sake of ideals or ambitions; mothers who cannot love their children, no matter how hard they try; mothers who love other people's children as much as their own.

I remember the nights in Dublin when I used to wake to the sound of my daughter crying for me, only to remember, when I was already halfway to the bedroom door, that she was asleep in another country. She was not here, or rather I was not there.

I think about the families we make for ourselves, the families we choose, and how love is the people who want the best for you, the people who text to see if you are OK, the people who pick up those who have been abandoned and hold them close, the people who make difficult choices in difficult circumstances, the people who cling on to hope, even as trauma rolls on, across generations, across divides.

MARCH

Journeys

Máel Dúin worked through his issues by going on a journey. By the start of March, with the semester in full flow, my students and I were exploring his encounters with fantastical islands, his search for vengeance and his discovery that forgiveness brings the greater reward. And we were going to other strange and wondrous places, tracing the fictional voyages of St Brendan, of Bran, of Connlae. As we read and analysed and discussed these stories it was becoming apparent that modern journeys were becoming filled with challenges and dangers too. A new form of coronavirus that had originated in China was spreading across the world through the movement of humans. Europe was about to become the new epicentre of infection, as cases – followed by deaths – occurred in Italy. Yet, although the World Health Authority had declared a public health emergency, that emergency had not yet been designated a pandemic.

I had been invited to give a keynote lecture in California at UCLA. It was unclear to what extent the virus was present in the United States, and the first case of the virus in Ireland had only been announced on the last day of February. My university's insurance policy cleared me to travel, so I flew from Dublin to Los Angeles. When I landed in the pleasant warmth of LA in early March there seemed little to worry about: a few mentions of infected passengers on a cruise ship off the coast; then, a few more mentions of confirmed cases in California.

How little we knew then, and how quickly we would learn

in this fateful month. At the airport those taking precautions were a tiny minority: there were no masks, no hand sanitizer dispensers. I had never heard of social distancing. But we all embarked on our own little journeys of epidemiological education, some towards knowledge, others finding islands of conspiracy.

When Máel Dúin is on his journey, he sails into a sea that is so thin, like mist, that it seems as though it will not support the boat. When he looks down, he can see a whole country beneath the sea. Amongst the strongholds, he sees a tree, and in that tree is a great and terrifying beast. It leans out of the branches to seize an ox, which it begins to devour. Máel Dúin is petrified, because he thinks that his boat will fall through this nebulous, insubstantial water, on to the land below, and into the jaws of the beast.

When I am in a plane, I too fear falling to my death. I am convinced that the aeroplane will acquire its own consciousness and decide to plummet to the ground. At the first hint of turbulence, my mind fills with desperate thoughts – not of my family or loved ones, but of the books I will never get a chance to read or write. Unlike Máel Dúin, I have no god to pray to, so I speak to myself and say that, if I am spared this time, I will work harder, read more, write more, be worthy of this second chance. And every time I land safely, I return to all my bad habits, unrepentant and unchanged.

These days, my fears are only slightly irrational. But a few years ago, they were crippling. I became consumed by anxieties that left me incapable of doing almost anything. I stopped flying, my passport expired, and for several years, my only journeys were to sail 'n' rail laboriously between Dublin and Cambridge to see my daughter. I would make my way to Dublin port and board the *Ulysses* or the *Jonathan Swift*, and read and mark essays and breathe and try to control my panic until I got to Holyhead. Then I would begin the long train journey via Chester, Crewe, London Euston and London King's Cross, to Cambridge.

Look at the coast, look at the mountains. Breathe. Breathe.

Sometimes I could get as far as Crewe before cracking under the weight of a heart that felt it was about to stop beating at any moment, at which point I would medicate myself with Valium.

Every other Friday, this twelve-hour journey to Cambridge so that I could spend Saturday with my daughter, and then early on Sunday morning I would turn around and begin the twelve-hour journey home. Cambridge, King's Cross, Euston, Crewe, Chester, Holyhead.

Read, breathe. Read, breathe. See how far you can get before your hand reaches for the Valium again.

Weekend after weekend, month after month, back and forth on the big, beautiful ferry, marking essays, preparing lectures, reading books, watching the rugged landscape of Anglesey emerging from the mist, panic attack in the ferry toilets, Valium, and then stepping off the boat with relief that we hadn't fallen through the sea into the jaws of a beast below.

I was working too hard and drinking too much. I missed my daughter. I walked into the lecture hall and performed, day after day, trying to convey my deep love for my subject, trying to dispel the preconceptions that my students brought to their study of it, often swallowing another Valium minutes before I entered the room so that I could make it through the hour intact.

I didn't get my hair cut, I didn't cancel direct debits from when I lived in the UK, I didn't complete change-of-address forms, I didn't open a savings account, I didn't buy new clothes, I didn't shave my legs. I got up, I worked, I drank, I went to sleep, and my life became increasingly disorganized, which made me increasingly anxious. My clothes were full of holes.

When Friday rolled round again, I got up at 6 a.m. and made my way to the port because – still – I hadn't renewed my passport, because – still – the thought of filling in the form was an obstacle too great to contemplate.

It took therapy – years of it – to overcome the anxiety. 'I can sing my own true story / of journeys through the world, / how often I was tried / by troubles . . .' as the Old English poet wrote. And then, suddenly, one day, after no great revelation and for no particular reason, I walked into a post office with my completed passport form, and accepted an invitation to give a lecture in Oslo. I started flying regularly again and stopped panicking about it.

I knew that I had finally overcome the anxiety, at least as much as I would ever be able to, in January 2019. I had travelled to Svalbard, a group of islands in the Arctic Ocean, located halfway between Norway and the North Pole. Before then, I would have avoided travelling somewhere new, for fear of unfamiliarity. One of the northernmost inhabited areas on earth, the temperature was far below freezing – though perhaps not as far below as in previous years; the signs of climate change were everywhere – and it was dark, dark, dark. I think, before I arrived, the concept of the polar night was an abstract one to me, perhaps involving gloomy afternoons when the sun never fully rises. I was unprepared for the pitch-black darkness, twenty-four hours a day, the disorientating inability to tell day from night. Until then, I would have avoided dark places, for fear of what lurks in the darkness. And I would have avoided cold places for fear of falling on ice. But here I was, in one of the darkest, coldest places in the world, and as I drove a dog sled over the Arctic tundra, feeling confident and exhilarated and brave, I could finally see how far I had travelled from the depression and anxiety of those earlier years. I knew that I had undertaken my own journey of redemption, and that I could make my way home to Ireland, having finally forgiven myself for some of my greatest sins.

And now, here I am, jetting off without much thought, to Los Angeles.

It's easy to assume that people in the Middle Ages didn't travel much. Over the years, I've encountered this popular idea of centuries filled with medieval peasants, born and raised and dying in the same village. That was certainly true for some people, just as it is now, but far from all. At the lower end of the socioeconomic scale, cattle fairs, markets and indigence could all take people quite considerable distances from home. For rich and poor alike, military campaigns and pilgrimages were causes for people to venture far from the land of their birth. Amongst the upper echelons of society, marriage alliances, studying abroad, becoming a bishop or papal legate in some distant land, or being sent on a diplomatic mission to a foreign king might all be reasons for long-distance travel. Raiders captured people and enslaved them in far-off places; traders moved ships full of luxury exports from one end of the known world to the other. Then as now, people were mobile for many different reasons: economic, political, social and educational.

In the first week of this month, the first round of negotiations on the future partnership of the United Kingdom and the European Union took place in Brussels. Negotiations covered transport and trade, energy and fisheries, law enforcement across borders and international co-operation in criminal investigations. For their own reasons, alien and unfathomable to me, a small majority of British people had voted in June 2016 to end freedom of movement for their own citizens through the European Union member states, and to end the freedom of people from those member states to live and work in the United Kingdom. However, because of the long and bloody and complicated history of journeys between Ireland and Britain, I was still free to move, week after week, between my loved ones and work, within the Common Travel Area.

In my journeying back and forth across the Irish Sea I was writing myself into a huge corpus of travel literature and occasionally having experiences that felt fictional in themselves. Once, due to a delayed train, I missed a tight connection at Crewe. The train company admitted fault and, since there was no way for me to make it to Holyhead in time to catch the ferry, they put me on a train to Chester and arranged and paid for a taxi to collect me from there and take me on to the port. As I waited in the Customer Service office at Crewe, there was someone else waiting too, and it emerged that we were to be put in the same taxi, since he was also heading to Holyhead to catch the same ferry. So the two of us, beginning as strangers, made our way together by train to Chester, by taxi to Holyhead, by ferry to Dublin, and we talked without ceasing. He was clever and good-looking and funny. A writer. It turned out that we both liked the same music, the same novels. We were both the same age, both born in the same deprived suburb of Dublin. If this had happened in some scuzzy bar on a Friday night in Dublin I doubt I would have thought much of it, but because it happened on a journey, while travelling, in that suspended reality of between-places, I invested it all with a weight it didn't possess. I felt thunderstruck. This must surely be love at first sight, something destined to happen, fateful and freighted with meaning. I didn't see our differences, the obstacles, the banality, our total incompatibility. This was surely an unworldly encounter on a journey, just as significant as Máel Dúin's, and, for a few hours, over a few pints of Guinness, the ferry was a fantastical island where time passed differently than in the real world and all things were possible, until we shuddered into Dublin Port and the mist evaporated. We met up again a couple of times afterwards, but without the supernatural space-time of a journey, there was nothing to bind us together.

I had spent a few years studying a group of poems and a theological tract that were all thought to have been written by a Bishop of Dublin named Patrick, who had drowned, along with his fellow travellers, in 1084, when his boat sank, probably while returning from somewhere in England (sailing, perhaps, via Bristol or Chester). I had spent my time 'subtracting from knowledge', as one colleague put it, as I pulled at the threads of what we thought we knew about Bishop Patrick's life and work, unspooling his biography and casting doubt on whether he had written any of the texts associated with him at all. Poor Bishop Patrick, in his watery grave, deprived even of poetry.

The poems are beautiful, no matter who wrote them, and many of them involve journeys, both physical and metaphorical. One little Latin verse sees the author sending a booklet of poetry to a monastic brother.

> Onward, my little book
> of halting poems!
> From Patrick
> of loyal memory.
> Duly request
> for my comrade,
> a thousand garlands
> of well-being.

This poem by a certain Patrick, whether or not he is the Bishop of Dublin, modestly sending his pamphlet to a friend, reminds us that books and ideas could travel as easily and as far as people – perhaps even more easily, since a single traveller could carry many books. Once, at Holyhead port, a security official who was searching my bag full of weighty hardbacks rolled her eyes at me and asked why I didn't just buy a Kindle. Servants, carrying the loads of medieval travelling scholars, might have wished for the same thing: a wondrous wax tablet that could hold an infinite number of words.

My favourite poem associated with this Patrick is a long one, beginning *Mentis in excessu* ('In Ecstasy of Mind'). It's not the most original thing in the world, but the way that it combines Classical Latin allegory with medieval Irish voyage literature to create something interesting intrigues me. Every time I read it I find something else to enjoy in it. The poet tells of a vision that he has of a woman, who represents studiousness. It begins:

> In ecstasy of mind through pleasant places in a wide
> countryside
> It chanced that I seemed to wander with hasty steps;
> Thus gazing at length on wondrous sights and things
> I was held captive. Then suddenly appeared to me
> A woman uttering a stream of lamentable complaints
> to the sky.

This fearsome woman, Studiousness, tells him that she has three sisters: Intellect, Memory and Eloquence. She escorts him on a journey across the 'wide countryside', and this land represents Holy Scripture. She takes him to an island, Archipolis, which represents the Church. It's simple allegory, but beautiful. At one point, he sees five horses galloping across the plains and the horses represent the five senses; one horse is faster than the others, and that horse represents sight, the superior of the senses, because it is with sight that we read the word of God. At another point, our visionary sees a forest with trees that are laden with fruit.

And by their odour many are sated.
This fruit preserves the unending salvation of him who eats:
Many are willing to breathe its odour, but few to eat.

The interpretation of this is that the 'fruit' is moral and ethical knowledge. Lots of people are willing to inhale the odour of morality, but few are willing to ingest it, deeply and profoundly. We all moralize freely about others, but few of us are truly ethical ourselves. Hypocrites, the lot of us. The whole poem is ultimately about the moral value of learning and reading and studying, the idea that perhaps – perhaps – we can improve ourselves through knowledge. And education is, of course, a journey: we start out knowing nothing and end up knowing that we know nothing.

Studiousness could be a ticket to exciting adventures and career advancement in the Middle Ages, and if a scholar excelled in a particular field he might be on the path to international fame. Irish scholars with good knowledge of Greek like Iohannes Scotus Eriugena ('John the Gael born in Ireland'), Sedulius Scottus ('Sedulius the Gael'), Martin

Hiberniensis ('Martin the Irishman') – the subtle clue is in their names – were respected intellectuals in the ninth century, who travelled to the Continent to pursue their careers: language graduates will always be sought after.

These guys were thinking about philosophy, poetry, language and translation. Eriugena (as he tends to be known) left Ireland and travelled to north-eastern France, where he became a prominent figure at the court of the emperor, Charles the Bald (who was not, in fact, bald), and was associated with major intellectual centres like Laon, Soissons and Rheims. He was quite simply one of the most brilliant philosophers of the Middle Ages. Just as his contemporary, the equally brilliant Islamic philosopher Al-Kindi, was translating Greek philosophical works into Arabic, so Eriugena was translating them into Latin. Both were Neoplatonists, which in highly simplified terms means that they viewed physical reality as less real than 'intellect', which in itself is a lower manifestation of the divine intellect that is the ultimate cause of all creation. Eriugena and Al-Kindi developed interesting metaphysical ideas of their own as a result of their reading, and in different ways they refined the Neoplatonic model. Eriugena basically saw our very existence as a kind of journey: for him, all of nature, the whole universe, is taking part in an epic voyage away from (*exitus*) and back to (*reditus*) the Divine.

As a terminally godless infidel, I don't think Eriugena is right, fundamentally, but his thought is so elegant, so precise, so rich. I have a sneaking admiration for the world view that underlies Neoplatonism. And I love the idea of existence as a heading out towards darkness on our wayward and ignorant voyage and, eventually, all of us returning home to wisdom and peace and unity. If you must have a metaphysics, there are worse ones than that.

Speaking of voyages towards darkness, there were two ecclesiastics who travelled from sunny climes to rainy England a couple of centuries before Eriugena and Al-Kindi embarked on their philosophical journeys – let's go back to the seventh century, which must have been a really exciting time to be a student in Britain or Ireland. Imagine being a student in Canterbury in the 670s or 680s. Students flocked there from all over Britain and Ireland to study under Theodore, who was born in Tarsus (in modern-day Turkey) and had come to England via Constantinople (now Istanbul) and Rome, bringing with him the latest scholarship and pedagogical methods. Theodore, who was appointed Archbishop of Canterbury in 668, arrived in England with his friend Hadrian, a North African scholar, who became abbot of a monastery in Canterbury. The two of them were experts in Greek and Latin, and they taught poetry, astronomy and maths, as well as interpretation of the Bible. Students who learned from them would have taken their new-found knowledge back to their own communities, and this is likely one of several routes by which the study of Greek was established in some medieval Irish schools.

Ireland was developing its own reputation for international scholarship in the seventh century. Just as Irish scholars travelled to places like Canterbury to study, English students reciprocated and journeyed to Ireland to learn from experts there. In the same year that Theodore and Hadrian had set off from Rome on their long journey to England, a group of English monks led by Colmán, the Irish Bishop of Lindisfarne, travelled to Ireland and eventually set up a monastery called Maigh Eo na Sacsan ('Mayo of the English'). Such English communities in Ireland – Rath Melsigi, Clonmelsh in modern-day Co. Carlow, is another well-known one – attest to ongoing exchanges of knowledge, religious culture and language between Irish and English scholars in the second half of the seventh century.

We know the names of some of the English scholars who studied in Ireland – Ecgberht, Chad, Willibrord – but there were innumerable individuals who are lost to history, who sailed back and forth across the Irish Sea, family in England, education and learning in Ireland. Just like me, in some ways, those sail 'n' rail saints of the seventh century. The Latin word is *peregrinus*. Plural: *peregrini*. Foreigners, travellers, exiles. They travelled *pro amore Dei*, for the love of God. I went for the love of knowledge, exiling myself from my most loved ones.

I like to travel now. I am happy in Los Angeles, this great sprawling, eternally sunny city. I talk to waiters and taxi drivers and they are friendly and open-minded. I visit the primordial soup of the La Brea Tar Pits; the raging, dazzling brilliance of the Los Angeles County Museum of Art. I see an intimate, earthly, gynic exhibition of work by the Venezuelan artist Luchita Hurtado. The exhibition is called 'I Live, I Die, I Will Be Reborn'. I couldn't know that although she lived now, she would be dead by the middle of August.

I buy the exhibition catalogue and eat an expensive lunch at the gallery restaurant. I go to the Westwood Village Memorial Park to see the graves of Ray Bradbury and Buddy Rich and Truman Capote. I look for Frank Zappa but his grave is unmarked. I pick up fancy chocolate souvenirs for my students. I am conscious of the stories I will tell when I get home, the headful of memories I am creating. I think of the Old English poem *Widsith*:

> . . . I travelled through many far lands
> over the wide world. I explored good and evil,
> journeyed far, away from my people.
> That's why I can compose and tell the story,
> report to the company in the great hall,
> how well I was treated by all these great nations.

I like to travel alone. I like solitary dining and solitary drinking and solitary walking and solitary reading, ignoring those who look askance at a solitary woman. For the most part, I have been treated well by all these great nations: the worst things that have happened to me happened not at the hands of foreign strangers but at the hands of family, friends, neighbours.

In the Middle Ages, it was never acceptable for a woman to travel unaccompanied. Male travellers could, in certain circumstances, face public vitriol, particularly if they were vagrants, but women faced far worse (plus ça change). A woman travelling alone was shameful. As one early medieval English writer put it:

a wandering woman engenders gossip,
she is often taunted with sordid sayings,
slandered, insulted, her complexion compromised.
A person nursing guilt must move in darkness
but one unashamed should not stay in shadow.

My travelling back and forth, back and forth, to see my daughter felt shameful because it was a consequence of my failure to mother her properly. If I were a good mother, surely she would be living with me. No one ever criticized me to my face for living in a different country from my child, but I have no doubt that many judged me quietly for my choice. I always saw myself as a wandering scholar, a *peregrinus* like Eriugena, albeit one 'nursing guilt', but perhaps the world saw me as a wandering woman who was morally 'compromised' by her desire for self-fulfilment.

Within the context of real historical journeys, we get a multiplicity of fictional journeys surviving from the medieval world. Many of these involve journeys through heaven and hell. We might be tempted to see these as metaphors for real life itself, with its highs and lows and tortures and rewards. But no: to understand the medieval Christian world is to understand genuine belief in heaven as a place that some would be welcomed into at the end of the world, and hell as a place that all others would be condemned to for eternity.

These days, once you beat your way past fuzzy ideas of a 'better place', or other platitudes about reuniting with loved ones in the hereafter, it is rare to find a Christian who believes literally in heaven as described in Christian tradition (hierarchies of angelic beings, ranks of the elect, and the big cheese, God Himself, on His triumphal throne forever and ever, amen). Rarer still to find one who'll buy in completely to the idea of hell. But while a few of the more rarefied theologians embraced the idea of hell as simply the absence of God, most medieval authors went for full-on horror-filled torture-porn.

In these guided tours of hell, the travelling soul, accompanied by an angel, traverses its many levels, each of which is devoted to a particular group of sinners. The torments for thieves, or the avaricious, or gluttons, or those corrupted by lust are precise and sadistic. Women give birth to birds with iron beaks who turn on them and devour their genitals. Men have iron spikes driven through their tongues. People are forced to stand in boiling water, or burning oil. Sinners are flayed, whipped, scourged, castrated and violated; their eyes are gouged out and their fingernails torn off. And all this is designed to, quite literally, put the fear of God into you. The audience is supposed to be afraid, so much so that they will give up their lying, cheating, fornicating ways, and turn to a more virtuous life. The authors only want the best for you, and the best is, of course, a place in heaven, a place so dull that the same authors rarely spend even half as much time describing it as they do hell.

I ended up writing my PhD thesis on these imaginary places that seem real to other people: heaven and hell. To me, they were expressions of a society's greatest hopes and fears, ideals and offences, a community's articulation of the in-group and the excluded. As ideological constructions, they fascinated me. But I had begun my doctoral research with a different topic in mind: I had originally wanted to write about real journeys to real places. The place that interested me was Regensburg, a small city in Bavaria, where the Danube and Regen rivers meet. I had never been there, but I had read everything I could get my hands on about the many Irishmen who travelled there from the eleventh century onwards. In 1067 a guy named Muiredach mac Robartaig, who would be better known by the Latin form of his name, Marianus Scotus, left Ireland, apparently intending to go on pilgrimage to Jerusalem. He made it as far as Bamberg and from there went on to Regensburg where he founded a Benedictine monastery dedicated to St Peter. Others followed, and a second Irish Benedictine house, dedicated to St James, was founded soon after. Marianus seems to have come from the north of Ireland but later the strongest connections of these Irishmen in Germany to their homeland was with the south. The third abbot of St James's was Christian Mac Carthaigh, a member of the ruling dynasty of Munster. His kinsman, Cormac Mac Carthaigh, King of Munster, was responsible for commissioning Cormac's Chapel, the stunning Romanesque chapel at Cashel, built in the 1120s and 30s. These were powerful men; connected across borders by ties of family and the exchange of ideas, personnel, books, patronage and prayers.

One of the things that caused me to shift from thinking about real people like Marianus and Christian in real places like Regensburg, was something that was written by one of those Irishmen in Germany, a monk named Marcus. He wrote in Latin because his audience was not (only) Irish, but was also a nearby community of German-speaking nuns. Latin, as an international language, was accessible to both Irish author and German audience, and eventually Marcus's work would be copied in innumerable manuscripts and translated into many languages, and read for centuries afterwards.

In the year 1148, Marcus wrote a fictional account of an Irishman named Tnugdal, who apparently travelled to heaven and hell while in a coma that lasted for three days. Tnugdal is a hard-partying, godless soldier, and is in Cork trying to retrieve a debt when he slips into unconsciousness and his soul departs from his body. An angel takes him on one of these guided tours of heaven and hell. And when they get to the layer of hell that is reserved for the avaricious, you'll never guess who he bumps into there: our old friend Fergus, Derdriu's failed protector. Fergus and his fellow Ulster warrior and exile, Conall, are propping open the jaws of a torturing beast for all eternity. So this was his punishment for having sold his honour for beer. The angel says to Tnugdal that Fergus wasn't all that bad: he lived by the standards of his time. But the standards of his time centred on greed and the relentless acquisition of wealth at the expense of others, and so he is excluded from salvation and sentenced to this unending fate. The torments that the angel shows to Tnugdal are pretty damn nasty. In the level of hell reserved for murderers, souls are fried in a giant cosmic frying pan, until they melt through a grate, 'like wax melts through cloth', and then the souls are reconstituted on the coals below and they're fried again. And again. And again. Forever.

Whenever I was reading medieval visions of hell, I would always skip through to find out what the punishment was for fornicators – thinking it would be good to know what I might be in for, if this Christianity stuff turned out to be true. In the 'Vision of Tnugdal', the fornicators are impregnated by a horrific beast. As the demonic foetuses grow within them they sting the sinners' innards so that they writhe with pain throughout their gestation. Then, when the time comes, men and women give birth to serpents: and they don't just give birth to them through their vagina – the beasts burst forth through the chests and limbs of the fornicators. The beasts they give birth to have iron heads with sharp beaks and they turn on the sinners who have just given birth to them and eviscerate their bodies. These beasts have hooks in their tails which make them unable to fully exit the body of their parent but they keep on attacking them with those iron beaks until they consume the sinners' bodies down to the nerves and bones. (This is just for regular fornicators: there are worse punishments involving genital serpents for monks and priests who broke their vows of celibacy, but that doesn't concern me.) The angel tells Tnugdal that he can expect to face this punishment when he dies, because he too has enjoyed sexual relations without moderation. I once explained all this in great detail to a married man that I was sleeping with, while I sat astride him, half naked: we engaged in our wicked fornication anyway, and it was great.

When Tnugdal finally gets to heaven, having been through all the sections of hell reserved for the thieves and the traitors and the repeat offenders, it turns out to be a Who's Who of Irish sanctity and hypocrisy. Cormac Mac Carthaigh, King of Munster, is there, in near-paradise. Although he was a bit of a fornicator himself, and had also ordered a murder while he was alive, Cormac is only punished for three hours per day and his punishment consists simply of wearing a hair shirt and sitting in fire up to his belly. What happened to the fried and melted souls? What happened to the hell-spawn beasts devouring the bodies that were forced to birth them? Cormac gets a reprieve for the other twenty-one hours a day, sitting on a throne, finely dressed, surrounded by riches, being offered gifts by crowds of visitors. Why? Because, of course, he had money to throw around when he was alive: building Cormac's Chapel, giving alms to the poor, welcoming pilgrims. I imagine those obscenely rich American mega-pastors plan on buying their place in heaven just like Cormac.

As he ascends to the highest ranks of heaven, Tnugdal encounters St Patrick, St Malachy of Armagh: this is an Irish heaven for Irish people, so I don't really know who would turn up in an American mega-pastor's heaven – Billy Graham, maybe. The angel tells Tnugdal that heaven is reserved for those who guard their bodies from the touch of carnal knowledge, and he sends Tnugdal back to his body to live a reformed and chastened life. I'll take my chances with the iron-beaked serpents and the sieved souls of the sinners.

After reading the 'Vision of Tnugdal' I never really went back to those Irish Benedictines who made their careers in Regensburg, and who founded related monasteries in

Nuremburg and Vienna and Konstanz and elsewhere. Instead, I dove into the journeys that non-existent people took to non-existent places. Imagined afterlives, imagined geographies, imagined punishments for real-life sins.

When I returned from my otherworldly journey to Los Angeles, where time and reality had been suspended in favour of hotel rooms and burritos, where it was possible to ignore the ever-increasing news reports of a spreading contagion, I gave two lectures to my students about the *Navigatio Sancti Brendani* ('The Voyage of St Brendan'), one of the most famous texts to emerge from medieval Ireland. Just like the 'Vision of Tnugdal', it was originally written in Latin and it was later translated into many of the vernacular languages of Europe, including Norman French and Middle Dutch. It survives in hundreds of copies in hundreds of manuscripts from all over Europe: a medieval bestseller. The Latin composition gave it an international reach that a text in Irish could not have hoped to achieve.

We're not entirely sure exactly when the author of the *Navigatio* wrote the tale, since – as with most medieval texts – we have no surviving authorial version, only later copies, but it seems most likely that it was sometime in the ninth century. In a conscious echoing of the story of Moses, Brendan goes off with some of his followers in search of a 'promised land', but rather than crossing a desert they must traverse an ocean. Giving themselves up to the will of God, they encounter strange creatures and great marvels, what the author calls 'varied secrets in the vast ocean'. But they never get to the promised land. They get so close – it's just there, right ahead of them – but they're told to turn back. They're told that God won't let them find the promised land straight away, because they needed to experience the journey itself, and now that they're on the verge of arriving, they need to go home so that Brendan can tell everyone what has happened and what he's seen. It's like a motivational poster: it's not the destination, it's the journey.

People get hung up on whether Brendan was real, whether he went on a journey, whether the walls of crystal that he encounters are really icebergs, whether he reached America. Whatever. I don't care. I'm more impressed by what the author of the *Navigatio* achieved: a literary masterpiece, full of allusions to the liturgical year, to the Bible, to religious life, to other voyages. And it was read by people who would themselves become travellers, heading off to the slightly less fantastical lands of England or France or wherever, to study or preach or teach or establish a monastery. Marcus, who wrote the 'Vision of Tnugdal', was writing after he had been on his own real journey from the south of Ireland to the south of Germany. So, there were vertical imagined journeys – down to hell and up to heaven – and there were horizontal journeys, both real and imagined, across oceans and lands and strange landscapes.

There was movement in the Middle Ages. Lots of it. But there is also stillness, as we shall come to see when we are stilled ourselves. The Covid-19 outbreak became an epidemic, which became a pandemic, and the world began to shudder and draw to a standstill in an effort to stop the disease's spread.

When my university locked down in March, I caught the first flight I could to the UK, which would lock down a week later. My ex-husband's partner was pregnant and potentially vulnerable if exposed to the virus, so I collected my daughter from her father's house and took her to my stepmother's, where we three – grandmother, mother, daughter – would observe a world grow still and delicate, its cracks exposed for all to see.

APRIL

Lockdown

One of the main objections to travel in the Middle Ages was that it led to sin. Even pilgrims, on their way to venerate holy shrines, would take the opportunity to have casual sex or indulge in drunkenness or partake of whatever fun was on offer on the road. It was often better, spiritually speaking, for people to stay at home. So it is in 2020: I discover very early on in lockdown that my stepmum's internet service has a porn blocker, and silently I curse my brothers, who are undoubtedly the ultimate cause of my enforced embrace of moral purity.

Those who espoused the view that staying put was best prized something called *stabilitas*. *Stabilitas* is the Latin word from which we get English 'stability', and it means a kind of immovability, a steadiness. What the anti-travel lobby in medieval Ireland really wanted was for monks to stay in their monasteries and not go gallivanting around being undisciplined. *Stabilitas* in the Middle Ages was about being subject to the authority of an abbot (for monks) or a bishop (for priests), subject to moral guidance, subject to rules. For those who travel, there are no rules and morality is, temporarily, suspended.

This month, almost every country in the world was implementing its own rules to keep its citizens still, under the authority of governments and public health officials. We were seeking *stabilitas* in the face of a still largely unknown disease as it swept across Europe and the Americas. Some people embraced the stillness as an opportunity for moral renewal, whereas others turned inwards to quiet self-destruction. Yet others saw themselves as above the law, the rules applying only to mere rank-and-file monks, so to speak, not to powerful spiritual advisers such as themselves.

One medieval Irish poem about the disadvantages of travel which every student of Old Irish learns is *Teicht do Róim*.

> Going to Rome:
> Great effort; small reward.
> You will not find the King you seek there
> Unless you carry him with you.

In other words, if you go on pilgrimage to the Eternal City you won't find Christ unless He was already in your heart when you set off. Contrary to the idea of the journey as a literal road to redemption, rather the journey merely confirms who you are; travel doesn't change you, because you always take yourself with you. You are your own constant companion, at home or abroad, and if you're a dickhead when you set off, you'll still be a dickhead when you get there.

In the tenth century, some Irish writers developed a whole genre of educational anecdotes about the moral hazards of travel. In one such tale, an Irish bishop heads off on pilgrimage to Rome. Once he gets there, he decides that, rather than returning to his episcopal duties in Ireland, he'll head on towards Jerusalem. On the way, he comes across a king who is looking for a spiritual adviser and confessor. The king invites the bishop to stay with him, builds a church for him, and goes to him for confession. The problem, the author tells us, is that the queen also starts to go to the bishop for confession. Very regularly. And while the king is away at one of his other royal residences the bishop and the queen start having an affair, which continues for some time. The king eventually hears about this and returns to his palace with soldiers, who surround the royal residence, where the queen and the bishop are in bed together. The bishop decides that this would be a good moment for some divine intervention, so he begins to pray and to perform genuflections. Although the physical exertion of shagging the queen doesn't seem to have bothered him, the physical exertion of prayer is a step too far, and he passes out. Luckily, God – who, we are told, always looks out for His own – steps in and angels miracu-lously transport the bishop to his church.

The unfortunate king thinks he has falsely accused both the bishop and his own wife. He pays compensation to his wife for slander, betraying the fact that, although the author may be setting the action somewhere in Eastern Europe, his mind is thinking in terms of early Irish law and the require-ment under that legal system to pay compensation for spreading false rumours about a woman's moral virtue. The king also abases himself before the sneaky bishop, who makes his escape and heads on towards Jerusalem. The story is comedic: the unfaithful wife and immoral bishop get away with everything and the cuckolded king is the one who (lit-erally) pays the price. The moral lesson of the tale is one aimed at kings – don't trust foreign bishops who turn up out of the blue on their way to who-knows-where – but it is part of a wider genre which outlines the opportunities for sin that await the traveller, the wanderer, the pilgrim.

I had lived a life of relentless travel over the past few years, so at first I was one of those people who thought that lockdown could change me for the better. I would drink less, exercise more, eat healthily, follow some modern version of a monastic rule – a diet, maybe, or a fitness regimen. I slept more regular hours, mostly, except at weekends when I would sit up until 3 a.m. getting hammered while watching Netflix. That's how I differentiated between weekdays and weekends: more booze and less sleep on Saturdays and Sundays.

I was disciplined Mondays to Fridays: I set my alarm for 7 a.m., got my daughter out of bed by 8 a.m., so that she could start her school lessons by 9 a.m. We worked quietly until about 3 p.m. and then she could do whatever she wanted after that. I would keep on going until my lectures were up online and students' anxious emails were answered. Psychologically, I didn't feel too bad, and the stillness helped me to process my grief for my father. At first, anyway.

Like a lot of medieval literature, the Old English maxims use journeys as a metaphor for interior, spiritual development.

> This world of hard days will make you weary, like a
> boatman
> who strains to row against the wind; yet you must
> keep on so that all will know you are a man of spirit.
> Be true of heart, be steady, never cease to be ready!

Our world has no haven. Ever since the blood of Abel
soaked into the dirt of the first farmland where Cain struck
   him down
there has been hatred, envy, greed afoot in this world.
That is where you must live, among thieves and killers . . .

We were living among a killer that was not human. The news carried images of overflowing intensive care units; doctors, nurses and hospital staff who were living in a world of hard days, straining to row against the wind; transport workers, supermarket staff, emergency services, true of heart. And we ourselves were still. A walk in the afternoon, perhaps – away from people, into the woods or the fields. One weekly trip to the supermarket, the shelves denuded of eggs, flour, yeast, pasta, rice and toilet roll.

My youngest brother's household joined ours: him, his girlfriend, and his two sons for whom he has shared custody with their mother. Their mother has a partner who has three children from a previous relationship, so sometimes my nephews are in a five-children household, and sometimes it's just the two of them. My brother lives in a tiny one-bedroom converted garage. For half the week it's just him and his girlfriend; for the other half, my nephews are there too – the boys have the bedroom and my brother sleeps in the little living/dining/kitchen room. For the purposes of lockdown, we counted them as part of our household, so that they could have access to the garden. Technically this was true, I think, because the garage doesn't have a separate address and our family home, a three-bedroom bungalow, is where he is listed as living.

For half of the week, then, we were three: me, daughter, stepmum. For the other half, we were seven. I'm not really sure how modern families were supposed to contain themselves within their bubbles with any degree of success: my two nephews would head home to be with their three stepsiblings who had themselves spent half the week with their biological mother . . . the webs of connections and contact were large and uncontrollable. But that's how blended families are, and since neither I nor my siblings are particularly good at staying in relationships, we all live in blended families of one sort or another. My nephews' mother and her partner are frontline workers; we did our best to limit all other contacts in order to contain the risk as best we could.

I put a cushion down on the living-room floor and sit cross-legged upon it, my laptop perched on the coffee table, and I begin to turn my lectures – usually witty, charismatic, compelling displays of knowledge and erudition: honest – into dull, annotated PowerPoint displays, point-by-point worksheets, online instructions. Not all of my students have broadband access; one is sharing a computer with his parents who are both now working from home on that computer; another is sharing a computer with her siblings. The library is initially closed and inaccessible to students, so I begin scrounging PDFs of articles and book chapters to share with them.

I simultaneously attempt to home-school my daughter, whose maths exercises defeat me. I can't remember Pythagoras' theorem and I can't remember how to calculate the area of an irregular shape. I can't help. I can't help.

I try to help my students instead: I shift their deadlines as late as I possibly can; I meet one small class synchronously on Microsoft Teams; another, bigger group gets a bunch of slides and my disembodied voice.

One Old English poet suggested that we should 'leave behind isolation, self-born suffering'. But, far from leaving it behind, some of the most religious people in medieval Europe willingly sought out isolation, whether by retreating to isolated places to spend time in prayer or by literally walling themselves into cells. A person who had themselves walled in was called an *inclusus* – one who is confined or enclosed – a form of anchorite. Ironically, one of the best-travelled Irishmen of the Middle Ages was also someone who spent a very long time as an *inclusus*. His name was Máel Brigte, although he also used the Latin name Marianus Scotus. (We have already come across another Marianus Scotus, who travelled to Regensburg, but this is a different person, although they were contemporaries.) Máel Brigte was educated in Ireland and became a monk there, but he travelled in the 1050s to Cologne, and then Fulda, and then Mainz. Fulda was a monastery that had been founded in the early eighth century by a guy named Sturm, who was a disciple of St Boniface, another missionary of the sort I told you about in March. Born in England, in what is now Devon, Boniface ended up being killed by a gang of armed robbers while attempting to convert the people of Frisia to Christianity. The thieves were reported to be disappointed to discover that his bags contained not gold and silver, but books. His body was buried at Fulda, where he was venerated. Three hundred years after that, an Irishman, Máel Brigte, would arrive in Fulda and choose to be walled into a cell, where he remained for perhaps as long as ten years.

Máel Brigte, like many medieval writers, liked language and word play and ciphers. He wrote a Latin chronicle of world history – though his body was trapped and still, his mind wandered widely – and came up with this puzzle for his chronicle.

> Multum ob excerptos legimus barbaricos
> reges iustificandos gestaque turbida egenos:
> <u>collige litterarum anteriorem: uoluito summam:</u>
> <u>existat numeratus auctor</u>: intra require –
> rectus omnes me tulit in nouem ordinem laudis.

The middle lines contain a set of instructions to the reader. They say 'gather the opening letters, roll up the whole: when enumerated, the author stands out'. So, let's do as he tells us. Let's gather the opening letters of each word of the poem: m o e l b r i g t e c l a u s e n a i r r o m t i n o l. Roll them up into a whole: *Móel Brigte clausenáir rom-tinól.* Voilà! That cunning little fox left a message for us in Irish, embedded in his Latin verse. Transmitted to us across the centuries, it says: 'Máel* Brigte, the enclosed one, compiled me.' The author stands out, and he is an Irishman who travelled to Germany, only to be walled into a cell for a decade

---

* That the puzzle spells out 'Móel' rather than 'Máel' is not a medieval typo: orthography wasn't stable in the Middle Ages so Móel and Máel were interchangeable. Máel is the standardized spelling we use today.

to think and pray and encode his native language, Irish, into his acquired, international language, Latin, in a poem in the chronicle that he wrote to tell the story of the entirety of history as he understood it. You can think big thoughts without leaving the room.

I had been angry at myself for failing to finish the book I had been writing before my dad died. I wanted him to see it. I wanted him to hold it in his hands, leafing through it gently, as though it were a holy object, even as strands of his tobacco tumbled on to the pages. This is what he had done with my other books, and my heart had glowed with pride. But my over-scheduled life, my constant activity, my travelling back and forth, back and forth, back and forth, had left little space for writing. Years had passed, the book remained unfinished and now it was too late.

Suddenly, though, I have *stabilitas*. My stepmum's house feels like a refuge, a place that is safe from the pandemic raging outside. So I begin to write. I read a book by Joli Jensen called *Write No Matter What* and I begin to follow her advice. Write. No matter what. One by one, I complete those chapters that had lain unfinished for a year or two or three. The time that I would have spent commuting to work or travelling to see my daughter, I spend polishing the prose, checking my translations, using whatever resources I can find online to fill in the last of the blanks. There is no secret message encoded in it, other than *I hope you would have been proud of me, Dad. I'm sorry I didn't finish it sooner. I'm sorry I didn't write no matter what.*

*

I write a letter to my students and post it on the crappy blog that I only ever intermittently remember to update. The letter says:

First of all, I miss you: those of you who never skip a lecture, those of you who always have a question, those of you who sit, silently, absorbing everything; those of you who seem to sleep through every class (do you have a long commute? Or an evening job? Or a Netflix addiction?); those of you who miss half of the lectures and then still write a great essay; those of you who invent an illness to excuse your absence (and I nod sympathetically, even though your classmates already told me that you were in Coppers until 3 a.m. the night before, because I too invented illnesses to excuse my hangover when I was nineteen, and that is part of life). I miss you all, and hearing your distant, overlapping voices on MS Teams, or the ping of a message incoming on Moodle, really isn't the same.

I have been thinking a lot about the pandemics that we have studied together. Last semester, for example, when we read the accounts of the plague which raged through England, Wales and Ireland in 664. We saw how contemporary commentators believed it to be an act of God, how it was linked in their minds with the solar eclipse of the same year – the *Annals of Ulster*, for example, hinting in its unassuming, laconic manner, that the eclipse in May was a portent of the pandemic that would arrive in Ireland in August. We read the account of the Northumbrian monk-scholar Bede, who likewise wrote: 'In the year of our Lord

664 there was an eclipse of the sun on 3 May about 4 o'clock in the afternoon. In the same year a sudden pestilence first depopulated the southern parts of Britain and afterwards attacked the kingdom of Northumbria, raging far and wide with cruel devastation and laying low a vast number of people [. . .] The plague did equal destruction in Ireland.'

We read how Adomnán of Iona used the fact that Scotland was seemingly spared the pandemic to argue that this was because of its people's devotion to St Columba. Columba's power alone had protected the Gaelic and Pictish communities of Scotland from the devastating loss of life which afflicted its neighbours to the south and west.

Studying the plague of 664 as an exercise in comparing differing accounts of the same event, and as an attempt to inhabit the minds of seventh-century observers, has a new immediacy, and I wonder whether you call any of this to mind when you see a DUP councillor linking the Covid-19 pandemic to Northern Ireland's abortion legislation, or simply when you read different interpretations of the same grim statistics.

The pandemic that I have most thought about in recent weeks is that of 1095–6. It compounded disaster upon disaster: plague followed famine which followed poor harvests which followed an exceptionally harsh winter, in a similar way to how the current pandemic has heaped sickness upon the disasters, displacements and uncertainties caused by man-made climate change.

In 1096, different communities across Europe responded to the pestilence in different ways, with appeals to God, to saints, to past kings, and to the distractions of 'holy war'. The Church in Ireland attempted to impose a national response involving regular penance, fasting and donations to the Church – did the latter of these line the coffers of already well-fed bishops? Or were they redistributed to feed the starving poor, to help communities already battered by poor harvests and extreme weather? We don't know. But when I see individuals raising money to fund state services, or homeless people in socially distanced queues for soup kitchens, I wonder how far we really are from those earlier responses to disaster.

I don't know when this will end. I hope we will meet again in person, so that we can continue our dialogue, our exploration of the past, our investigation of human experience. But in the meantime, I hope that you are putting your education to good use, treating newspaper reports and press conferences and internet conspiracies with the same careful and methodical approach that you study historical sources. I hope that your decision to study medieval Ireland is giving you some depth of perspective, which connects you to humanity in its broadest sense, and gives you empathy, and horizons which extend far beyond Ireland. I hope that you are safe, I hope that you are well, I hope that you remain so. I miss you.

Somehow, this letter comes to the attention of a publisher and she contacts me to ask if I would be interested in writing something longer, a book-length work that intermingles the personal, the modern and the medieval. The idea for this book starts to take shape in my mind. I begin to think about which parts of my own story I could tell and which parts would be too painful, too damaging for others. I ask my stepmum and two of my brothers whether they would be OK with me writing about them, about Dad. They give me their blessing and I open a fresh notebook, lined, with a soft binding of bright yellow.

I grew up in a male-dominated household, by sheer force of numbers of brothers. For half of each week during lock-down, though, we have become a house of women – my stepmum, my daughter and me. We call ourselves the 'lock-down ladies' and take it in turns to pick the films and TV shows that we watch together. We eat together: my stepmum cooks, I clean up afterwards, my daughter is into baking and keeps us supplied with cakes and biscuits.

We know very little about women's inner lives in medi-eval Ireland, but the archaeological evidence shows that their outer lives revolved around food preparation, domestic labour and textile work. As we saw with the poem *Ísucán*, women could be highly educated if they entered nunneries, but most women were fated for a life of pots and pans rather than ink and vellum. We know of Englishwomen who had impressive international careers, such as Leofgyth, who travelled to Germany under the protection and mentorship of Boniface to become abbess of Tauberbischofsheim, but most women spent their early life in the house of their father, and their adult life in the house of their husband.

When St Patrick was working as a missionary in Ireland,

probably sometime in the middle of the fifth century, he claimed that women in particular were flocking to Christianity. He said that their fathers were unhappy about this, and it seems likely that religious life – for all its surrendering of autonomy to live under rules and regulations governing behaviour – did, in fact, offer women a choice that they hadn't previously had. The choice not to marry. The choice not to have children. That decision to live as perpetual virgins for Christ was, at least, their own decision, in a way that their marriages would not have been, since fathers arranged marriages for their daughters in negotiation with the family of the prospective husband. If a man's daughter chose to enter religious life, he would indeed be unhappy, as he would have lost an important resource, useful for consolidating alliances as well as perpetuating a lineage.

According to St Patrick's own testimony, it was not only women to whom Christianity appealed in disproportionate numbers, but also enslaved people both male and female. An offer of salvation for everyone, from a religion that claimed that it was easier to pass a rope through the eye of a needle than for a rich man to gain entrance to heaven, must have been revolutionary, and a source of solace for those who were oppressed in life. Maybe there was even a moment when all sorts of radical opportunities for real social change were there for the taking, but if so they must soon have vanished because Ireland emerges into the well-attested historical record of the seventh century as a fiercely hierarchical and unequal place, with wealth still accumulated from the labour of the unfree.

A fairly wealthy household in early medieval Ireland would have comprised the nuclear family – husband, wife, children – but would have also been bustling with other people of a variety of social statuses: there may have been enslaved people providing domestic labour; there may have been children or adolescents in fosterage, being prepared for adult life. Hospitality may have been offered to passing travellers, and at certain times of the year there may have been gatherings of extended family. (In April we had no visitors; there was no hospitality given.)

The structures of the houses in Ireland, at least before the year 800, were circular. (From the ninth century onwards we start to see the fashion for rectangular houses, perhaps influenced by the architecture of the new Scandinavian settlers, perhaps by the design of churches.) If you outgrew your house and wanted to build an extension, rather than converting a garage into a little one-bedroom residence, you would add on another circular structure to make a kind of figure-of-eight-shaped house. These circular houses were enclosed by ditches and are still visible in the landscape all over Ireland. Sometimes, over the centuries, these raised circles in the land have been invested with a spiritual significance that they don't possess – they were just homes, like yours or mine.

When I was very little, no more than three or four years old, I had already moved house so often, amidst so many permutations of my shifting family unit, that I told my stepmother that I didn't know where my home was. She told me that my home would always be wherever my teddy bear was.

Now, this bear might, to the casual observer, look a lot like Sooty, the mute yellow puppet whose various shows were broadcast on children's television for most of the second half of the twentieth century. Indeed, if you asked the manufacturers of this bear, which I have had all my life, about his identity, they too might have claimed that he was Sooty. But I know better. To me, he was and still is 'Poodle' (don't ask). So, from that day forward, my home was wherever Poodle was. Today, Poodle lives in my bedroom in Dublin. He has a hole in his arse from when one of my brothers anally raped him with a pencil. His head has been sewn back on twice, badly, and stuffing sometimes falls out of his neck. But he is home.

I miss Dublin, locked down as I am in the English countryside, but there is something about Suffolk, its familiar flatness, that feels reassuring. I'm hardly the first Irish person to spend time in East Anglia. Fursa, a seventh-century Irish monk, ended up less than forty miles from where I am, at one of two Roman forts, Caister and Burgh Castle, which sit either side of the River Yare, defending the flat lands of the Waveney Estuary. In the 630s, according to Bede, who I wrote about in my letter to my students, the King of the East Angles, whose name was Sigeberht, had given the land inside one of these forts to Fursa when he arrived from Ireland and permitted him to found a monastery there.

Fursa had, like me, first arrived in East Anglia with two brothers. Fursa, like me, saw visions. When I was nine years old, distraught and hysterical with grief, after something had happened to me that I cannot tell you about, the Virgin Mary appeared before me. She looked, of course, exactly like the statue in the local Catholic church: pale-skinned, clad in white and blue, rosebud lips and sorrowful eyes. But she was huge, hovering slightly above me, with light radiating all around her. She put out her hand and touched my head and said, 'Everything will be OK.' To a nine-year-old Catholic girl, this was the stuff of miracles. The Blessed Virgin herself had visited me to reassure me; and I felt reassured. I became incredibly pious, I began reading the Bible, I served as an altar girl, I prayed (oh God, I prayed) throughout my teen-age years. About a decade later, when I went off to university and began to read about neuroscience, and the things a brain can do in moments of acute trauma, I realized what had really happened. Mary hadn't protected me, I had protected myself.

What Fursa saw was heaven and hell. In hell, he said, there were four fires: the fires of falsehood, covetousness, discord and iniquity. A demon recalled that Fursa had once accepted an unclean offering – gifts from a sinner – and threw Fursa towards the flames, but an angel countered that Fursa had accepted these gifts not through greed but through a genuine desire to save the sinner's soul, and pulled him out of the fire. A moment too late, it would seem, since we are told that, when Fursa was restored to life, he had severe burns on his shoulder and jaw, and for the rest of his life 'his flesh outwardly showed what his soul had inwardly suffered'.

Bede reports that an elderly brother in his own commu-nity had heard from someone (the medieval equivalent of 'a friend of a friend') who had seen Fursa himself recall his experiences that, even in the coldest winter, Fursa would break out in a sweat when telling people what had happened to him. Whatever happened to Fursa to scar him, to cause those sweaty flashbacks, we will never know. But perhaps his brain protected him from something by letting him see a vision of angels and demons, battling over his soul. Perhaps that experience, whatever it was, was a greater motivation for him to leave Ireland than the desire to preach among barbarians. Either way, he and his two brothers made it to the territory of the East Angles and set up their monastery, 'pleasantly situated in the woods, with the sea not far off', where he could 'with more freedom indulge his heavenly studies'. But East Anglia went through a period of political turmoil in the early 640s, and so Fursa headed on towards France, leaving one of his brothers in charge of the English foundation. Fursa established a new monastery at Lagny, now a suburb of Paris, and died in Péronne, the town in the Somme valley of which he is still the patron saint.

But I am back to talking about travellers and we're supposed to be staying at home.

That's the thing about staying still – thoughts are always on the move. Medieval monastic thinkers spent a lot of energy trying to deal with wayward minds. There's no point in your body embracing *stabilitas* if your brain is stuck in the pub or the brothel. One English poet put it in terms that feel familiar to me.

> . . . No man knows
>
> none of the warriors under heaven, how my mind becomes
> > weak,
> busy in the pursuit of books. Sometimes a burning rises
> > in me,
> surges oppressively near my heart.

This is it. One moment I am concentrating on what I am reading – focused, still, present – and the next it turns out that I have been day-dreaming for the past fifteen minutes about what I'm going to eat for dinner, the bottles of wine in the kitchen, what I would like to do with the hot guy I fancy, and a burning rises in me – hunger, cravings, lust – and my mind is weak. Even now, walled in as I am, my body prevented from straying, my mind is undisciplined. I am reminded of the Sinful Greek Girl.

A tenth-century Irish story tells of the daughter of the King of Greece. Like Derdriu, she is brought up isolated from civil society, 'in a house apart', attended only by a maidservant, but she is educated in 'learning and wisdom and art', perhaps a dangerous thing for a young woman. She begins having an affair with a good-looking young man who is part of the king's household. One day, the king knocks on her door when she is in bed with this young man, so she quickly hides him under a quilt. Unfortunately for the young man, the king decides to sit on the quilt while he talks with his daughter and by the time he gets up to leave, the young man has suffocated to death. A herdsman happens to pass by, and the girl asks him to take away a bundle – the body of the young man, wrapped in the quilt – and throw it over the cliff. However, when the herdsman gets to the edge of the cliff, the girl pushes him in the back so that both he and the corpse tumble 'into the abyss'.

The Sinful Greek Girl's crime spree has just begun. She had been betrothed at birth to the son of a nobleman, and the time has come for her to marry him. However, she doesn't want him to know that she isn't a virgin, so she asks the maidservant to go in her place to sleep with him. The maid agrees but after the sex has taken place she refuses to swap places with the princess, declaring that everyone should see that she, in fact, is the one who has slept with the nobleman and thus has the right to be recognized as his wife. This enrages the Sinful Greek Girl, who sets fire to the bed-room in which the maidservant and the young man are sleeping. When the maid runs to the water barrel to fetch water to quench the fire, the Greek Girl pushes her head under the water and drowns her. And then the Sinful Greek Girl goes away with her new husband.

The Greek Girl is guilty of lust, deceit, arson and double murder. That's a litany of sin even worse than mine. But for reasons that are never made clear she seems to undergo a total spiritual conversion and repents of her past actions. After the death of her father, she goes to the new king in search of atonement. The new king turns her into an *inclusus*. He builds an oak house for her at a crossroads, a building with small windows but no door, and he walls her in. Pious locals bring scraps of food to her, while she is locked into this cell for seven years.

Seven years to remember her past self, to think about what she has done, to pray, repent, seek absolution. How far did her mind wander while her body lay still? How far did she travel on her spiritual path and how often did straying thoughts bring her back to her lustful, violent youth?

At the end of her sentence, she is reformed and forgiven. She asks the king to build a church and hermitage for her. This place becomes, we are told, 'the Greeks' greatest city of refuge'. The Girl lives a long and holy life and, after she dies and goes to heaven, miracles occur because of her. She must not have thought too often about the body of the young, handsome lad who suffocated in her bed.

The flightiness of thought, its tendency to leap in a moment from intellectual things to worldly temptations, is a daily problem. For me as for medieval monks. My good intentions for lockdown quickly crumble. The drinking days start to outnumber the non-drinking days. Bedtime gets later, exercise less frequent.

There is an Irish poem, probably composed in the tenth century, which begins *Is mebul dom imrádud* – 'I am ashamed of my thoughts'. The poet says that he feels embarrassed by how his mind strays while he is supposed to be engaged in study or reciting the Psalms. Even contemplating God, his thoughts misbehave. He thinks of crowds of people, of the company of loose women. He knows that he should try to bind his thoughts, shackle them to prayer, but they slip from his grasp, unrestrained. He berates himself. Christ and His companions were constant, but the poet is not.

I understand how he feels. I marvel at my colleagues who

seem to be able to sit at their desks and focus. I click between email and online news, scroll down my social media feeds, return to my blank document, start thinking about tenth-century Ireland and end up looking at today's death toll, studying graphs with local infection statistics, watching distressing videos of grieving families and isolated individuals, thinking about the occupants of prisons, care homes and hospices, walled in, no way in or out, waiting for redemption. But I owe it to my students to prepare another online class for them. They have chosen to learn something from me. I click back to the Word document and begin to type.

MAY

Learning

The first time I ever took drugs – by which I mean proper drugs: alcohol, caffeine, nicotine and cannabis don't count, because they're just essential food groups – I was fourteen. I was visiting my biological mother, in a market town in the midlands of England, and one day I headed off to the squat that my older brother was living in with some other addicts in the same town. We dined on speed, washed down with cans of Kestrel Super, and started listening to 'Bela Lugosi's Dead' by Bauhaus. We listened to it again: there was something really interesting about it which we had never noticed all the previous times we had heard it, so we listened to it again. And again. And again. Somehow six hours passed and, while we were engrossed in the insistent tapping of the song's artificial drum sound, someone stole the door of the squat. Nobody noticed until the next morning.

Within a year or two, my brother was in prison. He was there for a long time on remand while his case was referred from the magistrates' court to the crown court, and after he was found guilty he remained in prison for many more months while psychiatric reports were prepared. He would send strange, rambling letters to me, written on thin, blue prison writing paper. Streams of consciousness populated with song lyrics and book titles and the occult inanities of Aleister Crowley. Eventually, he was sentenced to be detained in a secure psychiatric facility for an indeterminate length of time – he could only be released when the Home Secretary deemed him no longer to be a threat to the public.

My father had attended the sentencing and, when he got home, he fell into my arms, crying. I had never seen him cry before, and while he sobbed, I determined that I would do something in my life to make him feel proud of me. Right in that moment, it hit me: I would act as a counterweight to my brother, and would somehow – I didn't yet know how, but somehow – mitigate the shame and sadness he had caused my dad to feel.

An eleventh-century poem addresses a student named Máel Brigte who has reached the end of his church school education and has a major life choice ahead of him. Before our friend Máel Brigte went to Germany and had himself walled into a doorless cell for ten solitary years, he had been a student in Ireland. He may or may not be the Máel Brigte to whom the poem is addressed, as Máel Brigte was a common name in medieval Ireland. It was certainly written for someone *like* him, someone who was a scholar. His choices are: does he take orders and enter religious life; or does he choose to become a professional scholar who is 'half-lay', that is, living under a semi-religious rule but not having made a monastic profession; or does he return to lay life and pursue a professional career, such as law or medicine? The poet, who is clearly his teacher, asks him:

> What is your course of action,
> o soft-nailed, soft youth:
> since you have reached the pure bright prime of life,
> is it folly or wisdom that you go with?

The poet calls Máel Brigte his 'star pupil' and tells him that all of his erudition and learning will be useless if he is a 'person of evil habits'. Intellectual achievement is bound up with questions of moral purity. The best students should not drink and take drugs. The teacher-poet warns about the temptations of sexual immorality, the risks of hanging around with decadent 'half-lay' students, with their long hair and 'their gowns over their heels' – the hippies of the Middle Ages, clearly. He tells him that instead he should be 'chaste' and avoid 'evil, shameless women'. He claims that the benefits of pure scholarship are a thousand times greater than sex. (I would dispute this claim.) He argues that there is no value to knowing what's going on between a woman's thighs. (I would dispute that too.) But, like Polonius's advice to Laertes, there is some wisdom in amongst the moralizing. He warns:

> Do not side with uncertain falsehood;
> always side with truth;
> do not gain the reputation of being
> an angry and ill-tempered arguer.

Always side with truth. Always.

He advises never to interrupt someone who is less able than yourself – hear them out, because 'an arrogant scholar is never good'.

> Do not laugh at a weak scholar;
> do not engage in jeering;
> do not be false, avoid arrogance;
> do not be quick to give advice.

And in a timely sort of way, as our pandemic lockdowns continue into May, he adds: 'do not leave your house without good reason; do not be given to going about and visiting'. If our Máel Brigte was indeed the recipient of this poem, then I guess he both did and didn't observe that counsel, since he went all the way to Germany to get locked in a room.

I travelled from East Anglia to the University of Glasgow to study for an Arts degree. I wanted to move from the countryside to a city, and I wanted to get as far away as possible from home, so I picked Glasgow, a city that looked a long way away on the map. I arrived there a month after my eighteenth birthday, and over the course of four years I studied subjects that I didn't even know existed before I got there. I chose to learn Scottish Gaelic because a hot guy I met at the Freshers' Fair was doing it. He turned out to be a complete douchebag, but I fell deeply in love with Celtic Studies and never looked back. I took courses in Medieval History, Scottish History, and Classical Civilization. I read Aristotle and Plato and Herodotus. I took evening classes in Arabic. And in my third and fourth years I studied the medieval forms of Welsh and Irish – and that was it: I was hooked. There was so much to be done – texts preserved in manuscripts that had never been published or translated, sources that had never been read or discussed – and the opportunities for new discoveries were endless.

My father, who had initially been disappointed that I hadn't pursued an immigrant-dad-approved course like Law or Medicine, was proud of my outstanding exam results. My lecturers at Glasgow told me about postgraduate degrees and suggested that I should apply to do a master's degree at Cambridge. They told me about the national funding body that offered scholarships, and they helped me to apply for one. I wrote that application from a position of total naivety and ignorance, but somehow I was awarded the scholarship and was admitted to Corpus Christi College in the University of Cambridge.

My undergraduate years had been a transitional time in UK higher education. The year I began in Glasgow was the first year that undergraduates had to pay fees. Fortunately for me, I was exempted from paying fees because I came from a low-income background. Indeed, my Local Education Authority even awarded me a small grant because of my family's financial circumstances. But that was the last year that such grants were made – and I took out loans to complete the rest of my degree – and thereafter many students would have to take on burdens of enormous debt in order to study at all. (Of course, that had long been the case in countries like the United States.)

If I hadn't been exempt from fees, if I hadn't received that small assistance from the local council, I genuinely don't know whether I would have gone to university at all. And I wonder just how many talented and motivated young people now are deterred from accessing higher education through a very reasonable fear of beginning their adult life with unfathomable levels of personal debt. Now that the UK has left the European Union, it is Ireland that has the highest university fees in the EU. It all feels a step closer to the Middle Ages, when education was expensive and only those who could afford to pay the fees were able to attend school.

In Tallaght, for example, an important church site near Dublin, the initial payment required for admission into its ecclesiastical school during the ninth century was one dairy cow or its equivalent value. On top of that, the annual fees were 'a heifer and a pig and three sacks of malt and a sack of corn' plus a food and clothing allowance for the student. That's a lot, and relatively few people could have afforded it.

Cambridge, itself a medieval foundation, had many strange and arcane customs, retained from previous centuries. For me, who had lived in various rented apartments with an assortment of housemates in Glasgow over the previous years, it was disconcerting to move into college rooms with 'bedders' – cleaners who were literally paid to change the bed linen of grown adults. A lot of Cambridge life – formal dinners in halls with vaulted ceilings, idiosyncratic rituals and terminology, silver service and 'college servants' – felt alien and excruciating. I never did bring myself to attend my department's annual 'black tie dinner' or a college May Ball. It just wasn't me.

But the lectures were fascinating, the libraries were amazing, the opportunities endless: some of the most famous intellectuals in the world were either working there or visited to give guest lectures. Through other Irish scholars I got to meet Seamus Heaney and Ciaran Carson and Mary

McAleese. In my first year I attended a lecture given by the great Edward Said, whose most influential work, *Orientalism*, I had read a few years previously and which had blown my limited little world wide open. As I listened to Said speak, I marvelled that I was here – me! – sitting at his feet in a classroom, learning, and the scholarship I was in receipt of meant that the annual heifer and pig and sacks of malt and corn were being paid on my behalf. I could not have been there otherwise.

The vast majority of people I encountered at Cambridge came from relatively privileged backgrounds and I felt passionate about making sure that the opportunities it offered were available to a more diverse range of people. I founded an annual summer school in the Department of Anglo-Saxon, Norse and Celtic. These summer schools were aimed at students from non-privileged backgrounds – teenagers who had got good results at GCSE or equivalent, who were attending state schools that did not have a history of sending pupils to Oxford or Cambridge, and who would be the first in their family to go to university. They were funded by the Sutton Trust, a philanthropic organization that seeks to advance social mobility through education, and they gave the students the opportunity to spend a week at Cambridge, living in a college, attending lectures and classes, visiting libraries, to demystify Cambridge and show that it was a feasible option for them. Yes, it was an alien world, but one that could be reached. One year, of the ten students who attended the summer school, four went on to study at Cambridge. It made the effort worthwhile.

I went to inner-city schools – in London and elsewhere – to give lectures to school pupils who might not otherwise think of applying to elite universities like Oxford and Cambridge. Eton ran a summer school for state school pupils and I went along for a few years to do Q&A sessions with teenagers who were hoping to apply to Oxford or Cambridge.

An expensive private boarding school like Eton – exclusive, all-encompassing, and seeking to shape character as well as to educate – is a pretty good way of thinking about the ecclesiastical schools run by the monasteries in early medieval Ireland. The relationship between a teacher and student was comparable to that of fosterage. The teacher was not only responsible for the student's education but also for making sure that they were clothed and fed, being the guardian of their body as well as their mind.

Scholars have written about the ways in which violence was embedded in medieval pedagogy, how the threat and possibility of physical punishment runs through depictions of the early medieval classroom. One legal text explains that 'teaching without negligence and correction without excessive harshness' is what is required and, in return, the student is expected to be 'meek' and show deference to their teacher. The fact that early Irish legal texts had to stipulate that a teacher should correct his students 'without excessive harshness' implies the existence of teachers who were, in fact, excessively harsh. Corporal punishment was in all likelihood a feature of some, if not all, schools.

One time at Eton, I was invited into the Vice-Master's

rooms for lunch. Silver service, Gainsborough portraits on the walls, it was something else. It was so far from my entire experience and understanding of school education that I could hardly even fathom that children grew up in this environment, so utterly divorced from anything approaching normality. And yet it was reminiscent of those many references in medieval Irish sources to students having their own servants and attendants. The ties of wealth and privilege binding the centuries together.

It was a world away from my own secondary school years. Once or twice a month, as a teenager, I would travel up to the secure psychiatric unit to visit my brother. Lighters and anything sharp to be left at reception. Through one set of heavy doors. The soft click of the doors shutting behind you while you wait in the small intermediary space. Then the next set of doors release and you enter the secure wards. Patients, sluggish from anti-psychotic medications, became increasingly obese with every visit, listening to music through headphones in their own individual worlds.

The man who saw diseases coming in through the windows.

The young lad who thought he had fought in Vietnam.

The guy who had murdered his own mother.

The solitary Black man, who a few months later would suffocate to death, pinned in a restraining hold by four psychiatric nurses.

Cigarettes were the currency and blank cassettes were in high demand, for recording music from the radio, making mix-tapes. Sometimes other families were there to see their sons, their brothers, but some patients never had any visitors at all. After a few hours, out again through the heavy doors, the quiet click behind me, and through the next set of doors, into sunlight and freedom and the road home.

The week after I submitted my PhD in Cambridge, I began a job as a research assistant on a project in Corpus Christi College to digitize the hundreds of medieval manuscripts that were preserved in their library. Again, I was a fluke beneficiary of chronology: this period happened to coincide with the Labour government's generous Working Families Tax Credit scheme, since decimated, which at least covered a couple of days of nursery. I could only afford two days a week of childcare for my daughter, but even working part-time I probably learned more about medieval literature and culture during the eighteen months I spent on that project than at any other time.

This was a once-in-a-lifetime opportunity to have unlimited access to some of the most important documents surviving from medieval Europe. To my amazement, my job was to read, endlessly. I was being paid to do what I loved. I was trying to find and read all the modern scholarship that mentioned these manuscripts in order to compile annotated bibliographies that would help and guide researchers who were looking at the digitized images. Anything that mentioned the manuscript, its date, its origins, the scribes who had written it, its contents, its history.

Because I was working in the room where the manuscripts were housed, I could take any of them down from the wall where they were shelved, open the lid of the wooden box in which each one was kept, and lift out – say – a 1,200-year-old book. I devoured these medieval books: copies of the Psalms, works of medieval science and history-writing, illuminated books of the Gospels, legal texts and theological tracts. My favourite book was not any of the spectacular manuscripts, dripping in gold leaf and exquisite illustrations, not the Bury Bible or the Augustine Gospels. My favourite book went under the name of 'CCCC MS 199'.

CCCC MS 199 is a youngster compared to some of the manuscripts in that library: it is only 930 years old or thereabouts. It's less than 28cm tall and just 18cm wide. Palaeographers – that is, people who study old handwriting – describe the writing of the scribe as 'a beautiful round, somewhat flat-topped hand'. His handwriting is indeed beautiful, and it is punctuated by lovely decorated initials in what one might think of as a typically 'Celtic' style, all knot-work and animal heads in black, red and yellow. The text is a copy of a work on the Trinity by the North African theologian (and repentant sinner) Augustine of Hippo. A scribe called Ieuan ap Sulien created this copy in mid-Wales, near to Aberystwyth, in a place called Llanbadarn Fawr. Ieuan died in 1137 and probably copied the manuscript several decades earlier, around the year 1090. One of the things I love most about the manuscript is that combination of the local and the international: Augustine's text travelled via multiple intermediaries from North Africa across Europe to Wales, where it was copied in a characteristically local style: the handwriting, the colours, the decoration making this particular copy of a North African text a distinctive product of medieval Britain.

Relatively unusually for the scribe of a medieval manuscript, we know a lot about Ieuan ap Sulien. Unlike me, Ieuan came from a whole family of prominent literary scholars. His father, Sulien, and his brother, Rhigyfarch, both became Bishop of St David's. Another brother, Daniel, became Archdeacon of Powys. Sulien had spent ten years studying in Ireland before returning to Wales, where he personally educated his sons. Rhigyfarch wrote poetry and a biography of St David, and Ieuan, as we can see from CCCC MS 199, became a talented scribe. But Ieuan was also a poet, and he wrote some of his verses – in Welsh and Latin – in the margins of this manuscript. Unfortunately, in a reminder of how fragile and incomplete are our sources from the medieval world, when Corpus Christi College sent the manuscript to be rebound in the 1950s, the binders assumed these marginal Welsh scribblings were unimportant, they sliced them off and threw away parts of some of the earliest Welsh poetry to have survived to the modern era. A discarded voice.

Like Máel Brigte in his cell in Germany, or Sulien in training in Ireland, I spent ten years in Cambridge, as a postgraduate student, then a research assistant, then a postdoctoral fellow. Two things I learned: one, you start with the knife and fork that are furthest from the plate and work your way inwards; two, port is always passed to the left.

Oh, and a third thing: the intellectual quality of dinner conversation is no higher at a Cambridge high table than it is in a squat full of junkies or on a secure psychiatric ward. Seriously.

Anyway, Cambridge wasn't the place for me and by 2012, with my divorce finalized, it was time to move on, to see what I could learn in Ireland. I was awarded a Marie Curie Fellowship – an EU-funded research position – and I headed to University College Cork.

There is a very funny eleventh-century Irish story called the 'Vision of Mac Con Glinne'. The eponymous hero, Mac Con Glinne, is studying at an ecclesiastical school in the midlands of Ireland when he decides that the life of a scholar is too hard. He figures it'll be easier to be a court poet, and he heads south to Munster – because he's heard that they have better dairy products there – and his first stop is the monastery at Cork. The monks of Cork, however, offer Mac Con Glinne truly terrible hospitality. I won't comment on that other than to say that the only time I have ever had really bad food poisoning was after eating at a restaurant in Cork.

Things spiral out of control with Mac Con Glinne and he ends up in a situation where the abbot of the monastery is trying to have him executed on very spurious grounds. Mac Con Glinne may be lazy, but he's quick-thinking, and he manages to gain a stay of execution. He claims to have had a vision. An angel appeared before him and showed him something marvellous. Now, the author of this story is extremely clever and he toys with his audience in a postmodern sort of way. Indeed, we never quite know whether Mac Con Glinne really saw anything at all. But one thing is for sure, Mac Con

Glinne manipulates his reports of his vision, recounting a radically different story every time he tells another audience what he claims he saw.

I really like Mac Con Glinne. Mac Con Glinne is presented as being as clever as his author – not studious, or dedicated, or devout (in fact he's extremely irreverent), but clever in a 'getting out of sticky situations' sort of way. He's not only a survivor, but he thrives, and by the end of the story his cunning and guile have led him to wealth and success and a position of influence, making more powerful people look very silly along the way.

If we lived in a more equitable society, it would not require extraordinary levels of quick-thinking, life-saving ingenuity to succeed. It would be a possibility for everyone. This month, students in England, Wales and Northern Ireland should begin their GCSE and A Level exams, but the pandemic lockdown has led to all exams being cancelled. Later in the summer, outrage will erupt when results are calculated based on algorithms that have classism written into them – the previous overall performance of a school being one of the factors used to come up with the GCSE and A Level results of individual students. Now, I went to a comprehensive school that was placed in 'special measures' while I was there. It was deemed to be failing to provide an acceptable standard of education, and a new headmaster was brought in to try to turn things around. If my A Level results had been calculated on the basis of my school's previous performance, they would have been markedly lower than the results I actually achieved.

Few students from my school went on to university. Attainment levels were low, while multigenerational unemployment was high. But I liked learning, I had a couple of really good teachers in History and English, I worked hard, and I did pretty well in my exams. Such is the case for many students from low-income backgrounds at so-called 'under-performing' schools, whose talent and hard work has the capacity to confound the expectations of those who write and approve the results algorithm. The government would eventually backtrack and restore the school-assessed grades, but not before some pupils had lost their places at prestigious universities.

I went on to confound expectations – other people's and my own. And now I am one of the fortunate few who can say that they have their dream job. Not simply a permanent academic post, which is already a privilege beyond measure, but a job at the university where I wanted to end up from the moment I first visited its campus. I remember walking into St Joseph's Square on Maynooth's South Campus, with its ivy-clad, nineteenth-century buildings and broad, open lawns, and thinking *I want to work here.*

I find it deeply satisfying to work at the Irish university with the highest number of students from non-traditional backgrounds, the highest number of mature students, the highest number of first-generation university attenders, the university with an outstanding disability service and a genuine policy of inclusion, the university with a strong relationship with the Traveller and Roma communities. My students go on long journeys of discovery and it is wonderful to see them grow and thrive, to see their minds opening to a world of knowledge. This is everything education represents to me: social mobility; changing the course of your life; perhaps outgrowing, but never losing sight of, your upbringing. Not just living the life that an algorithm might predict for you, but truly making your own path.

I frequently ruminate on how I have managed to arrive at the position I am in, and whether I deserve to be here. A senior male academic once told me in a pub that my transcriptions from medieval Irish manuscripts were inaccurate, my translations were 'shit', that I was unqualified in Old Irish and that I didn't deserve to hold an academic post.

Another senior male academic in another pub heckled me from across the bar, verbally abusing me in front of my friends and colleagues.

Yet another senior male academic vetoed my application for a place on the editorial board of a journal because he just didn't like me.

And another senior male academic (you may be noticing a pattern here) called me 'a stupid cunt who doesn't know anything about anything', just a few months after I was appointed to my job.

Maybe he was on to something. Maybe I am a stupid cunt who doesn't know anything about anything. But do any of us here know anything about anything? Surely we are all floating in a sea of ignorance whose waves might overwhelm us at any moment. My guess is that at least some of these men are floundering amidst the magnitude of the unknown just as much as I am. I regard my three degrees as simply the beginning of an apprenticeship and now, after twenty-two years studying medieval history and culture, I still learn new things every day and still have much yet to learn. That's the whole damn point of it: there is so much still to learn.

There is an Old English version of a Latin text called the 'Life of St Mary of Egypt'. In her youth, Mary of Egypt gave her body freely to men and was consumed by lust. But she had a moment of conversion, embraced God, and now in the story she wanders through the desert as a religious ascetic. In the parched desert, Mary encounters a monk named Zosimus. Zosimus thinks that he is something special. He asks himself:

> Is there any monk on earth who could teach me anything new or support me in any matters that I did not myself know, or that I had not accomplished in monastic works, or is there any among those who love the desert which is better than me in his deeds?

Arrogant prick. But an angel appears before Zosimus and tells him: *nis nan man þe hine fulfremedne aeteowe* – 'no one can reveal himself to be perfect'. And this is it: we are all flawed. Like Mac Con Glinne I am quick-thinking rather than studious. The men who have been most viciously savage to me seem to revel – at least outwardly – in a sense of their intellectual superiority. These modern Zosimuses of academia, convinced of their own superiority, of the perfection of their knowledge, are just as flawed as I am. And Zosimus realizes, in the end, that he can actually learn a lot from Mary. Not about education or monastic works, perhaps, but about human frailty, mortality, and what we can learn from others.

On 25 May, in Minneapolis, a Black man suffocates to death under the knee of a white police officer. The next day, protests against systemic racism begin to spread across the United States, and from there across the world. Black lives matter.

It is much harder to listen and to learn than it is to speak, especially for those in positions of influence. It is more difficult to change one's mind in the face of new information than it is to distort that information to fit one's pre-existing world view. I had thought that there was no possible way that *I* could be racist. Not me, with my multicultural family, my Black nephews and Asian nieces, my Black and Asian friends, my liberal world view. I had never had a racist thought in my life. But then I read some of the work of Ibram X. Kendi, on the idea that it is not enough to consider oneself 'not racist': unless you are actively anti-racist, then you are complicit in upholding racist systems. I realized, with a jolt, that I needed to listen more, I needed to learn.

The mother of my nephews, an old school friend, a friend from university . . . people who had not previously spoken at length about their experiences of racism begin to say things that I had not heard them say before – because they thought, at long last, that people might actually be listening, or because they felt an irrepressible need to share their stories right now, because they thought they might finally be heard by non-Black audiences.

I watch the films of Ava DuVernay, Steve McQueen and Jordan Peele. I read novels by Colson Whitehead, poetry by Jericho Brown and revisit old essays by Toni Morrison and James Baldwin. I read works of history, like W. Caleb McDaniel's *Sweet Taste of Liberty*, and contemporary non-fiction, like Akala's *Natives*. I stream stage productions of Inua Ellams' *Barber Shop Chronicles* and Andrea Levy's *Small Island*.

I try to listen and learn. I realize that I have been wrong about some things and that I have misunderstood others. I change my mind. My eldest nephew is becoming aware of his own Blackness and my subtle realignment of some of my ways of understanding coincides with his youthful awakening. One day he comes home from school with BLM written on his hand and I feel his glowing pride.

I think back to the man who died in the psychiatric unit while my brother was detained there. I remember him as quiet, lonely, always listening to music on his headphones. My brother had told me at the time that a fight had broken out between him and a white patient, and the white guy had repeatedly abused him with racial slurs. The nurses decided to move the Black patient to another ward. Why him? Why not move the white patient? He understood this as racial discrimination, adding insult to the verbal injuries he had already received. He resisted violently, punching one of the nurses. He was pinned to the ground by four ward staff for more than twenty minutes, until he lost consciousness and the life drained out of him. In those final minutes he uttered the familiar refrain: 'I can't breathe.' No individuals were found to have acted illegally, although eventually an inquiry identified racism as a key factor in his death. Ever since my brother told me what happened, this man's face has flashed momentarily into my mind every time I hear about a Black man being shot by police or dying in custody or taking his own life in his cell.

'Race' is a human construct, not a biological reality, and conceptions of what constitutes 'racial difference' have varied across time and place. A decade or so ago, it would have been fairly uncontroversial to say that the racialization of humans was an invention of the modern era. That is, 'race' as a concept (and therefore racism) is inseparable from the growth of the transatlantic slave trade, capitalism and modern colonialism. The pseudoscience of race served to justify and legitimate the kidnap, sale and exploitation of human beings on a monumental scale. But one consequence of identifying the seventeenth or eighteenth century as the time when 'race' was invented is that it situates the Middle Ages in a time before race and therefore before racism. Surely, if medieval peoples did not conceive of race, they could not be racist? But then how do we understand discrimination by one social group or ethnicity against another in medieval societies?

Recently, scholars such as Geraldine Heng have argued that 'race is a structural relationship for the articulation and management of human differences, rather than a substantive content'. For example, when Jews in medieval England were identified as different to Christians in some fundamental way, and suffered structural discrimination and persecution as a result of that perceived difference, then that is racism.

And the anti-Semitic discourse which delineated and articulated the ways in which Jews were perceived as different is racist. And the violence that Jews suffered at the hands of their Christian persecutors is the manifestation of racism. These recent scholars therefore regard the phenomenon of racism as existing even before the invention of 'race' as it would be framed by modern societies.

By contrast, there are others who would rather speak in terms of 'xenophobia' or 'prejudice', or some other less anachronistic term, since discrimination in the Middle Ages, for all its ugliness and vitriol and hatred, was not conceived or expressed in racialized terms. I'm grappling with these ideas in relation to medieval Ireland and Britain and still don't know where I stand: the work of learning is never done.

This month I continue to work on the book that has been languishing on my desktop for years. In one chapter, I look closely at anti-Semitism in medieval Irish sources. Some of it is the formulaic anti-Judaic rhetoric that medieval Irish authors read in earlier Latin sources and parroted in their own writings: nasty but predictable. But other examples are gut-churning in their virulence. Blathmac, son of Cú Brettan, who was mourning Jesus so eloquently back in January, also wrote at length about Jews as a lesser people. Much of what he and others wrote would be recognized as racist if it were written now, and it certainly feels racist to me as a modern reader. But the question of whether or not historians like me should classify it as racism is thorny. We inevitably inscribe the past in our own image, and therefore it is unsurprising that a society as racist as ours should see its own sins reflected in the Middle Ages.

What makes early Irish anti-Semitism all the more peculiar is that all the available evidence tells us that there were literally no Jews in Ireland before the Norman invasion. They were railing at an invisible enemy, just as today some of the communities that fear immigration the most are those that have the least experience of it. One chronicle records the arrival of five Jews at the court of Tairdelbach Ua Briain, King of Munster, in 1079. We are told that they came from overseas, bearing gifts, but Tairdelbach sent them back to where they'd come from. Ignorance breeds intolerance, and hatred grows from lack of knowledge.

Just as history is not predetermined, neither is an individual's fate. We may be battling all the forces that confront us – societal disadvantages that intersect in complex ways. For me, there were only a few factors standing against me: I am a woman and I come from a fractured immigrant family with a background of crime, addiction and exclusion from education. But there are many, many others for whom other factors – systemic racism, poverty, homophobia, transphobia, religious prejudice, ageism – form a series of interlocking barriers, yet more difficult to overcome. But we can work together to overcome them.

As May ends, so does the semester, and I send out into the world another generation of students who have read, and learned, and thought, and changed. They will continue to face challenges as they stagger through the desert of life, but I hope that their learning will guide them on their journey and give them a clearer, bolder voice. No one can reveal himself to be perfect, but we can all do a little better. Zosimus needs to know that he is not infallible and neither is he omnipotent, that he can be toppled from his plinth, and that the more people we listen to, the more we all learn.

JUNE

Inheritance

When I moved from Cambridge to Dublin, in 2013, I got a lift in the van with the vegan raw-food-eating Latvian guy the removals company had sent to move my stuff. On the way to Holyhead to catch the ferry, I asked him to stop by the side of a road in north-east Wales so that we could traipse across a field to see the Pillar of Eliseg. This stone pillar, originally the base of a great inscribed cross, was erected in the first half of the ninth century by a king of Powys named Cyngen ap Cadell, in honour of his great-grandfather, Elisedd ap Gwylog. The site of the pillar has suffered great violence over the centuries, not least by antiquarian excavators in the seventeenth and eighteenth centuries, trying to get at the Bronze Age burials that lie beneath. The Latin inscription on the pillar is badly weathered and illegible now, but from seventeenth-century transcriptions we know that it invoked Elisedd's military victories against the English and asked people to pray for Elisedd's soul. It also asked for God's blessing on Cyngen, who had commissioned the statue, on his household and the kingdom of Powys.

I tried to explain the significance of it all to the removals guy, but he was visibly unimpressed by something that is now, let's face it, just a broken stump in a field, and he took vengeance for my time-wasting diversion by playing Hari Krishna CDs on the van's stereo all the way to Holyhead. I tried to drown out the incessant chanting with thoughts about Cyngen – this powerful king, who ruled his kingdom in north-east Wales for more than forty years. In 854, he travelled to Rome, where he died: perhaps it was an end-of-life pilgrimage to expiate the sins of his violent royal career, or perhaps the international journey was a public display of his political status. Perhaps it was a bit of both, just as the Pillar of Eliseg is: a statement of power and of prayer. Despite the irreparable damage done to the pillar over the centuries – by forces both human and natural – neither Cyngen nor Elisedd have been forgotten.

June sees the removal and effacing of a number of statues in the UK and in the United States by Black Lives Matter protesters. Monuments to slave traders, Confederate soldiers, people whose wealth and reputations were built on the exploitation and suffering of others. A statue of the brutal King Leopold II is pulled down in Belgium. June also sees a chorus of voices claiming that removing a statue from a public square equates to an erasure of history, as though the world had instantly forgotten who Lenin was when his statues tumbled with the fall of Communism.

Back in January, when I was drowning in grief for my father, I told you a story about another father and his own dangerously disproportionate response to grief. According to the author of the Book of Wisdom he had commissioned an artist to build a statue in the likeness of his dead son. The artist created something so true to life that people began to worship it, and thus was idolatry unleashed on the world. The author of this story – and the medieval Irish poet who later adapted it into verse – intended it to be a warning of the risks of memorializing someone in bronze or stone: the danger that instead of simply remembering them, we might venerate them.

A statue tells us a lot about those who erect it, those who fund its creation and provide space for it – a public square, perhaps, or a park, or the side of a building. A statue says: *We admire this person, you should admire this person, this person has qualities that we wish to magnify through commemoration, this person embodies our communal identity*. In many societies and many eras people have regarded military success or the amassing of great wealth as markers of moral virtue: people conquered the lands of others and became rich because God, or the gods, favoured them. So Cyngen wanted people to remember Elisedd because of his great military victories, his defence of Powys against English incursions.

However, public statues are not history; they are an inheritance that we can choose to accept or reject. We can tear statues down and make new ones, just as we can refashion our society with different values. Instead of battles and gold, we can commemorate justice and peace. Far from seeing history as being erased, as I watched the news footage of the statue of slave trader Edward Colston getting pushed into Bristol harbour, I knew that it was being written.

History is not the same thing as the past. The past is everything that has ever happened before this present moment: history is the stories we choose to tell ourselves about that past. It is the voices, events, trends and forces that successive generations decide to remember and amplify. History is not a finite space. Just because you add something in, it does not mean that you need to remove something else to make room for it.

Churchill, Roosevelt and Stalin played undeniably important roles in the Second World War. You do not have to take that out of the history box when you also add in Churchill's culpability for the Bengal Famine, or Stalin's gulags.

There were many white men and women who fought bravely during the war: they are not removed from the history box when someone adds to it by writing a book, or making a documentary, about the experiences and contributions of Black soldiers, noting that they too should be remembered and their stories told.

During the Blitz, many British communities banded together to support and protect their neighbours in the face of devastation and loss. You do not have to take that out of the history box when you also point out that, at the same time, crime rates in the UK soared and the blackouts provided cover for increased levels of rape, murder and burglary.

History isn't heroes and villains, good guys and bad guys: history is human stories, and humans are complicated, contradictory and multifarious.

In the ancient and medieval world, history was perceived as moral example: it was often the actions of 'great men', whose deeds the readers should wish to emulate. This morally freighted approach still carries weight in all sorts of pernicious ways. We see it most clearly in the idea that history is something to be 'proud' of – a notion that is most dangerously applied to national histories. Something I inherited from my father is the idea that having been born in Ireland is nothing to be proud of. It's nothing to be ashamed of either, of course. It just is what it is: a result of the chance events of birth; a line on an official document or application form; a harp on the front of my EU passport rather than the heraldry of Germany or France or Sweden. Happenstance.

I love living in Ireland, I have loved living in Britain, but when I have visited Belgium or Thailand or Slovenia or the United States, I have thought it would be nice to live there too. Perhaps it's just a symptom of my rootlessness, but I don't understand flag-waving and exceptionalism and 'national pride' because, of all the things to be proud of, the place where you happen to have been born seems the most random thing to choose. Because many people do place great value on their national identity, they see the statement 'Your country is not perfect' and understand it to mean '*You* are not perfect'. 'People from your country have done bad things' is heard as '*You* have done bad things', because they have tied their personal identity so closely to that line on their birth certificate, to the colour of their passport.

There are British people who seem to think that history has a duty to be a record of all the great things that Britain has done, just as there are Irish people who seem to think that history has a duty to be a record of all the bad things that Britain has done. But history owes no loyalty to public opinion or national pride; it owes only fidelity to the past. Historians have a responsibility to tell as many of the stories as they can reconstruct from the records of the past, and we can hear whomever we choose to listen to. There is an important place for battles and kings and emperors and nation-building. But they are not removed from the history box when we also add in the experiences of oppressed and minority groups, the history of women, the history of Travellers and Roma people, the history of LGBTQIA+ individuals and communities, the history of ideas and emotions and ecosystems and the environment, the history of erasures and what we know to be lost from the archives.

The history box has space for many voices; indeed, the great thing about it is that there is room for everyone. The more voices we listen to, the more stories we hear and retell, the more reflective history becomes of that vast, undifferentiated mass that is the past. Because the past includes everyone and everything.

In 2011, I gave a lecture at an inner-city school in a deprived area of London. One teenage boy, who had listened attentively but sceptically, put his hand up at the end and asked me whether there was any value to studying history at all. He said, 'What's the point, Miss, when it's already happened? There's nothing you can do to change it.' At the time, I answered by trying to explain some of the ways in which the past works to shape the present. I explained that the reason why he and his classmates had the precise diverse ethnic make-up that they did, in a school in twenty-first-century London, was in large part because of history: colonialism, post-colonial economic and political history, and so on. Historical forces which had led his parents' families to emigrate to London rather than, say, Berlin. Why the ethnic make-up of a school in Paris would be different, but for the same historical reasons: colonialism and post-colonial history. In short, I said that studying history helps us to make sense of the present.

It was a reasonable enough answer in the heat of the moment, although it was far from perfect and I doubt he ran off afterwards to apply to do a History degree. What I wish I had said to him is that there's nothing we can do to change the past – the past is what has already happened – but there is everything we can do to change history. Because we can go into libraries and archives and communities and retrieve or record or publish the stories that have not yet been heard; we reinterpret causes and effects on the basis of new information that we have uncovered; we consider phenomena which we hadn't previously realized might have played a role in leading X to become Y. Historians change history every day: that is our job.

We inherit both history and the past, in complicated and intersecting ways. And we inherit other things too. In medieval Ireland, you could only attain the top rank of poetic scholarship – the status of *ollam* – if your father and grandfather had also held that status. This worked to prevent social mobility and exclude people from more humble backgrounds, or outsiders, from the most socially prestigious positions.

At the other end of the social hierarchy, another thing that could be inherited was enslavement. As it happens, Irish history – written stories about the past – begins with slavery, with one of the most famous enslaved individuals in early medieval Europe: St Patrick. Patrick was taken from his British homeland by Irish slave raiders as a sixteen-year-old boy. He eventually escaped, and his account of his experiences – his *Confessio* – is the earliest written narrative to survive from Ireland.

International slave-raiding expeditions such as the one that took Patrick went hand in hand with domestic enslavement. A person could become enslaved through three main processes in early medieval Ireland. First, through cross-border raids – for example, armies from, say, Munster, going into Leinster to steal cattle, women and children (the men would usually just be killed). Second, through an inability to pay fines imposed as compensation to victims of crime: if you and your family could not pay the fine, you could be enslaved as punishment. And third, by being born the child of a woman who was already enslaved. Enslavement was a common, everyday consequence of inter-territorial violence in Ireland, and once enslaved, a person had no human rights or standing in early Irish law: they were simply property.

Early Irish slave raiding was focused within Ireland itself and along the western seaboard of Britain. The arrival of Scandinavian settlers in the ninth century broadened the international scope of the Irish slave trade, with slaves being sold as far afield as Russia and North Africa. It was the coming of Anglo-Norman invaders in the twelfth century that brought about the end of slavery in Ireland. After that, whatever the sufferings and injustices of Irish history, there was no enslavement, no matter what right-wing sites on the internet might tell you otherwise.

I have had to battle – in my lecture hall as well as online – the myth of 'Irish slavery': the idea that, in the Early Modern period, Irish people were enslaved in the Caribbean or the Americas. This is untrue, and no one has done more to refute this falsehood than the Limerick historian Liam Hogan. Impoverished Irish people did indeed sell their own labour, as indentured servants. Indentured servitude was awful, inhumane and cruel; penal servitude even worse. But it was finite. A standard term, for example, was seven years, and at the end of that period the person was free.

Enslaved people were almost never freed; and for the vast majority the only end to their inhumane treatment was death. The phenomenon of indentured servitude simply cannot be compared with the massive enterprise that saw millions of Africans kidnapped and transported across the Atlantic – vast numbers of them dying on the journey – to be sold into an enslavement that would outlive them, and their children, and their grandchildren, and their great-grandchildren. The effects of the inheritance of slavery for Black communities in the Americas and the Caribbean continue to be felt today in a way that the effects of indentured servitude for Irish people are not. They are very different stories.

Just as those who built statues to kings and princes believed that their successes were the result of God's favour, so those in the early medieval world who were enslaved could often conceive of their condition as a divine punishment. St Patrick himself engaged in what we now call 'victim blaming'. He writes:

I was taken into captivity in Ireland, along with thousands of others. We deserved this, because we had gone away from God, and did not keep his commandments. We would not listen to our priests, who advised us about how we could be saved. The Lord brought his strong anger upon us, and scattered us among many nations even to the ends of the earth. It was among foreigners that it was seen how little I was. It was there that the Lord opened up my awareness of my lack of faith. Even though it came about late, I recognized my failings.

This kind of thing enrages me, whether it's happening in the fifth century or in the present day. Human beings kidnapped and enslaved Patrick, just as human beings kidnapped and enslaved millions of Africans for the transatlantic slave trade, just as human beings continue to discriminate against and mistreat their fellow humans today. There is no divine punishment behind it, any more than there is divine favour behind those who win battles and grow rich from the spoils of war. But Patrick was so immersed in his biblical world view – even in that passage he adapts biblical quotations to fit his story – that he simply could not conceive of a world in which it is human, not divine, agency that determines our experiences.

But this is all to conceive of history as big, sweeping forces: the great historical injustices which have shaped the lives of millions of people across centuries. We also inherit small things, personal stories that are unique to us. Even Patrick, who saw himself as part of a great, divinely ordained movement that would bring the word of God to the end of the known world, knew that he was also an individual. He wrote: 'Although I am imperfect in many ways, I want my brothers and relations to know what I am really like, so they can see what it is that inspires my life.'

And herein lies a central tension of the medieval Christian world. On the one hand, this world view sees the epic sweep of God's hand across history, in the rise and fall of political powers, in conquest and conversion; but on the other, each individual expects to have a singular moment of reckoning with God at the end of time: *Did you feed the hungry? Welcome the stranger? House the homeless?* Each person expects to be judged on the basis of their own, individual actions in their lifetime. Every time they did something good, every time they did something bad – all weighed in the scales of justice on Judgement Day.

My individual inheritance, my small story, revolves around alcoholism. When my father was unconscious in hospital in 2008, his liver failing, I had, in a moment of the kind of unthinking stupidity we experience in stressful situations, said to the hospital consultant, 'My father's father died of liver failure too – is liver disease genetically inherited?'

The consultant looked at me with a combination of pity and exasperation and said, 'No – alcoholism is.'

What my brothers and I inherited from our patrilineal line was a propensity for addiction more generally, not necessarily alcohol. Crack and heroin for one brother; in the case of another, the potent high-THC skunk that flooded our

community in the late nineties, leading him to teenage para-
noia and breakdown.

I am a girl of simple tastes, so I settled for good old-
fashioned booze. I am an alcoholic. Alcohol, first and
foremost, silences the raging cacophony in my head, transforming it into a dull and pleasant buzz. I love drinking, I
love being drunk, and passing out unconscious at the end of
the night pauses my overactive dream life and gives me a few
hours of peace. (Incidentally, if you are reading this hoping
for a redemption story – where I learn the error of my ways
and come to understand that a sober life is a better life –
you're going to be sorely disappointed: I still love to drink
and indeed am writing this with the fuzzy-headed, foggy
brain that is my regular morning-after punishment.)

My genetic inheritance is poor: my father's brothers and
sisters, who predeceased him, died in their teens, thirties
and early fifties respectively. I carry with me an expectation of a brief window of life and immerse myself in
exploring all its self-destructive pleasures accordingly. I go
through phases of commitment to a particular drink: first
was cheap lager, then I had a precocious Guinness phase at
the age of fifteen, like a prematurely old man. This was followed by cider, then Jack Daniel's, then whiskey, then red
wine, then white wine, then red ale, then gin, then lager
again. I am currently back on wine, alternating between
red and white.

Addiction to alcohol is a timeless problem. One early
English poet wrote, in Kelly Cherry's translation:

Drink swallows others; diabolic reversal,
It maddens men to mindless volubility
And vehemence, provoking swift swords,
Or, if not, it dazes them night and day
And they drink away their drear, reduced lives,
Slow suicide for sure say those who know them,
Though some will save themselves in time
To prosper and take pleasure in a separate peace . . .

When I was younger it certainly maddened me to mindless volubility. I would argue – politics, religion, history, literature – with anyone who wanted to cross swords with me. As I get older, it dazes me more and more; settles me into silence and sleep.

Many medieval Irish sagas open with the main protagonists being or getting drunk. Previous generations of scholars, if they commented on that at all, regarded it as part and parcel of a heroic warrior ethos: you fought, you fucked, you feasted. Keeping an ear open to the saga writers' cultural expectations casts literary drunkenness in a rather different light. It can be read as condemnatory of the life of excess, the un-Christian life. Medieval authors set the action of their narratives in a pre-Christian period, and drunkenness in the sagas often leads to 'mindless volubility / And vehemence, provoking swift swords'. In one story, 'The Intoxication of the Ulstermen', the warriors of Ulster drunkenly get lost on their way from one part of the province to another: so lost, in fact, that they end up at the other end of the island, in Co. Kerry. Which reminds me of the time that my middle brother went to a party in Belfast and woke up in Liverpool.

One of the central challenges for a historian is to get the balance right between telling the stories of individuals and those of broader trends, to find that point somewhere between the story of one individual soul facing God's judgement, and the great sweep of forces that are often beyond any single person's control: economics, political ideologies, social inequality. It is often the case that the more centuries separate us from those whose stories we are telling, the harder it can be to see the individual, the particular. If for some strange reason a future historian chose to tell my story, would they say that I was an alcoholic because of things that lay beyond my control, such as genetic inheritance, or because I personally chose to drink? I might become a single data point in a broad assessment of rising alcohol consumption by women in early twenty-first-century Europe. I might become an anecdote about how nature and nurture combine to create an addict. Then again, I might disappear into the great abyss of the future and be forgotten.

I've never had any particular interest in exploring my own family history. Perhaps I just don't want to know what I'd find. I can go back as far as my great-grandfather – a pastry chef at the private Kildare Street Club, preparing desserts for Ireland's wealthy elite – but no further. I know that I am Elizabeth daughter of Patrick son of Ernest son of Reginald, but I know nothing more. What long line of drinkers might stretch beyond?

Genealogies are amongst the most copious sources to survive from early medieval Ireland: tens of thousands of names. X son of Y son of Z going all the way back to Adam. Some of the names are real – individual people with individual lives, some that we know about from elsewhere, others diminished to a single name in a list, otherwise unknowable – but others are not real at all. Genealogies were markers of familial identity and allegiance, and as political realities changed, genealogies did too. New ancestors could be created; new branches of a family grafted on to the tree of a bigger, more important dynasty. And the ultimate falsehood: the sleight of hand that allowed Irish families to trace themselves back to Japheth and therefore to Noah and therefore to Adam and therefore to the creation of the world. The particular and individual binding itself to great, sweeping forces of history.

One of the things I have learned as a historian is that most things aren't as old as you think they are. Innovations become traditions with remarkable speed. In Ireland, many things are described in the popular imagination as 'ancient' when they're barely even old. Take ringforts, for example. I see people posting Instagram photos of these circular remains in the landscape with hashtags like 'Pagan' and 'Prehistoric Ireland'. But they're products of a medieval Christian society; the seventh-century equivalent of a detached house. And the idea that they are 'fairy forts' is a modern development which emerged after the settlements were abandoned: within a few generations something can be so lost as to seem more distant (and less real) than it is.

It is losing sight of the individual and the particular that leads people to describe as 'ancient', 'mythical', even 'mystical', many aspects of Ireland's early history. It is by uncovering individual stories that we can begin to add clarity, precision and detail to what is often presented as an undifferentiated mass of Irish pastness.

A colleague recommends a Don DeLillo novella to me, called *Point Omega*. I really enjoy it and pass it on to one of my students to read too. At one point, DeLillo writes: 'The true life is not reducible to words spoken or written, not by anyone, ever. The true life takes place when we're alone, thinking, feeling, lost in memory, dreamingly self-aware, the submicroscopic moments.'

How, as a historian, can I get to those submicroscopic moments? Just because it is an impossible task doesn't mean I shouldn't try, because maybe, just maybe, I might reach a close approximation of a handful of the innumerable submicro-scopic moments that make up a single life, the infinitesimal submicroscopic moments that make up the past.

If all that survives is a single name in a genealogy, at least we have that name. Lists of names in biological relationship to each other are genealogies. But there are lists of names of other kinds too. Litanies. Litanies are names spoken in prayer. The medieval Irish 'Litany of Confession' calls out the names of Hebrew Scripture.

> O Abel, first martyr,
> O Noah of the sacred Ark
> O faithful Abraham,

O meek and gentle Moses,
O Aaron, first priest,
O noble David
O mystic Solomon . . .

There is a power in those names, in speaking and remembering them. Calling on them to forgive or protect or save us. When I read Jericho Brown's *The Tradition* I find another litany in the title poem.

Where the world ends, everything cut down.
John Crawford. Eric Garner. Mike Brown.

We could write a too-long litany: Philando Castile, Stephon Clark, Breonna Taylor, George Floyd. There is power in knowing their names, but they will not be confined to a list. Their stories will be known and told and remembered. Their personhoods added to history. We know this genealogy: discrimination, son of hatred, son of segregation, son of injustice, son of enslavement, son of death. What reckoning is needed before there can be healing?

It seems to me that there are three practical things that I can do towards bringing about healing in my job as a historian of medieval Ireland and Britain. The first is in relation to those around me: ensuring that my university, for example, is a diverse and inclusive space. Supporting and citing and listening to students and colleagues from marginalized communities. Proactively encouraging diversification of the curriculum. Calling out discrimination and racism wherever I witness it. The everyday work of anti-racism.

The other two things involve my approaches to the past. First, I can find and tell the stories of previously marginalized voices, such as those of immigrants to medieval Britain and Ireland, to counteract the whitewashing of British and Irish history.

And, second, I can educate myself on the important work being done by colleagues specializing in areas beyond my own geographical limits: I can read the work of experts on medieval Ethiopia and Japan, West Africa and Central America, and perhaps incorporate some of their methodologies, make use of pertinent comparisons, look for solid connections, and better understand where the small bit of the world that I study fits within the global Middle Ages. By these means, I can find the stories about the past that speak to, and represent, the greatest number of people.

What can you do? What is the nature of your voice? Who are you listening to? What stories can you tell?

In 1875, an English soldier donated a small brooch to the British Museum. He said that the brooch had been found in or near Ballycottin Bog, near Youghal, Co. Cork. The soldier's name was Philip T. Gardner, and his account seems plausible, since his regiment, the 14th, was stationed in Fermoy, Co. Cork, in the 1860s. The brooch, however, like its finder, does not appear to be Irish. From its appearance and decoration it would seem to have been made in Carolingian Francia in the eighth or ninth century. The brooch is a gilt copper-alloy cross, decorated in a continental style. In that alone it would seem to be physical evidence of the kind of movement between cultures that I have already

146

described to you: like Máel Brigte, like Sedulius Scottus, like Eriugena, except rather than moving from Ireland to the Continent, the brooch has travelled from the Continent to Ireland.

What adds an extra layer to this story, though – the kind of story that needs to be heard to counteract the notion of a 'white, European' Middle Ages – is that in the centre of the cross is a black glass gemstone, a product of the Abbasid Caliphate, with an Arabic inscription that either reads 'as God wills' (*sha'a allah*) or 'we have repented to God' (*tubna lillah*). A tiny piece of medieval Islamic history preserved on the southern coast of Ireland. How the stone came to be part of the brooch and how the brooch came to be lost in a bog in Ireland is not known, but we should not be surprised by the intermingling of Islamic and Christian, Arabic words and Carolingian manufacturing, making its way to medieval Ireland to add to our store of history. The colonialism that led a young soldier from Cambridgeshire to be in Cork in the 1860s is also part of the story.

We are living at the beginning of a digital age that is currently giving voice to more people than ever before. The great shift of recent decades is the advent of social media. This has brought about – amongst many other consequences, both desirable and undesirable – an avalanche of claims about history on websites, blogs, Facebook, Twitter and discussion forums. False claims and unevidenced assertions vie with genuine insights and valuable information: people can feel confused and unable to distinguish one from the other.

Differing interpretations of the same evidence can be equally valid: one historian might claim, for example, that economic factors were the key determinant in the Anglo-Norman invasion of Ireland. Younger noble sons, left without inheritances with the rise of primogeniture, sought out new lands and territories to conquer: they wanted land and wealth, and those who followed with them desired their own cut of the profits – new trading centres were established, leading to changes in manufacturing, exports and supply chains. It's a plausible story, with plenty of evidence to support it. But another historian, equally well versed in the surviving sources, might say no, it was religion and ideological forces which were the key determinants in that same invasion. Twelfth-century ecclesiasts had constructed the image of the 'barbarian' Irish, in need of civilizing, their churches in need of moral and administrative reform, the English Church egging nobles on, after long competition with Armagh for jurisdiction over the churches in the Scandinavian-ruled towns of Ireland. Yet another historian might say, well, it's a little of both: economics and religion are inseparable anyway, and these forces interacted in tandem.

These kinds of interpretive differences – which are trying to get to the heart of why humans act in particular ways – are not the same as 'fake news' or false claims.

In recent months, I notice on Irish social media that right-wing commentators are using the word 'revisionist' as a pejorative term for the kind of history that I write. I'm not sure what they think I should be doing: perhaps I am supposed to say, 'Yes, everything you have read in already-published history books is accurate and correct and that's all the history there is and there is nothing more to be discovered or said or written about anything else.' Perhaps I am supposed to stop looking for new evidence, new voices, new stories. My history is revisionist because I think the stories need continual revising.

Writing new history, based on evidence (whether old evidence reconsidered, or new evidence freshly brought to light), is what historians do every day. Unfortunately, social media has given rise to increasing numbers of people making claims about the past that are not supported by evidence. The most famous example of a false historical claim is probably Holocaust denial, and this gives us a simple way of explaining the difference between competing, but valid, historical interpretations, and outright untruth. To claim that the Holocaust did not take place is a lie. To consider differing reasons for *why* the Holocaust took place is valid historical enquiry. Again, different historians might veer between economic, ideological and psychological explanations in attempting to understand how otherwise 'normal' human beings were able to oversee and enact a systematic attempt to exterminate entire groups of their fellow humans, and to understand where culpability lies, how reparations can be made, and how healing can be advanced.

The historian is not some sort of conservator of the past, passing on an increasingly dusty torch in a stagnant relay race through unchanging time. The historian is an active seeker of unheard voices, a writer of new stories about the past, stories that consider – and reconsider – how and why things happened, how humans have treated other humans. We might hold a single life up to the light and examine it in all its complexity, as though it were a black glass gemstone inscribed in Arabic and set in a gilt copper cross. Or we might gather up innumerable stories, genealogies, litanies, and place them in conversation with each other so that many voices gather in a chorus that speaks to us of change or injustice or hope.

Towards the end of June, as I am half writing this book in my head, pondering how to tell you about my life, my job, the history that I study, I also get closer to the finishing line with the dry, academic book that I have been writing for the past few years. In it, I translate medieval Irish writings about Assyrian and Persian history, about the cities of Babylon and Jerusalem. I'm trying to understand how one culture – that of medieval Ireland – understood and spoke about the cultures of others. The last bits I have to check are in the chapter on medieval Irish ideas about idolatry. There I have written about the father who commissioned the image of his dead son. I have written about statues: idols venerated by people who are portrayed by these Irish writers as misguided; people who have been fooled, deceived, because the statues are inhabited by demons that the ignorant have mistaken for gods.

The evenings are warmer and lighter now, so I take my bottles of wine out to the back garden to drink. My daughter attends a Black Lives Matter protest. I think about statues being pulled down by young protestors in different countries; teenagers and students and workers filled with a zeal for equality and justice. Those statues are inhabited by demons from the past: racism, slavery, cruelty. They are venerated by those who have inherited a privilege shaped by monumental injustices. They are destroyed by those who bring a new message of hope and change: a legacy of light. And history is written again.

JULY

Nature

I am an indoor person. I like pubs and libraries, sofas and beds. I like cities and the people who live in them. I have my revelatory experiences in bars, not on mountainsides. (Youngest nephew just read these sentences. 'That's because you're lazy, Auntie Lizzie.' He's not wrong.) On a hot summer day, I look up from my laptop and through the window I can see blue sky, a hedge of plum trees entangled in ivy, a bird taking flight. I look back at my laptop and continue writing.

Other people are outdoor people. I'm glad that outdoor people exist, because I like sitting inside reading the stuff that they write about the outdoors. I like books about unfamiliar landscapes and the histories of rivers or trees.

Tallaght, where I was born, is now pretty much another suburb of Dublin. People often sigh wistfully, recalling that just a decade or two before I was born it used to be a village. 'I remember when this was all fields,' and that sort of thing. I prefer Tallaght as it is now: houses, communities, occasionally witty graffiti, and a tram connecting it right to the heart of Dublin.

Before Scandinavian settlers arrived in Ireland in the ninth century, Ireland had no cities. The nearest things there were to urban centres were the major churches, like Armagh, Clonmacnoise, Emly: these sites could include monastic communities, both male and female, guest houses, schools and scriptoria. Communities living in the surrounding areas, such as tenants who farmed church-owned land, would gather at the church, especially on major feast days like Easter. Farmers sought to tame nature, to master it. Dairy farmers paid rent to their ecclesiastical landlords in the form of cheeses and butter; those tenants who were farming crops paid in wheat and oats.

What lay beyond royal land and church land, cultivated and populated land, was wilderness. Borderlands. One eleventh-century Irish writer, when writing about hell, described it as an infernal monastic community, with the Devil as abbot, and the wilderness beyond as a dystopian swamp of ice and fire. From the perspective of a community, whether large or small, it was from the wilderness that raiding parties came: approaching from the horizon to torch buildings, steal cattle and enslave women and children.

In medieval stories featuring Finn mac Cumaill, he and his gang of violent men – the *fían* – live outside the confines of civilized society, on the edges of acceptable behaviour and the 'natural' social order. They roam the countryside, engaging in acts of violent warfare, which are depicted with the rose-tinted spectacles of nostalgia. Whereas the authors of earlier saga narratives like the *Táin* seem horrified by senseless violence – Cú Chulainn murdering his foster-brother was a cause for grief – by the time the great epic about Finn, *Acallam na Senórach*, was being written, literature had become infused with images of knights and 'chivalry'. Violence seemed nobler. Even though the tales of Finn are set in a pre-Christian Ireland, the thirteenth-century author of the *Acallam* casts him in such a light that he bears more than a passing resemblance to a crusading Knight Templar.

A bit like Chaucer's *Canterbury Tales*, the *Acallam* has a framing tale – an overarching narrative – into which numerous sub-tales are slotted. The framing tale has St Patrick arriving in Ireland with his retinue of priests and churchmen and encountering one of the last survivors of Finn's gang: Caílte, son of Ronan. Caílte and his warriors are giants whose imposing physicality frightens Patrick's followers. But Patrick offers them hospitality and asks Caílte to tell his stories. The stories of Finn's exploits with his war band are the sub-tales.

I think of the character of Patrick in the *Acallam*, recording Caílte's tales for posterity, as being like a modern-day crime journalist writing about ageing gangsters. He is sometimes enthralled and sometimes appalled by the tales of violence. He takes seriously the world that these men inhabited on the fringes of society, even while holding them at arm's length, mediating their voices, and regarding his own world view as superior.

If the thirteenth-century author of the *Acallam* paints Patrick as an intrepid reporter, bringing news of violent pagans to his Christian audience, he casts Finn as a hero, a proto-Christian, his violence justified and necessary. As Caílte reflects on their glory days he says: 'We were, Patrick, in our own estimation, such that, from Ceylon in the east to the Garden of the Hesperides in the western part of the world, one could not find four hundred warriors that we would not trounce in battle or in combat.' It's possible that the author might have been reading a bit too much Arthurian literature, with his claims that Finn and his righteous warriors were the international equal of the Knights of the Round Table.

The *Acallam* is a much-studied tale. I don't know why so many academics are so into it: I find it deeply tedious and have only managed to get all the way through it once (the author could have done with an editor). But it is a useful text for thinking about medieval ideas regarding nature, and how people understood themselves in relation to the ecosystems they inhabited. Its engagement with the natural world is one of its most striking aspects. Caílte, along with his old gang mate Oisín, who is Finn's son, takes Patrick on a guided tour of Ireland. They travel around the island and at each place they stop, they tell Patrick their stories of Finn's adventures there. And they tell him about islands beyond – Britain, the Hebrides – and the *fian*'s foreign adventures.

The whole story, therefore, is deeply embedded in geography. It's almost a psychogeography – arriving in a place triggers the memories from which their stories emerge, but the journey itself is what holds the tale together. But there's more than that. Alongside the fighting and the romanticized bloodshed, there is a greater concern for landscape and biodiversity than the plot necessitates. It is as though every bird, every mammal, every plant, every tree in Ireland and its neighbouring islands, is contained within the tale. We stop at hills and plains and rivers and cliffs. And Oisín and Caílte recite poetry – endless poetry – about them all. Bright sprigs of cress, trout, red-breasted fawns, green-wooded streams . . .

Arran blessed with stags, encircled by the sea,
Island that fed hosts, where black spears turned crimson.

Carefree deer on its peaks, branches of tender berries,
Streams of icy water, dark oaks decked with acorns.

Greyhounds here and beagles, blackberries, fruit of sloe,
Trees thick with blackthorn, deer spread about the oaks.

Rocks with purple lichen, meadows rich with grass,
A fine fortress of crags, the leaping of fawns and trout.

Gentle meadows and plump swine, gardens pleasant beyond
    belief,
Nuts on the boughs of hazel, and longships sailing by.

Lovely in fair weather, trout beneath its banks,
Gulls scream from the cliffs, Arran ever lovely.

At first glance it all seems, as the poet puts it, 'lovely' –
the gentle meadows and plump swine, the streams and trees,
the deer and fish. But Finn and his gang weren't there to
commune with nature, they were there to hunt it. Just a few
lines previously, Caílte has said to Patrick that every August
they used to go to Arran 'with three battalions and have our
fill of hunting'.

Who is in those longships sailing by: another war band
from Ireland? And look again at that first couplet with its
'black spears turned crimson'. This is about death as much
as life.

Just a few pages later Patrick enters the kingdom of
Becán, King of Brega and Meath. The kingdom is being plun-
dered by Becán's own brother, Fulartach. When Becán
refuses hospitality to Patrick and his retinue, Patrick curses

him: 'Let not one of his livestock or his household survive until tomorrow.' We are told that 'at that very moment the earth swallowed up Becán, together with his household and his goods, both animals and people'. Patrick gives the kingship of Brega and Meath to Becán's marauding, pillaging brother. Perhaps his time with the warriors is rubbing off on him; the reporter is going rogue.

For all the gushing streams and fruit-laden trees in the *Acallam*, it is nature red in tooth and claw. And for all that Finn and his men are dressed up like chivalrous knights, with their deer-hunting parks and their musicians, yet they steal and kill. You can buy a nice house in Spain and wear expensive suits, but if you're still smuggling heroin into Dublin, profiting from misery, you're what Chaucer would call a *queynte*.

I was glad when, a few years ago, my dad and stepmum had moved off a housing estate and into the bungalow. The kids on the estate weren't as bad as Finn's warriors but the low-level anti-social disruption – throwing eggs at houses and crap like that – was annoying. My brothers and I had rounded on one gang of kids outside the kebab shop one night and I told the ringleader that if he ever threw eggs at my parents' house again I would stick a knife in him. No more eggs were thrown. But it was still nice when they moved to somewhere with a big garden, where my stepmum could grow fruit and vegetables.

After a few months of lockdown, I am relieved that I made the decision to get back here in March. If I was cooped up in my second-floor flat in Dublin – without even a balcony, let alone a garden – I would have gone out of my mind by now.

We tend to exercise alone: my daughter likes taking her headphones and listening to music by herself while she walks. I have a couple of walking routes around the perimeter of the small town, sometimes heading into the fields of the farms that surround it, sometimes wandering into the small patches of woodland. On one of my favourite routes, I can hear the traffic on the A12 rushing past on my left and the sounds of families on the housing estate echoing on my right, while I walk along the thin slice of wilderness that cuts between the two. A fence of forest towers over me. And I can hear birdsong: blackbirds, cuckoos. There's a small stream in amongst the lichen-encrusted trees. Out of the wood, into the light, and up towards the coppiced field maples that have marked the field boundaries for a couple of centuries. Then over a stile, across the playing fields, and back through the housing estate to the main road and home. Daily government-mandated exercise.

OK, not actually daily. But once a week. Maybe.

I return from my walks sweating and sticky. This month is one of the hottest on record, with global land and ocean surface temperature 0.92°C above the twentieth-century average. Torrential rainfall causes flooding in Bangladesh and fatal landslides in Nepal, but Australia's precipitation is 43 per cent below average. There are tropical cyclones in the Atlantic. Extreme weather phenomena become ever more frequent as we experience the effects of man-made climate change.

The monotheistic religions, Christianity, Islam and Judaism, which dominated medieval Europe, viewed the world as God's creation. Within that basic tenet lies a multitude of ways of understanding humanity's role within, and relationship with, that creation. One strand emphasizes the passage in Genesis in which God gives mankind dominion over creation. Ever since, that's been read as a licence to exploit natural resources. It is less easy for humanity to give it an alternative reading: that God wants humans to be stewards, or guardians, of the world, not its masters.

Of course, human exploitation of the landscape long predates monotheistic religions – Ireland's landscape was already being shaped and managed by humans way back in the Neolithic period, six thousand years ago, when cattle farming led to deforestation and the spread of grasslands, then as now. And humans continued to shape their landscape across the centuries, with fresh rounds of deforestation coinciding with economic growth and building booms. But what the man-as-lord-and-master reading of Genesis offers is a moral justification for the exploitation of natural resources. You needn't feel bad about what you're doing if God wants you to do it, right? You can believe that this world is God's creation, even as you destroy it.

Another way of understanding mankind's relationship with creation was shaped by the kind of Neoplatonism espoused by thinkers like Eriugena and Al-Kindi. This involves seeing the material world as a dark imitation of the Divine; a less-than place, inhabited by embodied beings weighed down by their corrupt corporeality, striving to get to the true glory of the immaterial world, the transcendent, the incorporeal reality beyond. The visible was only useful insofar as it could be used to understand the invisible. As the writer and cartographer Tim Robinson put it: 'for centuries the material world was seen as a quarry of metaphors to describe the glories of a spiritual world.'

A Latin tract that was long associated with poor old Bishop Patrick of Dublin, still lying dead at the bottom of the Irish Sea, says that this world is not real, but is merely the shadow of what is real. It says that chasing after worldly things is crazy, because worldly things aren't real. The author asks:

What could be more stupid, or more insane, than to be deceived and overcome like children by the shadow and image and similitude of true glory and true pleasure, true beauty, true decency, true honour, and not to seek after, or desire, the true glory itself? Who would choose the image of gold in water, neglecting the gold itself, and would not immediately be believed by all to be an idiot or a madman? Who would love the orb of the sun reflected in a mirror or formed in any other material, more than the sun itself, and would not be derided by all?

What the author thinks is that this world, the people and things we see around us, are mere reflections of reality. Physical pleasure is only a shadow of spiritual pleasure. Earthly glory is just an inadequate likeness of heavenly glory. Our relationship with the world is the image of gold in water, the reflection of the sun in a mirror.

Is that who we are, then: fools splashing in the shallows, trying to grab on to an insubstantial reflection?

I am wading out, knee-deep, reaching down to seize this illusion . . . of what? Truth? Redemption? Love? Cupping my hands in the water, I let the image slip through my fingers again and again. That is what constitutes a life.

Philosophers can consider whether reality exists beyond our own perceptions of it, and I enjoy the rhetorical skill of these medieval writers, but ultimately I can't embrace the idea that life is nothing but the image of gold in water. There must be something tangible.

Tim Robinson died in April after contracting Covid-19, and this month I read his last book, *Experiments on Reality*. Robinson was one of the outdoor people I mentioned earlier – someone who loved to be outside, in nature, and I am very glad that he did, because I take such pleasure from his words about the outside world, as I sit inside, curled up in a chair, reading them. He writes about his birthplace, Yorkshire, and the various places he called home: Istanbul, Vienna, Connemara, London. He writes that 'reality is endlessly more complex than investigation at any level can reveal'. He's right about that: historical research; scientific research, both macroscopic and microscopic; literature; the social sciences; they all provide some answers but they also create new questions. I hope we never get to the bottom of this mystery of reality, because it's in the very investigation of its nature that all the fun lies.

If some medieval writers thought nothing around us was real, others took a more materialist view of the world. One of the most interesting was a writer known in Latin as Augustinus Hibernicus, 'the Irish Augustine'. We don't know his original Gaelic name, but let's call him Augustín to avoid confusing him with Augustine of Hippo. This Augustín, who was writing in the middle of the seventh century, had a novel way of thinking about the natural and the unnatural, reality and the unrealistic. He began with the premise that God had indeed created the world in six days, as described in Genesis, and had rested on the seventh.

But what did that rest mean? Had he stopped working? Surely not, because God is eternally active in the universe. So Augustín stated that on the seventh day God ceased the work of creation, but continued the work of steering, or managing the universe. Like a divine pilot, he continued to keep the universe on course, just not creating anything new after that sixth day.

So far so good (if you accept the whole God thing). But, Augustín says, you then have a problem. Because if God stopped *creating* after the sixth day, and simply continued *piloting*, then how do we explain miracles? How do miraculous things appear or occur if God hasn't created anything new since the sixth day?

Augustín's solution to this admittedly rather arcane problem is this: if we see something that appears to be completely new to our understanding of reality – that is, something miraculous – we should not understand that thing to be newly created; rather, when a miracle happens, God is merely bringing forth something 'from the hidden depths of its nature' which already lay concealed within that thing before it was transformed.

In order to see what he's getting at, an example might

help. There's a famous passage in the Book of Exodus where God inflicts ten plagues on Egypt in a bid to force the Pharaoh to free the oppressed Israelites. The first plague turns the waters of the Nile into blood. So, did God *create* a river of blood with this miracle? Augustín says no:

> Water, the basis of every fluid, is by its daily operations in various creatures changed into different things, modified ceaselessly and naturally so as to provide nourishment and sustenance for every nature. For when it is infused into the wood of the vine, it is changed to the savour and colour of wine; and when it mounts to the top of an olive tree, the same water produces the fatness of olive oil; and when it is gathered by bees into their combs, it takes on the sweetness of honey [. . .] and when it is assigned to different animals as nourishment, it is divided into the several kinds of blood throughout the body. For it appears in the breasts with the white colour and mild sweetness of milk, for the sustenance of infants; but in all other parts of the body it has the red colour of blood. There are many other fluids in the body apart from blood: natural philosophers put their number at twenty-three, identifying them as urine, semen, black and red bile, saliva, tears, etc.

You can see where he's going with this: if water turns into blood in the human body, then a river turning into blood isn't something that is created out of nowhere; it's simply God taking a naturally occurring process and making it happen instantaneously, somewhere unexpected.

Or take the manna, or bread, that falls from heaven, with which God sustained the Israelites during their long journey through the desert. Since we don't have any problem with the idea of something quite substantial, like snow or hail-stones, falling from clouds, Augustín asks whether bread could fall from the clouds too? He thinks it can, without requiring any new creation from God, because the air shares some properties from the earth (which grows the grain nec-essary to make bread). He knows that air has some earthly properties, because, he says, 'How could air support the bodies of birds in flight, if it did not have something of the solidity of earth?' Therefore, we can say that, although clouds raining bread is indeed a divine miracle, it is not contrary to the created order of things. It is evidence of God governing nature however he chooses, not creating it anew.

Augustín's model is quite ingenious, with a logic that I can't help but admire. In our own age we create arbitrary and arti-ficial distinctions between what is 'natural' (Fruit! Mountains! Neutral make-up!) and what is 'unnatural' (Drugs! Bestiality! Colourful make-up!). For the medieval world, that tension was directed more towards thinking about what belonged to the world and what was above or beyond it. What was the stuff of the knowable natural world, and what consisted in the unknowable and ineffable, belonging only to God?

One medieval Irish poem, on the knowable natural world, begins *Dom-fharcai fidbaide fál*, 'A fence of forest towers over me'. The poet goes on to write of birdsong – blackbirds, cuckoos – and of studying beneath an idyllic woodland canopy. The lines, likely a fragment from a longer poem, are copied into the margin of a page of a ninth-century manuscript: the main text is a copy of the *Institutiones Grammaticae* ('Institutes of Grammar') which was written around the year 500 by Priscian, a Latin grammarian from what is now Algeria. Priscian's *Institutiones* is a classroom text. An indoor text.

The verses in the margin are grammatically and linguistically elaborate, with extensive use of first-person infixed pronouns: that 'm' in *Dom-fharcai* is 'me'. I. The self who is sitting in the forest, listening to the blackbird's song.

The page of the grammatical text that the poem is copied into also deals with pronouns. Me. You. He. She. They. The words that can take the place of things. In recent years, amongst my students, my friends, my daughter's friends, I have witnessed a greater variety and fluidity in the use of pronouns, as many people become more open to saying: *this is my nature*. Yet others seem threatened by the idea that a person can determine their own identity. He. She. They. According to some, this is not 'natural'. It's 'against nature'.

There's a tenth-century Irish story about shifting pronouns — he and she — and it is set on two neighbouring church estates: Drimnagh and Crumlin. It was written as a kind of pedagogical joke, but it raises questions about what is or isn't natural. The head of the church at Drimnagh, after feasting at Easter, goes out for a walk. He climbs a nearby hill and, when he reaches the top, he sits down and falls asleep. When he awakes, he discovers that he has turned into a woman. He passes his hand over his face, but finds no trace of his facial hair. He puts his hands between his legs, and 'found the sign of womanhood there'. Nevertheless, he refuses to believe that he is a woman, and thinks that some sort of magic is at work.

A hideously ugly woman passes by and asks the newly female abbot why he is alone on the hillside when night is drawing in. The abbot of Drimnagh replies that he doesn't know where to go. He can't go home, because his community will not recognize him; he can't stay on the hill, because 'I'm in danger as a single woman going around on her own'. He says that God has passed judgement on him 'for it is He who has distorted my shape and my form and made me disfigured and repulsive'. He offers up a cry of sorrow and lament and heads off in the direction of Crumlin.

When he arrives at Crumlin he meets the head of that church's estates. The *airchinnech* (best translated as 'ecclesiastical land manager') of Crumlin is consumed with lust for him and pressures him into sleeping with him. The abbot marries him and bears him seven children in seven years. The church of Drimnagh invites his husband and himself for an Easter feast, but as they head in the direction of Drimnagh, the abbot falls asleep on the same hill as seven years previously, while his husband heads on towards the church. When he awakes, 'it is thus she was, a man'. He has resumed his original form.

He arrives at Drimnagh and when he tries to explain the events of the previous seven years, he is told that he has only been gone for an hour. The whole thing has been a dream. Except it wasn't a dream, because the seven children in

Crumlin exist. And a case has to be taken to decide their legal and financial status.

For its original audience the tale was a humorous one, told at the expense of the community of Drimnagh, to set up a legal quandary, the sort of exceptional case that students could debate and learn from. But it also tells us something about what was regarded as 'natural' and what lay beyond nature. Ideas of what is natural delineated themselves against ideas of what is supernatural. The abbot's initial reaction to his gender-bending experience is to suspect 'magic' is at work, but he soon accepts it as some sort of divine punishment. It is a hardship to become a woman, and he does not know what he has done to deserve such a penalty from God.

The author of the tale shifts their use of pronouns: he, to she, to he again. Me. You. He. She. They. Words that take the place of things. In the author's world view physical appearance is enough to make him a her. Gender is based on genitals. There are, of course, more nuanced ways of understanding sex and gender, and it is clear that the abbot of Drimnagh sees himself as male, even when he has the physical attributes of the female sex. He adopts medieval conventions of femininity – marriage and motherhood – because it is clear to him that he has no choice, as he laments on the hill. It was a man's world. For him, to be a woman was to be 'disfigured' and 'repulsive'. To be less than a man. For my students, to accept and embrace their identity is to be more than a pronoun. It is to be true to their nature, whether him, her, them, or none of the above.

*

Early medieval thinkers knew more about the natural world than they often get credit for. They knew perfectly well, for example, that the earth was a sphere and not flat. They engaged in attempts to measure countries, predict eclipses, and understand the universe. Early Irish scientists used the term 'atom' to describe the smallest possible unit of matter. In the seventh and eighth centuries Irish scholars engaged in advanced study of computus, that is, calendrical science, and the calculation of time. Information circulated which represented the best knowledge of the age, regarding botany, geography, cosmology. People were curious about the world around them, and no more stupid then than today. And yet there is a gap between us and the minds of the people of the pre-modern world, a kind of irreversible shift caused by modernity, and the discoveries of Copernicus, Newton, the Herschels (brother and sister), Ada Lovelace, Charles Darwin, Marie Curie, Einstein, Alice Ball, Alan Turing.

The modern scientific method has changed our relationship with nature, not least in the understanding that we are simply animals ourselves, not created from clay but evolved, like our fellow primates, from our ape ancestors. The infinitesimal odds of life on earth having evolved in the first place, let alone the minuscule chances of us having our brief moment on this planet, mean that life remains a near-miraculous thing, and yet we are beginning to understand why we are not contrary to the natural order. We are nature. I like to think that our Irish Augustine would have appreciated this knowledge, learned from it, changed his world view in response to new information. But perhaps he would have continued to insist that it is the air's earthly qualities that keep birds from falling to the ground.

Just as there are people now who would swear that our natural world includes creatures such as Bigfoot or the Loch Ness Monster, so the natural world in the early Middle Ages incorporated creatures whose existence we might well doubt. Bestiaries, the zoological encyclopedias of the Middle Ages, gave as much space to dragons and griffins as to lions and elephants. However, that is not to say that the people who created bestiaries believed that those mythical creatures ever existed. Some did, perhaps, but the animals in bestiaries carry with them moral and theological lessons that had a greater significance than the reality or unreality of the animal under consideration.

The symbol of my former Cambridge college, Corpus Christi, is the pelican, because in medieval Christian thought it was believed that the pelican would cut open its chest with its beak in order to feed its own blood to its young in times of scarcity, just as the Eucharist commemorated Christ's sacrifice of his own body and blood for the salvation of mankind. It didn't really matter that pelicans don't, in fact, feed their own blood to their young; what mattered was the lesson about sacrifice.

One of the most beautiful surviving Old English poems is about a non-existent animal: the phoenix. It tells us of a place where there are clear streams in the woods, enriching the soil with their moisture. This fertile land of sweet herbs is Syria, and that is where we will find the phoenix. The phoenix dies and is born again. As it grows old, it makes a nest in that lush forest, in which it sits as the flames engulf it. And when the conflagration settles, a new life begins to form from the ashes.

The image of the phoenix's resurrection was used for a variety of purposes across the medieval world, including as a metaphor for the Resurrection, but for this early English poet it represents being reborn into salvation, the corrupted body purified by the flames, the newly redeemed penitent emerging from the ashes of sin, radiant and transformed. The poem is about the possibility of renewal, whether the phoenix exists or not.

My daughter returns to her father's house. A new life punctuates this year of death. My daughter becomes an older half-sister to a little boy and greets this development with all the enthusiasm one can expect from a hormonal teenager.

I wander around in my stepmum's garden, where she is growing lettuce and courgettes, corn on the cob and raspberries. Walking amongst the beds with my two nephews, the sun high above us, we pick a few sparse blueberries and check to see how the potato plants are getting on. There are multitudes of peacock butterflies, four spots on their wings like targets at a shooting range.

In a surreal development, I sign with a literary agent, who negotiates the contract for this book, which I shall give birth to. But I continue with my academic work too – a couple of articles come back from their respective publishers, all typeset and ready for publication, for me to give them a final check before they go to print. My teaching and examining is finished until the August resits, so I finally have some good, solid research time. The dry book is done at last. I send it to the publisher and drink a bottle of champagne on the patio with my stepmum, amongst the birdsong and the distant alarm of the level crossing near the train station, and the garden feels like a sanctuary.

The idea of a safe, idyllic space is a potent one. A place to take refuge, if only in the mind. Medieval poetry abounds with the literary construct known as the *locus amoenus*, the ideal place, where one is safe and comforted. The *locus amoenus* might be the Syria of the phoenix, or the Irish landscapes of the *Acallam* or Tim Robinson's books, or the fence of forest that overlooks the wistful scholar. Or, if you're really lucky, it might be your home. The Old English word *eþel* means both 'one's true home' and also 'paradise'. To be *eþel-leas*, is to be without a homeland, exiled from paradise. When I am in England I am exiled from Ireland; when I am in Ireland I am exiled from England. Never really home.

One early Irish poet imagined a *locus amoenus* that created for him a church within nature. He contemplates a little hut in the wood, beside a pool to wash away his sins, surrounded by woods that 'nurse many-voiced birds'. He would grow leeks and raise chickens, catch trout and keep bees. He would have twelve other monks with him, to make that holy number of thirteen, like Christ and his disciples. And at the centre of it all will be a church, with its linen altar cloth, candles and book of the Gospels; and just as the hut will be his dwelling place, so the church will be God's.

The dream of escaping to the country to be a smallholder

has long roots. What did this poet want to escape? His monastic brethren, perhaps, or onerous responsibilities in the monastic scriptorium or schoolroom.

Another early Irish poet dreamed of his retirement – and he too wanted to spend it getting away from whatever it was he wanted to get away from.

> All alone in my little cell,
> Not a single person with me.
> That would be a dear retirement,
> Before I go to die.
>
> A little hut, hidden and secluded,
> For the repentance of sin.
> A conscience, upright and untroubled,
> Turned towards holy Heaven.
>
> With a body sanctified by good habits,
> Trampling like a man upon it.
> With eyes, feeble and tearful,
> For the forgiveness of my desires.

All these monks, dreaming of little huts in the woods, all of them feeling burdened by sins that they needed to be washed clean of, weighed down by corrupt corporeality, but finding a place for God in the world. Phoenixes looking to be reborn.

These guys might have wished to escape their cares or responsibilities, but they were doing pretty well, all things considered. The ability to write and compose poetry is a privilege that was afforded to few in the Middle Ages.

Arguably, it still is. As the historian Donnchadh Ó Corráin once observed, all this beautiful poetry, these medieval meditations on the idyllic, these philosophical musings, are the products of:

> . . . a small artistic and intellectual cadre, supported and patronised by a much larger and powerful extractive elite that lords it over a wretched mass of toilers, some free, many slaves, all exploited, the sweated and bloodied under-belly of a profoundly unequal society.

The sanctuary can only ever be temporary, the safety illusory, the serenity hard-fought: to write about paradise, one must first pluck feathers from birds to make quills; crush gall nuts for ink; flay calves to make vellum.

And homes are not always paradisiacal. My family's house was not always a safe place for me. Our cat kills the birds, voles and insects that inhabit the garden. A snake takes up residence in our pond for a few days and eats the newts. A pandemic rages beyond our walls. The idea that we can isolate ourselves from the world is the image of gold in water. The world is what we inhabit always, alive or dead.

AUGUST

Time

In August I turn forty. At the start of the month, a couple of weeks before my birthday, my latest relationship ends. Yet another one. Three years ago, I was dumped shortly before my birthday – perhaps there's something in the humid summer air that helps small resentments to fester like mould. As a present to myself I take a trip to a history-laden English town, where I stay in a late medieval hotel, all wooden beams and uneven floors. An old friend of mine who lives in that town had asked me if I would be interested in a threesome, and that seems like just the thing to soothe my broken heart. He and a dark-haired woman with milk-white skin arrive at my hotel room: at first, I just film the two of them, the lens a barrier, keeping me distant, observant. Then I switch off the camera and lose myself in it all. After the orgasms, we clean ourselves up and leave the hotel – they walk off together into the beginnings of the warm summer night, and I head in the opposite direction to a death metal gig at a deconsecrated church. Cryptopsy play the whole of their classic album, *None So Vile*, in the sanctuary where the altar once was. It is my best birthday ever.

This year, I had booked a resort holiday in France for me, my daughter, my eldest niece and my (then) boyfriend. We were going to stay somewhere lovely for a week, and I would celebrate this landmark birthday in style. The pandemic put an end to that plan; the holiday was cancelled. And then we broke up. I hadn't seen my boyfriend since March and, although nothing in particular had happened, our relationship had not been strong enough to bear the weight of long separation, and when he was finally able to visit at the end of July, instead of running into each other's arms, joyously reunited, we bickered and found each other's quirks annoying. So I asked him to leave.

My stepmum tells me, 'You're just not built to give fully of yourself to another person. You never were. Even when you were two, you were already like this. It's not that you're not loving – you're the most loving person ever – but you just can't give yourself to someone else.' My now-ex said in the course of one argument that he was sure – no matter what else happened – that I would come up with some 'bullshit narrative' that justified my actions and made me look good. (I had briefly hoped that people might be nicer to me once I signed a contract to write a book about my life, but no one was any different, which is probably for the best.) I think it would take more words than I have at my disposal to even begin an attempt at making myself look good. James Baldwin wrote that 'the only real concern of the artist' is 'to recreate out of the disorder of life that order which is art'; this includes turning emotional chaos into bullshit narratives, to justify myself to myself, if not to you.

So I am facing forty, single and alone. There is an Old Irish poem, composed perhaps in the ninth century, known as the 'Lament of the *Caillech Bérri*', that commences 'Ebb-tide comes to me, as to the sea'. Ebb-tide was coming to me, as to the sea.

Back in January, I mentioned medieval poets using other

voices – 'I am Colm Cille', 'I am Eve', 'I am Heledd' – to mediate their own. The *Caillech Bérri* is one such poetic persona. The Lament says 'I am Buí, the *caillech Bérri*' and the poetic voice is female. That is no guarantee of who the poet was, or if they were indeed a woman.

Caillech means 'veiled woman'. In medieval Ireland, all adult women would have covered their heads, but for different reasons. Married women and widows wore headscarves of some kind, and one fragmentary law text tells us that women could be fined for going out in public with their head uncovered. Another kind of veiled woman was the nun. Women who entered religious orders wore veils, and so, depending on context, *caillech* can mean a married woman or a nun or a widow or, in other contexts, a married woman who has embraced celibacy – a penitent wife. By extension, it also came to mean 'old woman'.

At first glance, the *caillech Bérri* could be any of these things. It requires a closer reading of her words to flesh out her character. We know that she is ageing. She opens her poem with the quatrain:

> Ebb-tide comes to me, as to the sea.
> Old age yellows me.
> Though I may grieve at that,
> It approaches its food gleefully.

Time has a fierce appetite; old age approaches to consume her, heedless of her grief at the ageing process. And then she speaks her poetic name:

I am Buí, the veiled woman of Beare.
I used to wear an ever-new tunic.
Today, attenuated as I am,
I have not even a cast-off tunic.

She looks back on her younger days, a time of pleasure and carousing. Her arms, once fleshy, used to embrace kings, were wrapped around handsome young men, but now they are bony and thin. Her grey hair too is thinning. Everything about her is diminishing, lessening, as age relentlessly devours her youthfulness. We start to see someone emerging more clearly: she covers that thinning, grey hair with a white veil. Where once she dined with kings, she now eats whey-water amongst other old women. This seems to be a woman who has entered a religious community in old age. Our *caillech* was once a privileged lay woman but is now a nun, or a penitent.

The poem is a shambles but an interesting one. All of the early copies are lost and it only survives in manuscripts of the modern era. Along the way, through the process of copying and recopying, other stanzas – other poetic voices – have become entangled with hers. Separate verses, perhaps added to the margins of earlier versions, have become incorporated into the main poem; at least seven of the thirty-five stanzas seem to be later additions. Interpolators have crept relentlessly into the body of the poem just as the ebb-tide of age has encroached upon Buí's youthfulness.

Should we just take the poem as it is – as messy and corrupted as a human life? Or should we attempt to separate 'authentic' verses from later interlopers, to recreate the lost 'original', to purify the veiled woman and restore her to her former youth?

I live in a society that prizes youth in its women and old age in its historical documents. Generations of scholars have picked over medieval Irish texts, trying to strip away any given document's accumulated experience, alterations and accretions, in an attempt to find a 'pure' and 'original' source within, the oldest parts, the sections of greatest antiquity. Texts that have undergone processes of revision and rewriting over the centuries are dissected in search of their earliest core. The older the better. Academic hands tear texts apart in a hungry search for something that might pre-date Christianity; pre-date literacy. Stripping away word after word until there is nothing left but unspoken ideology. Bullshit narratives.

Historical sources, like life, are messy and complicated. They are not pristine, wearing an ever-new tunic. They are cast-offs, ageing and attenuated. And they have problems; sometimes serious ones. Scholars working on Roman history used to confidently deploy the information supplied by the first-century historian Tacitus. He provides us with vital intelligence about the events that occurred during the reigns of the first Roman Emperors – Augustus, Tiberius, Caligula, Claudius, Nero. His narrative is rich and juicy. However, the earliest surviving manuscript of the first part of his major work was copied, probably in Fulda, in the middle of the ninth century; and the earliest copy of the rest of it dates from the eleventh century. Seven hundred and fifty years between the date of composition and the earliest manuscript of the first half of the text; almost a millennium between the date of composition and the earliest manuscript of the second half. That's a big gap, and a lot of things can happen in the intervening period – mistakes, additions, revisions, erasures. The same is true for a great many medieval texts: the earliest surviving copies might date to seven, eight, nine hundred years after the date of composition. What lives might those texts have lived in the intervening period? We must be attentive to the whole lifespan of a source, not just its moment of birth.

Buí, the veiled woman of Beare, crept from white skin and yellow hair to yellow skin and white hair, from a love of men to a love of God. I am, if I optimistically award myself the average life expectancy of a twenty-first-century woman of Irish birth, at a midway point between youth and old age. The Middle Ages. I have created a great deal in my forty years – memories, friendships, a child – and I have destroyed a great deal too – hopes, relationships, marriages (other people's and my own). The insecurities of youth have faded and I am comfortable in my skin, which has not yet started to yellow. I don't mind that my hair is now more silver than black. I grow thicker, stouter, stronger with age. I am not fading away; I am more substantial. I buy my own ever-new tunics and, at least until the pandemic struck, I still used my arms to embrace handsome men. I don't even mind that much about being single again, because I am otherwise happy. I have a sprawling network of people I love, especially my daughter, and I am successful, doing a job I love. The anxiety is mostly under control – certainly, it attacks me less frequently than before – and the drinking has not yet caught up with me. From this perspective, the midpoint of my life appears to be an apex, a zenith. But perhaps that is an illusion, because I cannot yet see the shape of what lies ahead, no matter how much I contemplate what has gone before.

I often feel as though I've lived my ages out of order. I was prematurely old in childhood, grave and troubled. I did the full maturity of family life in my twenties, then wild and unbridled youthful lasciviousness in my thirties. It wasn't supposed to be this way. I don't know what my forties will bring. Women who have lived middle age often speak about enjoying a sort of invisibility that creeps up on us as we are no longer the object of lust. I think that lack of distraction might be good for my work. One of the academic men I slept with in my thirties – one of the nice guys, pillar of the community, loved by his students, attending Mass with his wife and kids before heading to a hotel room to sleep with me – once said that he wished more female academics would dye their hair. He hated seeing the rows of grey heads at conferences, so drab and unattractive. I wonder how many of those grey heads feel joyfully relieved of the burden of being the object of his gaze. He's starting to go grey himself now, but I guess he doesn't feel the need to dye his own hair.

People today tend to misunderstand the nature of life expectancy in the Middle Ages. Because the extremely high infant mortality rates pull the overall average down, you hear statements like 'people in the Middle Ages only lived until they were forty'. That's misleading. There were peaks and troughs of risks to life, and if a child made it to their fifth birthday there was a pretty decent chance that they would live to old age. The major barriers in adulthood to reaching old age were death in pregnancy or childbirth, death as a result of violence, and disease. These things all happened: there were bloody battles and lethal pandemics. But, statistically, if you made it past those crucial first five years, you stood a pretty good chance of seeing your sixtieth or even seventieth birthday. Lots of people would have experienced the victory that is survival, the mixed emotions that constitute ageing.

The idea that life arced from childhood and adolescence, through robust adulthood, peaking in maturity before declining into old age and senescence was an influential one in Western Europe throughout the Middle Ages. And the human lifespan was used as a way of thinking about all of human history. A microcosmic way of understanding the macrocosmic. Augustine of Hippo, the North African theologian whose work we encountered in an eleventh-century Welsh manuscript, working in the decades either side of the year 400, was the most influential advocate of this view of history: he delineated six ages of history analogous to the six ages of man – infancy, childhood, adolescence, young manhood, maturity and old age.

Augustine believed that he was living in the old age of the world, the sixth and final age, that the apocalypse promised by the Christian Bible would come soon, and that Christ would return to judge the living and the dead. Many Irish writers adopted his model, and one Latin text written in Ireland in the early tenth century tells us that:

> The first age of the world was from Adam to Noah; the second from Noah to Abraham; the third from Abraham to David; the fourth from David to Daniel; the fifth age until John the Baptist; the sixth from John until the Judgement when our Lord will come to judge the living and the dead through fire.

The world, like the veiled woman of Beare, is in its old age. Its virile young manhood was the fourth age, the age of kings – David, Solomon, Hezekiah, Josiah – just as Buí, the veiled woman of Beare, used to feast with kings in her youth. Now, though, the world turns its mind towards its end, which will come in fire and judgement and salvation (for a few) or damnation (for many).

Travel restrictions are a little less strict this month and the family of a friend of my daughter's unexpectedly invites her to join them on their camping holiday in France. They are already in France; I simply have to get her to a meeting point where they can collect her. So we go, masked and armed with hand sanitizer, by train to London St Pancras, and on a half-empty Eurostar to Paris. We get a taxi from Gare du Nord to Montparnasse: the streets are deserted. The taxis sitting in long, unmoving lines each contain a driver waiting hopefully for jobs that don't come. We're still masked, and it is hot and sticky at Montparnasse, where we board our train. Upon arrival, my daughter heads off excitedly to the campsite with her friend and his family. I walk to a hotel, sweating, exhausted. I take a cold shower and lie on the bed in air-conditioned bliss. I might not have my week-long family holiday in a resort, celebrating my birthday, but I get something just as good: a few days, alone, in a deserted hotel in Tours. It feels revelatory to be somewhere else.

I stand at the foot of the Tour de l'Horloge. There's a clock at the top of the tower now, hence its name. The tower was built in the eleventh century, replacing the Roman-era building which preceded it. Beneath the clock are five storeys of windows, built in a Romanesque style. A simpler, more rounded, architecture was in fashion then, before it was abandoned in favour of the sharper edges of the Gothic style in which the tower was later reworked. Layers upon layers.

In the shadow of the tower, I'm surrounded by groups of food delivery guys, mostly migrants from Francophone Africa, smoking, chatting, laughing together, and then heading off on their bicycles as jobs come in. They're much busier than the taxi drivers of Paris, as increasingly people choose to eat restaurant food at home. I wander on towards the Basilica of St Martin, a nineteenth-century building on the site of much older ones: once inside, I descend towards his tomb and the smack of incense pierces my senses in spite of my mask. There are only a couple of visitors, heads bowed in the cool silence. I light a candle for my father and think about how many people have prayed here over the centuries, throwing out their hopes and fears and wishes to this ex-soldier.

St Martin lived in the fourth century and had served in the Roman army before entering religious life. An account of Martin's life, or more specifically of his miracles, was written by one of his followers, the highly educated lawyer Sulpicius Severus. Sulpicius had given up his wealthy and privileged secular life for the sake of God, in accordance with Christian teaching, apparently at Martin's urging. His account of Martin's life and deeds was highly influential across Western Europe in the Middle Ages, and it was read by writers in Britain and Ireland, shaping the way they thought about sanctity and what it is to be a holy person.

In early medieval Ireland, the key driver of sanctity was founding churches and monasteries. To be honest, you could pretty much be the most awful human ever to have lived, but if you had founded a monastery, you'd be considered a saint. A pretty low bar, but it's the main reason why there are so many hundreds of 'saints' from early medieval Ireland about whom we know nothing other than the name of the church they allegedly founded.

Once someone had a church – or, even better, a group of churches and monasteries – associated with them, they had people who had an interest in promoting their reputation. The more miracles that could be attached to your saint's name, the more people would want to donate land to your churches, offer money for your pastoral services, pay to be buried in your cemeteries. Your saint needed to have bigger and better miracles than the founders of neighbouring churches. It was best of all if you possessed your saint's body, their relics, on-site – like they do at the Basilica of St Martin of Tours, which is built over his rediscovered tomb. If you had bits of other saints – an arm, a finger, a lock of hair – then that simply added to the potential of your place for intercession, for salvation, for more miracles. If a saint became famous enough, you wouldn't even need to have any real connection with them; you could name your church after them anyway (maybe acquire a dubious body part to bolster your claim) and get in on that saint's reputation for sanctity.

These churches hoped to create a kind of salvific feedback loop between heaven and earth, healing bodies in this life and souls in the next, storing up treasure in heaven while conveniently accumulating a healthy profit here too. The churches that failed to do this are the ones whose founders are only sparsely attested in the historical record: a saint without a life, without miracles, without a body. The ones that were successful are well known to this day: and when it came to hagiographical propaganda, none were better in early medieval Ireland than the churches associated with St Patrick.

Unusually, Patrick's early biographers didn't draw on Sulpicius's 'Life of Martin' as their model. They were more ambitious than that: they modelled Patrick on none other than Moses who, like many of the great biblical figures, is said to have lived to an incredibly old age. In the early ninth-century Book of Armagh, there is a note that states that Patrick was like Moses in a number of ways, one of which was that he lived to be a hundred and twenty years old. Now, human beings can, potentially, live for that long; the best-documented case is a French woman, Jeanne Calment, who lived to be a hundred and twenty-two. However, the lifespans of the figures of Genesis and Exodus are mythical and symbolic rather than real. Likewise for Patrick, whose lifespan is invented in imitation of Moses.

One of the unusual aspects of Patrick's cult is that his chief church, that of Armagh, long the most powerful and influential church on the island of Ireland, does not possess his body. The Book of Armagh states that, just like Moses, no one knows where Patrick's body lies. This is one way of dealing with the lack of corporeal remains (there is some evidence to suggest that he was buried at Downpatrick, but that is also late and unreliable). Shaping this absence to be one of many ways in which Patrick is 'like Moses' is clever propaganda on a number of levels. Since Armagh doesn't have the unique selling point of a place like Tours – *here is our saint, this is his body, pray to him* – they surpass mere sainthood as an attraction and instead put Patrick on a par with the long-lived, legendary leaders of God's chosen people.

One of our wandering medieval scholars came from England to Tours in the ninth century. By boat, of course, in those pre-Eurostar days. We don't know exactly when Alcuin was born, but he seems to have lived to the age of about seventy. He was born in York and had an illustrious career at the court of Charlemagne. He moved back and forth between the north of England and Francia and was hugely admired for his intellect and writings. Like many of the poets I was talking about last month, Alcuin jumped on the *locus amoenus* bandwagon. He too wrote poems featuring little monastic cells, encircled by trees, with streams and birds. And he contrasts old age and youth: 'While the devoted youths hunt stags across the fields, / the tired elder now leans upon his staff.' Life can be long and journeyed. Late in life, he was placed in charge of the Abbey of Marmoutier, which had been founded by St Martin, just outside Tours. Alcuin once wrote *interrogare sapiente est docere* – to ask questions wisely is to teach. That's something that's always stuck with me.

I visit the Musée des Beaux-Arts and have a panic attack amidst the portraits of civic notables and displays of romantic nationalism. The anxiety still flares up from time to time, and I wonder if I am feeling guilty for having travelled at all. I take a Valium and head downstairs to the ground floor, to look at the medieval art.

The Valium kicks in as I'm contemplating a twelfth-century, polychromatic carved wooden head of Christ, from Aragon or Catalonia. Christ is long-eared and sad-eyed. I wonder what has happened to the rest of his body – not Christ's body, scourged and crucified and resurrected, so they say – but *this* Christ's body. I see the decapitated body of John the Baptist in a fourteenth-century depiction of his funeral by Lorenzo Veneziano. I've seen lots of paintings of John the Baptist's head on a plate over the years; here, at last, is the rest of him. I stand in front of a tempera on poplar portrait of Joseph of Arimathea, made in the second half of the fourteenth century by Niccolò di Tommaso. Joseph is depicted with wrinkles, crow's feet around his eyes, grey hair, grey beard. An old man. In the words of the early medieval English poem 'The Seafarer':

Age creeps up on him,
his face grows pale; his head,
grey-haired, bewails old friends,
sons of princes, already
given to the earth . . .

I think about these aged artefacts, some of them now incomplete, diminished, gathered together in these empty rooms. Heads without bodies, bodies without heads. Objects which depict human bodies age and crumble and flake over time, more slowly than those bodies did themselves, perhaps, but in a way that makes them as fragile and vulnerable as we are. There is a fragment of an eleventh-century fresco which depicts St Florentius. It was discovered just down the road, in Charlemagne's Tower, in the centre of Tours, in 1938, and moved to the museum. It tells the story of some of the artistic influences of the Eastern Roman Empire on Western European art.

I could spend all day amidst these pieces, but I'm sluggish now, and hungry, so I abandon the icons and statues in search of food. There is a street full of restaurants. It's raining heavily but I eat my meal outside anyway – because although I am trying to escape the pandemic, I have not escaped it. There's a canopy to keep me dry as I eat cod ceviche with sliced radish, nectarine, samphire, cut through with something sharp and acidic. It's light and complex and delicious. I wash it down with white wine as thunder rumbles. Tours is endlessly layered: the Roman and the medieval, the pre-Revolutionary and post-Revolutionary, the ancient and the modern, all sit amidst each other, jumbled and inseparable, a place that has been used and reused over time.

Historians attempt to separate some of these overlapping layers in order to create order from the chaos of the human past, and in doing so we tend to label eras and peoples and things. I say that something is 'medieval', but when does the medieval begin and end? The Romanesque arches of the Tour de l'Horloge but not the clock at its top? Should I write 'Francia', which might be an unfamiliar place to you, or should I write 'France', which would help to situate it for you, even though the extent and borders of the Frankish kingdom do not map on to modern French borders?

I get the train back to Paris, and the Eurostar back to London, a day before the UK government changes its travel guidance and imposes a fourteen-day quarantine period for people returning from France. I self-isolate at home for fourteen days after I get back anyway: those few days being able to reach out and touch a tangible and visible history have fortified me, given me the strength to go nowhere for the foreseeable future. Four days later, I am forty.

In the early Middle Ages, comparing the arc of history to the human lifespan was just one of many ways to view the passing of time. Calendrical science was a big thing then, and there are complex and interesting writings from the seventh and eighth centuries about the calculation of time. Ireland made a big contribution in this regard, as did good old Bede of Northumbria. Much of this intellectual activity was prompted by the need to calculate the date of the movable feast of Easter, the most important day in the Christian year. Its trickiness lies in the reconciling of the solar and lunar calendars, because, ever since the early Christian era, Easter is always the first Sunday after the first full moon after the spring equinox – the equinox pertaining to the sun, and the full moon to, well, the moon. Christians wanted to be able to predict when Easter would be next year, and the year after that, and the year after that.

There were multiple competing systems in different regions because, while everyone agreed on using the so-called Julian calendar to calculate the equinox, there were various different lunar calendars in play. This led to unfortunate situations, such as the infamous one in the Northumbrian royal court recorded by Bede, where the king, Oswiu, ended up celebrating Easter when his wife, Eanflæd, was still observing Lent. This scheduling problem had to be resolved so, at the Synod of Whitby in 664, it was decided that the calculation observed by Eanflæd was correct. Churches in the south of Ireland were among those that had already adopted this so-called Dionysian system in the first half of the seventh century. Yet some of the churches in more northerly parts of Ireland did not switch to the new method until a century after their southern counterparts.

This fragmentary, piecemeal process of change is understandable: it was asking people to rethink how they thought about time, and the way that their predecessors had thought about time. The monasteries associated with St Columba were being told that their founder saint, their great man with his great reputation for sanctity, might have celebrated

Easter on the wrong day. This got to the very heart of thinking about sacred time. And yet, other places in Ireland and Britain had been more willing to move with the times, as it were, and adopt more mathematically accurate systems of calculation. Some people embrace change as others resist it.

People often feel nostalgia, either for their childhood or, more often, for a time they can't even remember, a time before they were born. We already saw it earlier this year, with the resistance to pulling down statues of slave traders and colonialists, because there are some who perceive Britain's empire as its golden age. These 'good old days' would be when women couldn't vote; people of colour had fewer, or no, legal rights; and only wealthy white men of property were enfranchised. People knew their place. Ah, those were the days, and it's all gone to shit since then. You see this too in the American nostalgia for the 1950s and early 1960s. The days of the all-American, shiny-white family, with the housewife in the kitchen, the breadwinning father in the office, the kids – one boy and one girl – excelling in baseball and needlework respectively. The days of Jim Crow and segregation and the KKK.

Nostalgia can be a very dangerous thing, and people have never been immune to it. In the works of Ancient Greek and Roman writers you can find plenty of 'young people these days . . . ', 'everything was better in the old days' and what have you. Likewise, in the Middle Ages, the idea of a golden age and a decline from some idealized past was a common way of thinking about time.

One eleventh-century Irish author, conscious of living in the old age of the world – judgement was coming, and coming soon – wrote a diatribe along these lines. For him (there's no conclusive evidence that the author was male but, let's face it, this gives off major 'grumpy old man' vibes), the golden age was the early centuries of Christianity in Ireland. Since then, he writes, everything had gone downhill. He condemns churches for their institutional failings and individuals for their moral failings. He says that the people of Ireland have become no better than heathens. Indeed, he says, they are worse than heathens because at least heathens abide by their oaths. He compares the corruption of his present-day society with the golden age of St Patrick, a man who had to escape enslavement before he could undertake his Christian mission. He articulates a narrative of decline and advocates a return to those good old days of the age of saints. Apparently, things have been going to hell in a handbasket for millennia – and yet, here we still are.

The author of the eleventh-century rant, which goes by the name of 'Adomnán's Second Vision', may have been writing during a pandemic: 1095–6, when those awful conditions of crop failure and disease that I wrote about in my April blog post to my students prevailed across north-west Europe, and so many died; when Pope Urban II called on Christians to go to war against Muslims, and the First Crusade was born.

In that time of crisis, then, this Irish writer seems to have searched for what he thought were better days, and he found a mythical golden age in fifth- and sixth-century Ireland when, he said, there was less crime, people were safer, Christianity was purer, people were quite simply better. A bullshit narrative. He thought that the way of returning to that better time was through penance and fasting and prayer. And, of course, people should give money to the church. If people didn't reform themselves now, then it was only going to get worse: there would be attacks by 'foreign races with avenging swords', the harvests would fail, there would be disease amongst livestock and among men. That is a view of the past and of the future that is shaped by fear of the present. And many still succumb to that today. I'm reading Miranda Doyle's *A Book of Untruths*, a gift from one of my academic mentors, in which she writes that:

> Our selves consist merely of a collection of moments, which we try to cohere through narration. We attempt to make permanent what is not. Like lying, memory is a process of (re)construction. When we remember, we assemble the fragments together, filling in the gaps with expectation and assumption. We construct our memories, in the same way that we build a lie.

We construct bullshit narratives of the past and of ourselves as a way of living with and in the present. Looking back clearly and honestly is difficult, perhaps even impossible. The poet who wrote the 'Lament of the *Caillech Bérri*' sees her youth as a golden age – everything was glorious then, everything was wonderful. Which is, of course, as fictional as her poetic voice.

There is something about reaching what feels like a midway point that impels you to take stock, to look back and look forward. Modern society tends to see one's prime, at least for women, as being somewhere in the twenties. Women are over the hill by thirty and all but done for by thirty-five. Augustine saw the peak of one's life as the age of virility and, for him, the age of full maturity – middle age, what he calls the age of *gravitas* – is characterized by decline, a gradual crumbling into old age and death. Funnily enough, when my father turns up in my dreams now, he is in his forties, his age when I was a young child, before the drinking overtook him, before the disease and the disintegration. Before his skin turned yellow and his hair turned white. He appears often in my sleep, black-haired and smiling, and we talk and laugh together as adults of the same age, both of us in our prime.

Life is not a simple arc, and neither is history. It is more like the printout of a heart rate monitor, telling the story of a heart palpitating with an irregular beat. There are innumerable peaks and troughs, sometimes even flat lines. The Old English poem 'The Seafarer' says that no man is wise without his share of winters, and that wisdom accumulates with age and experience. Maybe so. But it accumulates in irregular and unequal ways, and we can be wise in one area of life even as we are foolish in another.

As the days reach their summer prime, I have an opportunity to reflect on where I have been and where I am going, not only because of this landmark birthday, but because at the end of this month I come to the end of a five-year period as the head of my university department. My reward for my service is a full academic year without teaching or administrative responsibilities; a year to read, and research, and translate, and think. From the first of September, I will have a year to write. Unencumbered by a relationship, a solitary scholar, for me forty will be a year of words, and I cannot wait to get started.

SEPTEMBER

Words

As a child I didn't have any burning desire to be a historian. I don't think I even knew that historian was an option. I did one of those careers quizzes at school and the job recommended for me was bricklayer (a very satisfying job, it strikes me, because a bricklayer can measure their day's work in walls built, just as I measure mine in words written). But I had a voracious appetite for learning: I could protect myself by living behind a fortress of books. It didn't really matter to me what I learned – in the end, it happened to be medieval history, but it could just as easily have been astrophysics, cell biology, Russian literature, economics. Anything. I just needed to find a discipline to dissolve myself into so that I could exist within a protective sphere of knowledge, its boundaries marking a point to which I can walk in order to reach out and make contact with the outside world – as when I give public talks, or write pieces for non-academic audiences – but at its centre a refuge to which I can retreat whenever the outside world harms me. Heartbreaks, assaults, grief and other trials are survivable because I can shield myself with education, use productive research to silence destructive thoughts, coat myself in an epistemological armour. This is not an ivory tower; it's a survival technique.

Now I have a full year to retreat as far as I want into the centre of my knowledge-sphere. I am no longer burdened by the administrative pressures that have governed my life for the past five years, worrying about student welfare, staffing issues, timetabling, HR disputes, workload allocations, budget overspends and curriculum reform. These are important things that affect people's education and their careers, and I took my responsibilities seriously, so to suddenly be relieved of them is a revelation. I feel ten years younger already.

I can really think about some of the historical problems that most interest me. I can read primary sources in medieval manuscripts that have never been published, never been translated. Through understanding and interpreting that material, I can create new knowledge; and I certainly will do a bit of that over the course of the year. But, uncharacteristically, thanks to the approach from my publisher, I will be spending a considerable chunk of the time out at the very limits of my sphere, writing this book, reaching out to you.

Writing this non-academic book frightens me a bit, leaves me vulnerable to attack from the outside world, like a poorly defended ringfort. But it also feels liberating. On the first day of my research leave, I am out of bed and at the only desk in the house, ready to write, by 8 a.m. The hard-fought knowledge I have accumulated over twenty-two years working in this field – all of the research for every scholarly article I have written, everything I have read or translated for a conference paper or undergraduate lecture, everything that has been stored inside me all this time – is suddenly ready to gush forth, a breach in my defences, and words start to scatter themselves upon the page. I write quickly and easily and more pleasurably than I have ever written before.

My stepmum's black cat strolls into the room, arches his back and jumps up on to the bed behind me, curls up and goes to sleep. I laugh to myself as I inevitably think of Pangur, the white cat about whom a medieval Irish poet famously wrote.

Pangur Bán, like any of the small number of medieval Irish texts that have reached the popular imagination, drives me mad. Don't get me wrong; it's a great poem. And I want to talk about it. But it's one of those things that has acquired a significance disproportionate to its creation and survival, primarily because a lot of people seem to really love cats. The image that the poem creates of a scholar and his cat, each engaged in their respective work of apprehending the meaning of texts and apprehending mice, appeals to a sort of cosy nostalgia about the past and gives a false impression of something that is 'just like us'. Hence, my own wry laughter when our family pet curls up near me as I settle into writing.

It's natural to feel that moment of connection. Greg Toner, the professor of Irish at Queen's University Belfast, has written very astutely about *Pangur Bán* and its appeal, noting some of the more eccentric interpretations of the poem by previous scholars (the writer Frank O'Connor's assertion that it represents 'the perfection of the Oxford common-room' being up there amongst the most idiosyncratic). Toner reveals how the poem has been seen as 'quaint' and 'childlike' and imbued with other such innocent qualities. To my mind this is part of a broader tendency to see early medieval Ireland in juvenile and simplistic terms.

What *Pangur Bán* really exemplifies is part of that mobile, scholarly world I come back to again and again. The poem survives in a scholar's notebook, dating from about the 840s, which has been kept in the monastery of St Paul im Lavanttal in Austria since the early nineteenth century, but which was previously preserved at Reichenau, the island monastery on what is now the German side of Lake Constance. This scholar's notebook is known as the 'St Paul Codex', and other items in this short book include some brief sections on Greek grammar, notes from a commentary on Virgil's *Aeneid*, bits of astronomical learning, something on biblical place names. The sorts of things that an advanced student or professional scholar would be expected to know at that time.

That this scholar was an Irishman is clear from the inclusion of various poems in Old Irish: some verses from a poem ascribed to St Moling, a poem in the voice of Suibne Geilt, a praise poem addressed to Áed mac Diarmata of Leinster. The local interests of these poems might be a clue to the geographical origins, and dynastic affiliations, of the book's owner. He may have started his education somewhere like the monastery of Tech-Moling (St Mullins in modern-day Co. Carlow) or Ferns (Co. Wexford), both within Leinster territory and both associated with St Moling.

It's impossible to know whether the owner of the book is the author of the poem about the cat, or whether he knew it from elsewhere, but there are a few clues that it was probably his own work. First, no copies of the poem exist elsewhere, which suggests that it's a one-off composition by the owner of the book. Second, the language of the poem fits the date of the manuscript – it's not an older text that has been recopied over centuries. Finally, the poem is written in the main body of the manuscript page, not in the margins.

Because the cat in the poem is called Pangur – not an Irish name – it looks like the author headed abroad after his Irish education. The best explanation of the name that has been suggested so far is that it's Welsh, derived from the Welsh word for fuller's earth, a kind of white clay – a fitting name for a cat who, we are told, is *bán* – white.

So perhaps after a sojourn in Wales, during which time he picked up some Welsh, and maybe even the cat, our Irish scholar headed on towards the Continent to further his career. And there, possibly, he writes a poem about himself and his cat.

> Me and white Pangur,
> each of us engaged in his particular profession;
> his mind is on hunting,
> my own mind is on my particular occupation.
>
> I love to sit – better than any fame –
> at my notebook – assiduous understanding;
> white Pangur does not envy me,
> he loves his youthful art.

While the cat pins a mouse under his claw, the poet rejoices when he pins down the difficult meaning of a passage with his own sharp mind. Perhaps he is referring to the very things we find in his own notebook: the study of Virgil's *Aeneid*, Greek grammar, theological tracts. For the poet, his work is an attempt to hone his mind, although he is, like most scholars, ever conscious of how little he knows. Again, he compares himself to Pangur.

> He sharpens his vision, the full bright one,
> against the interior wall;
> I myself sharpen my clear vision,
> though it is inconsiderable, against keen knowledge.

Our scholar-poet studies, and strives to understand, what he reads but he doesn't tell us – and nor does his surviving booklet suggest – that he is engaged in the production of new knowledge. This is something that some of our earliest Irish sources on the nature of education distinguish: the difference between those who learn, and those who have reached a sufficiently advanced stage that they create new knowledge. It was at some point during my PhD, I guess, when I published my first academic article, that I crossed that boundary. I never cease learning, of course; I too know that my knowledge, my vision, is limited and inconsiderable. But I know enough to say new things about some small and insignificant area of human enquiry. Enough to write.

It is one of the most rewarding parts of my job to see my own PhD students cross that knowledge threshold, as they present their first conference papers or publish their first articles. Although I am on leave this year, I continue to supervise these advanced research students. One of them is due to submit her thesis at the end of this month, so I devote long hours to reading the final draft chapters of her study of the life and cult of St Abbán. Another is beginning his fourth and final year working on kingship in Ireland either side of the

Anglo-Norman invasion. A third is entering her third year, researching Latin and Old Irish ideas about language and cognition, the relationship between thoughts and words and grammar in early medieval Ireland. And my 'youngest', going into her second year, is looking at medieval Irish paternity law and the concept of illegitimacy.

They are four very different people, from very different backgrounds, from three different continents, with varying social, ethnic and personal identities. All of them clever and interesting and likeable. Their intellectual journeys towards their chosen research topics, and how these have been shaped by their life experiences, fascinate me. And as with my previous – and, no doubt, with future – PhD students, I feel a strong maternal protectiveness towards them. My first ever PhD student was actually older than me, but I still felt like his second mum. I've seen them go through heartbreaks and grief, illness and homesickness, as well as triumphs and successes, alongside the quiet, continuous work of research.

Perhaps the nature of the relationship between a supervisor and research student is such that the early Irish idea of education as a form of fosterage persists. One medieval Irish text describes a teacher as a *féthathir*, a 'knowledge-father'. Perhaps I am my students' knowledge-mother. Eventually, they will fly the nest, sometimes to a job that will involve writing new knowledge, rewriting history.

Not everything I write is scholarly, though. I am addicted to social media, and I post incessantly on Facebook and Twitter: what I have read, films I am watching, where I have been, how much I have written today. Ephemeral thoughts and words, really, although they persist in the digital realm. It's as though I feel compelled to leave behind as many traces of my life as I can, as many words and documents and records as I can create in my brief existence, in the hope that some future historian will find my story and confirm that I existed. That I was. Sometimes I wake up in the morning and delete the worst of the previous night's drunk-posts, but other times it's too late because I have already initiated an online argument with my clumsy, booze-addled brain-farts.

My phone is never far from my hand and I tap away at it at all hours. For my academic writing, though, I still write by hand before I type it up. Pen and paper. I have these gel ink rollerball pens, and their black liquid spills smoothly and easily on to soft paper. If the ink runs out, I toss the pen into the bin and pick up another. It was different in medieval Europe. For transient writing – schoolroom notes, hand-writing practice, (social media posts) – people used wax tablets. The wax was set in wood and once the writing was no longer needed it could be scraped away, leaving the tablet ready for the next day's work. Some of the earliest writing to survive in Ireland is the Springmount Bog wax tablets, preserved from rot and destruction for centuries in a bog in Co. Antrim, containing passages of Psalms 30 and 31, etched with a metal stylus into the wax. An astonishing glimpse of the vast reservoirs of words that are gone. Ephemeral and forgotten.

For more permanent writing, people in Western Europe chose vellum, made from animal skin, usually calves. Medieval

Ireland was a dairy economy, so there would have been a regular supply of male calves slaughtered each year, whose skin could be prepared for transformation into a book.

One of the poems ascribed to Bishop Patrick of Dublin tells us how the physicality of the written word was something that would outlast the fragile human body.

> Alas! The writer will die before the written page –
> unless it is consumed by fire or drowned in heavy water.
> This skin which I have scored briefly with my own hand,
> ah! It will outlast my brief life.

His own skin will decompose, but the skin on which he has written lives on as testament to the fact that he existed. That he was. Ironically, little verses that say how the page will live longer than the writer become quite commonplace, especially in the later Middle Ages. They become a cliché and, although they may feel like they are drawing us closer to a real person, their generic nature means that such intimacy is an illusion.

Scribes did, however, leave signs in the margins of their manuscripts that they had existed. That they were people. Complaints about the quality of the ink or of the parchment are the most common interventions. But we also find notes about the weather (usually cold), about the time of year, or sometimes just a name. Quite a few of these are what we call 'pen trials' – writing something inconsequential to make sure the ink is flowing before beginning writing. But despite their functionality, they can be little windows into the world of the scribe. Perhaps the best-known such note simply says, in Ogam script, *latheirt* – 'ale-slain'. Hung-over. I know how he felt.

One eleventh- or twelfth-century Irish poet tells us that they are just tired, whether simply from the physical exertion of writing, or from something more existential. Old age, perhaps:

> My hand is tired from writing –
> my keen nib is not blunt.
> My slender-tipped pen vomits forth
> A draught of blackest ink.
>
> A torrent of hard wisdom flows
> from my tanned right hand.
> It spills its liquid upon the leaf;
> ink of green-coated holly.
>
> I stretch my dripping little pen
> ceaselessly across great, gathered books,
> for the sake of the storehouse of the skilled;
> suddenly my hand is tired from writing.

The fact that this poet, like so many others from the Middle Ages, is now anonymous suggests that words have life outside and beyond their author. There are a fair number of writers whose careers we can trace and whose work we can identify, but many more works have no individual identity attached to them. How do you imagine the poet who is tired from writing? An old man, a monk, with a long grey beard? A woman flexing an arthritic hand as she stretches out her back? A young man who didn't sleep well last night?

My ink, too, gushes on to the page as I set down my thoughts, hoping that these words might outlive me. Yet, one of my colleagues reads a draft of one of these chapters and tells me that I am reticent, holding back, that you could read all this and not really know who I am. Should I flay myself and display my viscera to you in the image of a martyred apostle? Do you want to read my confession? That wouldn't get you very far: the confessor is always in control of their narrative.

In his *Confessio* St Patrick tells us exactly as much as he wants us to know, and no more. He tells us that he committed a grave sin in his youth, but he does not tell us what it was. Gallons of scholarly ink have been devoted to speculating: was it sex? With another man? With a woman? Masturbation?

Patrick's sin is whatever you want it to be. He never gives himself to the reader, because he reserves that part of himself for God. He is not even confessing to us: he is justifying himself and his mission to those who have ecclesiastical authority over him.

As satisfying as it is to tell you these things, this book won't count as what universities charmingly call a 'research output'. Because I am telling you stuff I already know, rather than discovering new things. I will also have to produce some research outputs during this year of writing, in order to justify myself and my mission to those who have authority over me. So in between bouts of writing this, I start writing something else. It's about a short medieval Irish narrative that's preserved in two different forms in two different places. The story is about a young boy – seven years old in one version of the story, fourteen in the other – who is developmentally challenged. In the first version, he is very small – no greater than a fist – and in the other he is very large, with a swollen, distended belly. In both stories, having never previously spoken before, he says something quite obscure and incomprehensible and, as a result of this mysterious utterance, he is sent to be educated as a poet, an unlikely outcome for such an unpromising character.

I initially became interested in the story when a student of mine was writing a dissertation on disability in medieval Ireland, and now I finally have time to look into it in more detail. I want to explore why the two versions of the story are different, and whether those differences have something to do with their intended audiences, or the functions of the texts, or the contexts in which they are found. When I start looking at the two versions of this story, I don't know why they're different. Nobody before me has even asked why they are different. So that's my research question for the next couple of months. A small question – inconsiderable, no greater than a fist – but I want to know the answer; and the answer might – or might not – tell us something greater, something more important, about medieval Ireland.

The first thing I need to do is to see exactly how each version is preserved. Digitization has revolutionized the study of medieval history. Just a decade or two ago, checking source material would involve expensive and time-consuming journeys to libraries to look at a manuscript in the flesh; or you could order up poor-quality microfilms or pay for photographs of the relevant pages, which might take weeks to arrive. Now, the vast majority of the manuscripts I work with are freely available online as high-resolution images.

Sitting at my desk in my pyjamas, I check images of the two manuscripts and note exactly how the story appears in both. Next, I check the published translations of the story against the manuscript text to see whether they are accurate and usable. Where I think the translator has made an error, I make a note of my own translation. These are my raw materials. I compare the two versions, noting the similarities and differences. And then I start to think about their broader contexts: what comes before and after the story in the manuscript; what might the author of each version be trying to say?

The boy's name is Amairgen and he lives, apparently in a single-parent household, with his father, who is a smith, and his sister. The sister cares for Amairgen, who is unable to look after himself. In the version of the story that I'm telling you, Amairgen is fourteen years old and monstrous. His belly is swollen and distended. Snot flows from his nose into his mouth. His eyes are sunken and dark red. His back is knobbly and bony and covered in scabs. Amairgen 'had for so long neglected to clean himself after defecating that his own shit rose up to his buttocks'. And he doesn't speak, until a man named Greth, who is the servant of a poet, turns up to have an axe mended by Amairgen's father. All of a sudden, Amairgen speaks. He says, 'Does Greth eat curds (i.e. cooked), blackberries, sloes, sprigs of wild garlic, pine nuts (i.e. nuts), sour apples, curds? Does Greth eat curds?'*This terrifies the servant, who runs off to tell his master what Amairgen has said.

The poet and his servant return to kill Amairgen, but his quick-thinking father has already created an image in the likeness of his son while his daughter hides the real Amairgen. Greth and his master strike the image of Amairgen instead of the real boy and, as compensation for this attempted murder, they have to educate Amairgen as a poet.

Why were Amairgen's innocuous words so dangerous and terrifying?

In part because of who spoke them. You see, what Amairgen said might not look like much more than some garbled words about food in English, but in Irish it's all complex poetic speech, with alliteration and metre. And people like Amairgen – mute and uneducated and disabled – aren't supposed to be able to speak like poets. Poetry was a hierarchical and exclusive profession in medieval Ireland: poetic language should not, from that perspective, belong to the deformed son of a smith.

My student who works on the relationship between thoughts and words in early Irish grammatical tradition decides that she will enter an essay into a competition. The prize is a book and £200 and the chance to have the essay published.

* Believe me, this is as strange and mysterious a statement in Old Irish as it is in English! The words in brackets are part of the original.

The deadline is at the end of this month, so I read a couple of her drafts and watch as her argumentation develops and grows. Her essay is on speech sound – that is, the sounds that emanate from your mouth when you speak, and how these relate to the idea in your mind that you are trying to express and the external reality that those sounds describe. Early medieval writers had quite a bit to say on this topic, and her essay explores the Irish contribution to this aspect of grammatical discourse.

Medieval Irish intellectuals thought in sophisticated ways about language. They inherited the theories of language and grammar that had been developed by Latin writers in previous centuries, but they also brought their own perspective on language that grew out of their particular relationship with Latin. Unlike much of Western Europe in the seventh and eighth centuries, in Ireland nobody's first language was Latin. It was not a native language, because Ireland had not been part of the Roman Empire, and people therefore learned Latin as their second language. They started young – often from the age of seven – and many went on to acquire an extremely high degree of fluency.

Having to learn Latin as a second language caused some thinkers to conceptualize it – and languages more generally – in interesting ways. So my student, whose own first language is Russian, writes in English about the Latin and Irish terminology that medieval Irish writers used to distinguish the sounds of speech from words-as-thoughts or words-as-writing. Her essay goes on to win the prize, and she is happy and quietly proud.

One of the most original Irish writers on the topic of language was a man named Virgilius Maro Grammaticus. We don't know much about his life, and some people have doubted whether he was even Irish, but he writes a kind of Latin that suggests that he was indeed an Irish speaker, since some of his more idiosyncratic Latin words can be understood as literal translations of Irish ones. He writes that letters are quite a lot like people because:

> . . . just as man comprises a physical portion, a soul and a
> sort of celestial fire, so is the letter also permeated with its
> body – that is, its shape, its function and its pronunciation,
> which are its joints and limbs, as it were – and has its soul
> in its meaning and its spirit in its higher form of
> contemplation.

This is heady stuff. The actual physical shape of a letter as you write it down, or the shape of the sound that you pronounce in your mouth, is, according to Virgilius, analogous to the physical body of a person, our outer body. But we all have a soul, he says, and that soul is like the inner meaning of a letter or word or statement. When you dig beneath the surface of the letter on the page, or the sounds emanating from your mouth, and get to the heart of what something really means, there is its soul.

But there is more than that – because Virgilius says that we have something even beyond the soul – what he characterizes as 'celestial fire', that spark which connects us with something divine, something eternal. And he says that words have that quality too, a spirit beyond the soul, which we can only unlock through the most profound sort of contemplation.

Virgilius's way of thinking about language is in part indebted to the Latin grammarians who preceded him, but it is also heavily influenced by the way that people read the Bible. Medieval Christians thought that the words of the Bible – the physical words on the page or in the mouth of the reader – were literally true, an account of things that had happened. They also thought that the Bible had other layers of meaning that could be unlocked through close study. Some of the events recorded in the Bible could be both literally true and simultaneously metaphors for, or prefigurations of, things that happened at other times. So Jonah being in the belly of the whale was a prefiguration of Christ's days in the tomb before his resurrection. Or the Israelites' time in the desert during their Exodus was a prefiguration of Christ's forty days in the desert. That, then, is like Virgilius's soul – the inner meaning of the words.

Yet, beyond all that, Christians believed that there was a way in which every bit of the Bible also possessed a fuller meaning intended by God, beyond anything its human authors could have known or understood – its 'celestial fire', to borrow Virgilius's phrase. Grammarians like Virgilius took a way of understanding holy texts and applied it to all words, all language. Everything has a capacity for meaning beyond the surface layer.

It's because of deep thinking like this that it irritates me when I see medieval Ireland being portrayed in simplistic terms, as though everyone was sitting around a fire telling stories about gods and heroes; as though the stories which emerged from medieval Ireland are folk tales without authors. These writers thought so carefully about words, and wrote with a consciousness of having meaning layered upon meaning, that to reduce it all to 'mythology' feels like an insult. The tendency to romanticize it seems disrespectful to writers who valued precise engagement with words and what they signify.

The sophisticated grammatical terminology attested in Old Irish shows how writers subjected their own language to the same rigorous analysis as Latin. Words could be broken down into syllables, and writers discussed why some vowel sounds were long and others short. They discussed why some nouns were feminine, others masculine and still others neuter. They differentiated between 'natural' and 'artificial' gender, noting that words were assigned genders in artificial and arbitrary ways: there's nothing inherently feminine about a stone and yet stone is a feminine noun; there is nothing inherently masculine about heaven, and yet heaven is a masculine noun.

Some of the most complex discussions of Irish grammar survive in the commentaries that were written on a text called *Auraicept na nÉces*, 'The Scholar's Primer'. The earliest part of the text has been dated to the eighth century, but it was heavily studied over the centuries, and bits were added to it in different versions at different times. One of the oldest parts of the text, though, tells a remarkable story about the creation of the Irish language.

Auraicept na nÉces says that the Irish language was invented by a man named Fénius Farsaid, ten years after the fall of the Tower of Babel. Fénius, we are told, remained at Babel, after the peoples of the world had dispersed, speaking their various languages. Fénius was asked 'to extract a language out of the many languages', that is, to create an artificial, scholastic language. So Fénius cut a language from the other languages, and it was named Goídelc. Irish.

This story persisted over centuries, and we find later texts all telling us that Fénius invented the Irish language. As Christians, medieval Irish people would have been conscious that they are not mentioned in the Bible amongst the peoples of the world. Nor is the Irish language numbered amongst the languages of the biblical world. By situating the invention of Irish in the aftermath of the fall of the Tower of Babel, it places Irish into the scheme of salvation history: Fénius was there when it all happened, and he created Irish from off-cuts of biblically sanctioned languages. This provides comfort to medieval Irish scholars – while Irish may be an abstract invention, rather than one of the natural languages of the world, this account sees Ireland written into the Bible.

But there's more to it than that. If you regard Irish as a language that has been created artificially, 'cut out of the many languages', then it gives you a way of analysing Irish words, because you can try to break the words up again into their constituent parts and use those parts to tell you something about the whole. This is called etymologizing, and medieval Irish authors were pretty obsessed with it.

As a practice, etymologizing goes something like this:

let's take a word – *eclais*, which means 'church'. One medieval author who etymologizes the Irish word *eclais* knows
perfectly well that it's a borrowing from the Latin word
ecclesia. Because he conceives of Irish as something that can
be broken up into its constituent parts and analysed to find
inner meaning – the celestial fire of the word – he experiments with breaking it apart in different ways. He says maybe
eclais comes from *ecan-chlais* 'assembly of wisdom', or *eclas*
'healing assembly', because the church heals people, or *eclais*
'need-enclosure', because churches provide for those in
need.

Those different ways of understanding the meaning of the
word *eclais*, 'church', tell us fundamental things about
what – in the eyes of this author – a church actually is: an
assembly of wisdom, a place of healing, a refuge for the
needy. And the author has revealed these things through etymologizing the actual word for church. He ends by saying
that the word comes from the Latin *ecclesia*. By modern
standards that is the 'right' answer and all his others are
'wrong'. But that misses the point of what he's doing: by his
own standards, all of his etymologies are right, because they
succeed in peeling away the body of the word and revealing
its soul.

Early Irish glossaries do this, over and over, for vast numbers of words, and they draw on Latin and Greek and
Hebrew and Welsh to etymologize Irish words – which is
valid, because they've said that Irish is created from bits of
all these languages. The word *catt*, which means 'cat', comes
from Greek, so they say, from *apa toi catesta* (= *apa tou*

kaiesthai 'from being lit up'), because of the burning light in the cat's eye which allows it to see so keenly in the dark. It doesn't matter that the Old Irish word *catt* is really a borrowing from the Latin word *cattus*, because the Irish writer's remark about the fiery glint of the cat's eye at night tells us more about cats than mere words.

One of the versions of my story about Amairgen appears in one of these etymological glossaries. Not the version that I told you earlier, but the one in which he is seven years old and tiny when he speaks his strangely meaningless words. The story, therefore, is contained within a work that is fundamentally concerned with words and meaning and language, the work of advanced scholars. When those scholars started out their educations, they too would have had to learn Latin as beginners and they would have had to learn vocabulary lists that included lists of food much like Amairgen's strange litany. For example, there's a manuscript that was probably compiled in Cornwall in the tenth century. In it, there's a colloquy known as *De Raris Fabulis*. This is a Latin text, in the style of a conversation or dialogue, all about quotidian life in the classroom and the regular activities of a monastery. The 'teacher' asks: 'What are the foods that you're setting down? Tell us the names that are familiar to you?' and the 'pupil' replies: 'Bread made of wheat and of barley, of darnel, of rye, of spelt and of millet; butter, lard or fat, and milk; and cabbage and again leek; whey, sausage, black pudding, potage, porridge, cheese . . .' and on it goes. Dialogues like this are how students learned the basic vocabulary that they would need to converse in Latin in the monastery. The stuff of daily life. When Amairgen spoke, it was also about food, but in his own native language, Irish, and he took a quotidian list of food and created poetry from it.

If you break sentences down into words, and words into syllables, and syllables into letters, you get the basic building blocks of language: the bodies that will be imbued with the soul of meaning. In teasing out the ideas of scholars who were working a thousand years before me, exploring how they thought about natural and artificial language, I am giving you an insight into my day job as a historian. It is what I love to teach and to explore, and I am at my happiest doing this. I end each day, like the bricklayer I might have been, exhausted but satisfied, having constructed another edifice of words, with deep foundations.

Language, especially poetic language, had the potential to exclude people in the Middle Ages; the story of Amairgen is an example of how startling and radical the idea of access to the world of language seemed to medieval thinkers. Today, more people than ever before can write. More of those who were previously silenced have found their voices. And yet we still need more, and different, stories. More translations of literature from one language to another. More diversity in publishing. More platforms to hear the unheard speak.

We can fill ourselves with words – stories, research, blogs, Facebook posts, tweets – with talk about food and daily life. We can also sit and contemplate words' deeper connotations, capturing difficult meanings as a cat catches mice. In the twenty-first century, that involves thinking carefully about how words can be used in dangerous ways: to divide, to mislead, to stir up resentment. We need to recapture language for good. Open the doors of poetry and let Amairgen speak. It is through words that we can do the vital work of recognizing each other's humanity. Set the world ablaze with the celestial fire of language.

OCTOBER

Bodies

I start measuring the pandemic in the quantities of my body that I am discarding: the number of times I have cut finger-nails, toenails; the hair that clogs the drain as I wash my hair, shave my armpits. How much of me have I thrown away since this started? I stare at my naked, forty-year-old body in the mirror before I step into the shower: long, greying hair; broad shoulders; large, heavy breasts; soft fold of belly fat, pocked and scarred with stretch marks and a Caesarean smile; a triangle of pubic hair, as black as the hair on my head once was; narrow hips, strong thighs, strong calves, slender feet. *A capite ad calcem* – from head to toe – this is how medi-eval Irish descriptions of bodies are often arranged, whether in tales or in medical texts: hair, eyes, teeth, shoulders, legs, feet.

The longest description of a woman's body in early Irish literature is at the beginning of a story called 'The Destruc-tion of Da Derga's Hostel'. The woman, whose name is Étaín, is washing herself. She unties her hair and her hands appear 'through the opening of the neck of her dress'. From this semi-clothed state, she is undressed with the words of the author, who describes her beetle-black eyebrows, her hyacinth-blue eyes, her Parthian-red lips, her smooth, soft shoulders, her warm, sleek thighs . . . Étaín is being watched the entire time: by the author, running his eyes over her body; by us, the voyeuristic readers; and by the king, Echu, who marries her in the story and then promptly dies.

Étaín and Echu's great-grandson is named Conaire, and

he too becomes a king. The account of his rise to kingship and dramatic fall from grace is the main concern of the rest of the story, but the narrative includes a vast array of bodies – ugly, beautiful, striking, deformed, athletic, repulsive – all described by an author who, as with his textual undressing of Étaín, was apparently fascinated by physical forms.

For reasons too convoluted to explain, Conaire and his retinue end up inside Da Derga's hostel, surrounded by a raiding force comprising Conaire's own foster-brothers and a monstrous Briton named Ingcél, who has a single, enormous eye in the centre of his forehead. Ingcél peers into the hostel and takes in the scene with a single glance. He proceeds to describe everyone his eye has seen, and Conaire's foster-brothers identify them from his descriptions.

Ingcél describes three enormous brown men, with brown hair equal in length both front and back, wearing long-hooded black capes that reach to their elbows, holding black swords, black shields and broad black spears. Conaire's foster-brothers tell him that they are three Pictish warriors who have left their country to join Conaire's retinue and they will fight bravely in battle.

Ingcél sees three flaxen-haired youths, with silken mantles and gilded brooches. They have concentric circles of gold upon their heads and no one can match them in voice and words and deeds. Conaire's foster-brothers tell him that these are the sons of Conaire, royal princes, who have the bearing of young maidens, monastic hearts, the courage of bears and ferocity of lions. They too will fight bravely.

He sees Da Derga, the owner of the hostel, who has

blood-red hair and wears a blood-red mantle. He has blue eyes and a green cloak, a hooded white tunic embroidered with red thread, and he holds an ivory-hilted sword. And Ingcél sees Conaire himself, and the long description of him echoes that of his great-grandmother, Étaín, whose body was so erotically articulated at the opening of the tale. Conaire wears a diadem and his skin is snow white; his hair is golden; his eyes are hyacinth blue, hedged by beetle-black eyelashes; his cloak is red; his brooch is ornamented, his tunic silken and many-hued; his golden-hilted sword sits in its silver scabbard. Conaire's foster-brothers affirm that he is flawless in his beauty, his proportions, his clothing and his weaponry.

In Ingcél's descriptions, and the foster-brothers' identifications, we see inequalities made flesh: the beautiful, the golden-haired, the men adorned with multicoloured clothing are high-status Irishmen; the black-clad, the dark-haired, the monstrous-bodied are foreigners, outsiders and low-status. This is a literary reflection of medieval sumptuary laws where the colour of one's clothes was an outward manifestation of social status: peasants could wear brown, dull colours; kings could wear multicoloured, richly embroidered silks and linens and brocades. Bodies could not be dressed equally, because bodies were not treated equally.

But the bodies are also metaphors. At this point in the story, Conaire's body is intact because his kingdom is still intact, but Ingcél and his warriors are about to attack the hostel. In the battle, Conaire's head is struck off, and so the body politic is left without its head. The warrior Mac Cécht pours a drink of water into Conaire's decapitated head and the head – a king who no longer has a kingdom – recites a deathly poem of thanks.

Another warrior, Conall Cernach (who we last saw in hell propping up the jaws of the beast of avarice with his comrade Fergus) escapes the battle and heads home to his father. At first, his father is worried that Conall has been cowardly: how could he get out alive when the battle had killed his king? But Conall reassures his father: 'My wounds are not white, old man,' he says. Conall displays his body: his shield arm bears one hundred and fifty cuts, his sword arm has fared even worse and is attached to his shoulder only by the threads of its sinews. This broken warrior, his body barely held together, represents Ireland, a broken kingdom.

Conall's father acknowledges, 'That hand injured many tonight, as it was much injured.'

'True, old man,' says Conall, 'there are many to whom it served draughts of death at the entrance of the hostel tonight.'

Medieval Irish sagas like 'The Destruction of Da Derga's Hostel' or the *Táin* are best understood as being similar to the Marvel Cinematic Universe. There's a shared cast of characters, so we meet Conall in this story of Da Derga's hostel, and in the *Táin*, and, in a cameo role, in the vision of heaven and hell given to Tnugdal. And Fergus, as we know, is central to the Deirdre story and to the *Táin*.

Yet each story has its own author and its own priorities in terms of character, plot and theme. You can place the stories in 'timeline order', but that doesn't always correspond with the order in which they were written. Just as *Iron Man 2* doesn't have the same themes, or purpose, or message as *Captain America: Civil War*, which in turn explores different themes and foregrounds different characters to *Black Panther*.

So it is with the sagas of medieval Ireland – a shared story-world used by different authors (the scriptwriters of the Middle Ages) to create works of literature that can stand alone in their own right or be read in the light of others. And the characters are indeed like superheroes, because just as they have superhuman strengths and proficiency in battle, they also have character flaws and weaknesses, which authors exploit in different ways to construct messages about the dangers of excess, or the fallibility of the proud and the vain.

Cú Chulainn is portrayed in medieval stories as performing heroic acts of violence, defending the people of Ulster from the military incursions of neighbouring provinces, but he is also portrayed as dangerously unstable, his violence a threat to his own people, a threat to the very fabric of society. If Cú Chulainn were real, and alive today, he'd be beheading journalists on YouTube videos, no doubt. In one part of the *Táin*, Cú Chulainn is so injured, his body – like the kingdom of Ulster – so threatened and depleted, that he constructs a kind of cyborg armour for himself from a chariot and goes into battle half-man, half-machine.

In some of the Marvel films, society reacts negatively to the collateral damage caused by the superheroes in the course of 'saving the world': the innocent bystanders caught up in the violence, the cities destroyed, the unintended consequences laid bare. Medieval Irish authors considered that too – how, when kings lead their armies across borders to fight their enemies, mothers lose their children, churches burn, and bodies are dismembered. Fragmented.

As you might be able to tell, this month my sister-in-law has logged me into her Disney+ account and I am making full use of it.

I have an American friend and colleague who is everything that I am not: she is elegant and slender and precise, where I am clumsy, fleshy and scattered. She regularly runs long distances, and is always impeccably dressed, and never finds herself berating people shit-facedly in a pub. I adore her. I think we get on so well because we're such polar opposites in personality and background, and yet we share this love of knowledge, and we both – equally accidentally – ended up working on medieval Ireland. We found ourselves sharing an office in Cambridge when we were postdoctoral researchers, and she sat at her desk, beside mine, as my marriage broke up and I embarked on ill-advised relationships and self-destructive drinking binges. I sat at my desk, beside hers, as she fell for the wonderful man from Monaghan who would eventually become her husband. We shared our research discoveries with each other and guided each other through grant applications and job rejections. Eventually, though, I headed off to Ireland and she to Oxford and for a while we were in separate places. A few years later, when a job came up in my department, I was delighted when she was appointed: we were colleagues again, her office the next-but-one to mine. We resumed sharing our ideas and problems and fears over morning coffees.

Around the time she joined my department, she'd begun researching some of the many medical manuscripts that survive from medieval Ireland. Even though they represent a significant proportion of the total surviving early Irish manuscripts, they've hardly been studied. They're full of really difficult terminology – words that aren't in any dictionaries – and some of them are incredibly hard to read, but as my friend quickly realized, they're rich with as-yet-unexplored evidence of how people in medieval Ireland understood human beings – what they made of our bodies and how they fail us.

She starts working on one medical instruction manual that begins by asking for how long a person will be healthy. *Ní ansa* – not difficult – is the manual's response: you'll be healthy as long as your heat and moisture are evenly balanced. Too much heat and you'll end up with urinary disease, pulmonary disease, haemorrhoids. Too much cold and you're facing headache, sciatica and other stabbing pains. This understanding of the causes of disease ultimately derives from Galen, the second-century physician and scientist, who was born in what is now modern-day Turkey and who had a long and prolific career during which he formulated influential theories of bodily 'humours' that would shape much of Western medieval medicine.

Another great influence on European medicine in the Middle Ages was the work of Arabic and Persian scientists, such as Ibn Sīnā, whose eleventh-century *Canon of Medicine* had another transformative effect on medical practice, almost a millennium after Galen. One late medieval Irish manuscript contains part of a translation of Ibn Sīnā's work, via a Latin intermediary, into Irish, and other texts are strewn with references to him and his ideas.

There were, of course, regional particularities to medicine as it was practised in different parts of Europe, not least because the kinds of herbs and fruits that, say, a Persian or Greek medical tract might prescribe would not necessarily have been freely available in England or Ireland. Or they might be available – spices and other products were traded internationally – but only sporadically and then at great cost. Either way, practitioners would need to source local alternatives in medical preparations.

We see other local substitutions too, some of which show us how ideas from one place could be repackaged as 'native' to another. Appropriated. One example, which I am stealing shamelessly from my dear friend's work, is the instance where an Irish medical text tells us that there are four humoral divisions in the head: red blood (associated with a sanguine nature) in the forehead; red humour (responsible for aggression) in the right side of the head; black humour (which causes melancholy) in the left side of the head; and white humour (which causes a phlegmatic nature) in the back of the head.

The text says that this medical doctrine originates with Dían Cécht in his 'Book of Instructions'. Now, Dían Cécht is a character found in medieval Irish historical tales, where he is portrayed as a medic with supernatural healing capabilities. You can see why he's an attractive choice for the source of this piece of information – if Dían Cécht said it, then it must be good medicine: he's a superhero of healing! Except that this particular understanding of the head and its humours doesn't originate in Ireland at all: our Irish medical writer has got it from a Latin text called the *Viaticum*, written by an eleventh-century North African scholar called Constantine the African. Constantine was born in modern-day Tunisia but spent his career in Italy. He used his linguistic skills to translate and synthesize the writings of many great Arabic-speaking scientists.

Mediated through Constantine's Latin work, then, this particular idea about the anatomy of the human head reached Ireland, and was not only translated into Irish but was attributed to a legendary character of Irish literature. Such is the way that ideas moved ceaselessly in the Middle Ages, between languages and cultures, and were absorbed and adopted, and sometimes disguised in more familiar form. Modern neuroscience has long displaced humoral theory, and yet it endures in the English language, in the idea that one might be a melancholic person, a sanguine person, a phlegmatic person.

October began wet and grey until a crisp, sunny day breaks through at the end of the first week. My mind breaks on that one bright day. Some people's minds and bodies respond dramatically to the changing year: they are the ones who dread the incoming darkness, the long nights of winter. I am an indoor person and I rarely notice what the light or weather are doing out there; as long as I am enclosed with my books, I enjoy all seasons in equal measure. But I am still part of this world; I cannot separate myself from it, no matter how hard I try. I am a member of this particular species and my mind and body exist within an ecosystem, just like every other organism. And my mind is an organ, a brain inside a skull, its functioning affected by how I treat – or mistreat – my body.

My stepmum finds me in my bedroom, hung-over and weeping after another major bender. She puts her arms around me and says, 'You can't keep messing up that wonderful brain of yours.' But it's this brain of mine that keeps on messing up. As Augustine of Hippo wrote, the punishment of the disordered mind is its own disorder. Usually, modern pharmacology helps to keep my unbalanced humours in check, but after the euphoria of the freedom that September brought, October has brought the crash that is its corollary.

In the Middle Ages there were various different theories about the relationship between the mind and the body, and where precisely within the body the process of cognition took place. The relationship between the mind and the soul was equally complex. Another of the Latin poems that got associated with poor, drowned Patrick, the Bishop of Dublin, is all about the structure of the mind. Following the influential theories of Augustine of Hippo, this poet thought that the mind was a single whole that also comprised three parts: intellect, memory and will. Augustine used his understanding of the mind as a way to characterize the Trinity: Father, Son and Holy Spirit. If the mind could be both one and three, then so could God. If God could be both one and three, then so could the mind. Our poet took the cognitive side of that analogy and ran with it, using Latin hexameter verse to expound his understanding of how the mind works. He says that a human being 'wills, understands and meditates / and later recalls in memory'.

You can see the influence of the theology underlying this idea of the mind throughout the poem.

> So indeed does one substance signify many things:
> our intellect is mind, our memory is mind, our will
>   is mind.

He says this because he's thinking of the model of the Trinity (the Father is God, the Son is God, the Holy Spirit is God), but he's not wrong on a cognitive level – our intellect and memory and will *are* all functions of the brain; they are all part of what we call our mind. And his theology leads him to say something interesting: he says that just as the Holy Spirit proceeds from the Father and the Son, so memory proceeds from both the intellect and the will. So, his way of seeing things is that if you are reading my words here, and not finding them very interesting, you will see the words – because your base perception, some low-level brain function, sees and reads them – but you won't remember them afterwards because, our poet says, it takes an act of will to concentrate sufficiently to commit something to memory. You have to want to remember. Each function of the brain has to work together harmoniously, and it takes both intellect and will to create memory.

Of course, neuroscientists now know that memory formation is more complex than that, but hey, give the guy a break – he was writing a thousand years ago, before we knew even a fraction of what we know now about the human brain (which is itself only a fraction of what there is yet to discover). All these centuries later, it remains an interesting way to think about conscious memory formation, such as learning information in preparation for an exam. It certainly takes an act of will in order to commit knowledge to short-term memory – whether or not we still remember it an hour after the exam is over.

Towards the end of his poem, he shifts away from thinking about memory, intellect and will, and moves into a discussion of another interesting Trinity: that of thought, word and deed. How does what we think relate to what we say, and how does that relate to what we do? Social media platforms are full of people saying a lot. Twitter is particularly designed for instantaneous connections between thoughts (hot take!) and words (tap, tap, tap on your phone!) and deeds (send tweet!), spewed out for all the world to read and react to. The more controversial the better, because controversy gets more reactions, and those reactions affect the production of neurotransmitters and hormones – and that's a relationship between thoughts, words and deeds that our poet couldn't possibly have known about, yet somehow he understood in a less scientific, more experiential way.

The American presidential election is reaching its tense conclusion and the President, reality TV star and failed entrepreneur, Donald J. Trump, appears to be governing by Twitter, and amplifying, to a geopolitical level, the small, sharp stab of every unkind online interaction. Thoughts and words lead to deeds: voter suppression, targeted social media adverts, the closure of polling sites, the purging of voter rolls. The FBI foils a plot by a right-wing militia group, the Wolverine Watchmen, to kidnap the Democratic governor of Michigan.

As the Holy Spirit proceeds from the Father and the Son, so deeds follow thoughts and words. Words can be a form of violence. Words can harm bodies, especially the bodies of the marginalized and vulnerable, bodies already damaged by the scourge of oppression. It is clear that this pandemic is not treating all bodies equally. Black and brown bodies are dying at a disproportionate rate. Those who live in cramped housing, those who have underlying health conditions – diabetes, heart disease, obesity – whose distribution are themselves indicators of social inequity.

Who are the superheroes now? The media speak of 'NHS heroes', the doctors, nurses and hospital porters who go to work every day to save the world, even though their bodies might be broken by it: because that's the thing about heroes – they have to die.

I'm reading a lot of poetry at the moment. It soothes my broken head. The Scottish poet Kevin MacNeil writes: *An ath latha, dhùisg mi le ceann goirt, le aodann lainnireach ùr ri m' thaobh, 's clach throm nam chridhe,* 'The next day I woke up with a sore head, a shining new face beside me, and a heavy stone in my heart.' The image is so familiar: there are no shining new faces beside me, but the sore head and heavy stone in my heart are always there.

I think about a poem that my friend uncovered and translated, which is a medieval Irish cure for sore heads (though it promises nothing for hearts). It starts by instructing the reader to gather seven bits of ivy growing around seven different trees and then (seriously, don't try this at home, people):

> The cleansing nectar of a willow:
> let there be boiled in it, without delay,
> juice of the seven herbs, without plunder.
> All is put into a single skin bottle.
>
> A handful of it on the top of the head
> when a strong shooting pain comes there.
> The sickness, though it were strong and severe,
> the seven ivies are healing.

Another American friend sends me melatonin to help me sleep – it's not licensed for sale in the UK or Ireland, so I can't get hold of it myself – but over the course of ten days it becomes clear that it is interacting with my other medications, to ill effect.

'You're going mad again,' says my stepmum, and she confiscates the pills.

She tries palming them off on my youngest brother, who also suffers from insomnia, but they screw with his head too, and the bottle gets squirrelled away in the medicine cabinet alongside all the other failed attempts at healing. Seven ivies; the cleansing nectar of a willow.

An American poet, Molly McCully Brown, writes: 'You cannot hear what I am saying / in the cathedral of my own head.' My mind settles itself once more – more sleep, less booze – and the words begin to flow on to the page again.

There was a type of prayer in medieval Ireland known as a lorica. It was like a verbal amulet, which could protect bodies from harm. Probably the best-known lorica, some-times called 'St Patrick's Breastplate', asks for:

> Power of God to support me,
> Ear of God for me to hear,
> Word of God for me to speak,
> Hand of God to defend me,
> Path of God to go before me.

With some loricae, you would request God's protection while making the sign of the cross on each body part in turn. One such lorica, by a poet named Mugrón, makes its way down the body, *a capite ad calcem*.

> Cross of Christ across this face,
> across the ear, like this.
> Cross of Christ across this eye,
> cross of Christ across this nose.
>
> Cross of Christ across this lip,
> cross of Christ across this mouth.
> Cross of Christ across this back,
> cross of Christ across this side.

Today, a ritual of protection.

> Wash your hands.
> Wear a mask.
> Stay two metres apart.
> Hands, face, space.

Questions are being asked in the UK about the companies that were awarded vast government contracts to provide healthcare workers with personal protective equipment (PPE); millions of pounds of public money handed to companies with no track record, for supplying the masks, gloves and gowns that were needed to protect the bodies of doctors and nurses, carers and undertakers.

I watch *Channel 4 News* every evening, and the litany of injustices piles ever higher.

The UK government votes not to extend a free meal voucher scheme to help some of the most disadvantaged children in the country (later, through the efforts of campaigner and footballer Marcus Rashford, it has to backtrack).

In the United States, heavily armed white people look like they are preparing for civil war.

In Nigeria, the police fire live ammunition at unarmed protesters.

In Pakistan, a deadly bomb explodes at an Islamic seminary, where students had gathered to listen to a lecture from a prominent religious scholar.

In Hong Kong, a pro-democracy activist is detained by authorities while trying to claim asylum at the US consulate.

Mo chridhe-si as crotball cro − 'my heart is shrouded in

blood'. In medieval literature, people perform acts of spectacular violence. An excess of brutality. Armies cross borders
and kill men, enslave women, rape, desecrate, and they are
protected by words: 'divine justice', 'the right of kings',
'holy war'.

Ngũgĩ wa Thiong'o writes in *Devil on the Cross*:

There is no difference between old and modern stories.
Stories are stories. All stories are old. All stories are new.
All stories belong to tomorrow.

One of the things I miss most at the moment is live music.
The ritualized violence of the mosh pit. I like heavy metal –
very heavy metal – death metal, grindcore, thrash. I like the
physicality of it, the brutality, the bass so down-tuned that it
makes your stomach churn, the blast-beats so fast that your
heart races. When I was young, I used to dive into the pit,
and push and pull and punch wildly amongst the other bodies.
Now that I'm older, I stand towards the back, or at the edge,
and observe, and feel that energy vicariously. It's this semi-
controlled space where you can give full vent to your pain,
your animal urges, without ever being in any real danger.

My entry into heavy metal as a young girl was through
fairly mainstream bands, like Black Sabbath, Pantera, Slayer,
but my tastes got heavier and more extreme over time. The
bands I loved most were political and radical: Extreme Noise
Terror, Brutal Truth, Carcass, Napalm Death. Screaming
cacophonies of rage. Early Sepultura calling for us to
'Refuse/Resist'. Brutal Truth telling us that 'Extreme

Conditions Demand Extreme Responses'. At The Gates defiantly declaring that 'The Red In The Sky Is Ours'. My brothers shared the lighter, more commercial end of my musical spectrum and, in the days when we all got on with each other, we'd go to gigs together: Machine Head, System of a Down.

I began a five-year relationship with the drummer in an iconic grindcore band and gradually fell in with an international crowd of musicians whose friendships would endure beyond that relationship. Over time, metal became as fundamental to my identity as my study of history.

Now, my musician friends are struggling from the lack of gigs, the cancelled tours. Part of their identity and purpose is stripped away. Some of them have financial problems; others retreat to their bedrooms to write new albums, recorded across continents in individual home studios. Their lyrics suggest personal crises. Some of them are drinking heavily, others just quietly crumbling inwards. Music is for them what books and learning are for me: salvation. This month I read Anne Lamott, *Bird by Bird*, and what she says about writing is also true of music.

> To be engrossed in something outside ourselves is a powerful antidote for the rational mind, the mind that so frequently has its head up its own ass – seeing things in such a narrow and darkly narcissistic way that it presents a colorectal theology, offering hope to no one.

I like to be engrossed in music almost as much as I like to be engrossed in words. There are certain bands that I find good to listen to as I write, mostly experimental drone and noise artists like Merzbow and Sunn O))), or avant-garde metal bands like Neurosis and Opeth. Volume low now that I am at home, so I don't inflict my music on my stepmum. They hold just the right amount of my attention so that I don't obsess about what I am writing, but not so much that I don't consider my words.

Heavy metal as a scene, as a social identity, seemed to me to be more accepting of non-normative bodies than some other subcultures. In some respects I suppose it is a genre of music that attracts misfits. There are some women in the scene who spend time honing particular gothic- or punk-inspired aesthetics, with elaborate hair and make-up, but it never felt necessary for acceptance. It was a choice you could make or not make, and it was always fine to be in a hoodie and a pair of jeans.

Aside from Étaín, with her slender-limbed eroticism, there are other women in 'The Destruction of Da Derga's Hostel' – among them Cailb, about whom we are told 'her pubic hair hung down to her knee', and Cichuil, whose labia 'hung down to her knee'. Unlike the radiant Étaín, the object of lust, these female bodies are too much, too hairy.

I read Virginie Despentes' *King Kong Theory*, where she writes of being 'too aggressive, too loud, too fat, too brutish, too hairy, always too mannish, so they tell me', and I recognize in it a description of myself. My body has always been abundant, my appetites fierce. There is no cure for being 'too much', no lorica to protect the body from taking up too much space. The mosh pit was a place where it was OK to take up space, although when I listen – really listen – to Lingua Ignota's *CALIGULA*, or Zeal & Ardor's *Devil Is Fine*, or Oceano's *Revelation*, my body doesn't seem to exist at all, as my inner self, my celestial fire, transcends the corporeal realm.

In one medieval Irish tale, the warriors boast about their previous attacks on each other's bodies: the loss of an eye, an amputated hand, a spear through the testicles. Injuring your enemies in other kingdoms was considered lawful and justified violence. But if you injured someone unlawfully, striking them down in a brawl or an unregulated act of aggression, early Irish law legislated for your obligation to pay their medical expenses. Needless to say, the amount you had to pay depended on the social status of the person you had injured: the value of fourteen female slaves if you seriously injured a king; less than a quarter of that if you injured a free farmer. On top of that, if you caused the injury you were required to take the sick person into your home and care for them there. There are exceptions to this rule: if you injured a king or bishop, for example, you'd have to provide care for him in his own home – at your expense, obviously.

The king and the bishop are exceptions because of their high rank. There are others too: the 'idiot', the 'fool', the 'lunatic'. Their 'lack of reason' is the grounds for their exemption, because it is 'difficult to control' them. These divergent minds had to be cared for by their own families because of their unpredictability, their existence beyond the bounds of what is acceptable.

There is another Old Irish legal text that deals with

injuries, this one (fictionally) associated with the superhero physician Dían Cécht, who we encountered earlier. *Bretha Déin Chécht*, 'The Rulings of Dían Cécht', deals with payment to doctors and the monetary value of medical fees and compensation that must be paid for particular kinds of injuries. The circumstances in which bodies might be damaged are indicative of medieval life: being wounded in battle, a ploughing accident, falling from a tree, being hit by a horse-racing chariot. As always, the higher the social status of the victim, the greater the payment. Values are set for the breaking of a bone, for the 'summoning of floods of arterial bleeding', for the loss of a tooth, for a wound that causes a facial disfigurement.

The United Kingdom feels deeply fractured, fragmented, a kingdom without a head. Each limb responding differently to the pandemic. The Mayor of Manchester, Andy Burnham, delivers an emotive speech in which he describes the north of England as the 'sacrificial lamb' for Westminster's failing regional lockdown policies. The brokenness of the body politic is manifested in real tragedies, real suffering, an ever-increasing death toll.

Across Europe, the voices of virus deniers blend a disregard for science with an incoherent mixture of nationalism, populism and conspiracy theory.

The United States looks irrevocably divided, by racism, injustice and a leader with no regard for the truth. The integrity of the body, broken by divisive rhetoric, structural inequality and white supremacy. Another headless body.

A story preserved in the twelfth-century Book of Lein-ster tells of a miracle attributed to St Ciarán. A woman accuses her husband of infidelity: he denies the charge and swears, under the hand of Ciarán, that he is innocent. But this is a lie, and immediately, in the place where Ciarán's hand had lain upon him, he is consumed by a cancerous tumour which swells until it causes his head to fall off. But he doesn't die – he just goes around without a head: 'a mira-cle through which God's name and Ciarán's were magnified'. Ciarán takes the headless man to Clonmacnoise, where he subsequently lives for another seven years. A Latin account of the same miracle says that 'the unhappy wretch begged for food with an open throat'.

A failing state can struggle on for years, without unity, without purpose, without a head, shovelling the cheap nour-ishment of nationalism into its open throat.

Towards the end of October, another body – modified for hate – makes itself known, as I am scrolling through my Twitter feed. I notice an advert for a forthcoming reality TV series, about carpentry of all things, and, to my astonish-ment, one of the contestants has neo-Nazi tattoos on his face – symbols praising Hitler, glorifying genocide. I tweet a response, outraged that hate symbols would be so unques-tioningly displayed in this way, and my remarks get picked up by various international media outlets. I'm invited on to RTÉ Radio 1's *Drivetime* to explain what this man's tattoos mean and why they are offensive, anti-Semitic, racist.

The next morning there is an email in my inbox from

someone who was born in Amsterdam during the Second World War. He tells me about his parents' neighbours who disappeared and never returned. He thanks me for speaking up.

I'm far from the only voice articulating how unacceptable this imagery is. The TV company cancels the show. I receive messages calling me pathetic, an email telling me that I should lose my job. The abuse is a fraction of what some of my racialized colleagues receive on a daily basis. Bodies are not treated equally.

There is one passage of Irish law, dealing with the callous abuse of vulnerable bodies, that causes my stomach to roll nauseously whenever I see it. This particular legal code is attempting to deal with every possible circumstance in which children might be produced, in order to assign legal responsibility along with liability for providing child maintenance payments. So, it's not entirely clear whether the circumstances outlined are understood as something common or as something vanishingly rare. It comes below the provisions for children born of rape. It is characterized as a 'union of mockery', and defined as a 'lunatic' or 'madman' being coerced to have sex with a 'deranged woman or madwoman' for the entertainment of onlookers. 'For fun.' Whoever organizes this abuse-as-entertainment is financially and legally liable for any child that might be born as a result of the union. Divergent people exploited for laughs. A freak show. As perverse and horrific as any headless body. The past was as barbaric as the present, and neither Cú Chulainn nor Iron Man will save us.

NOVEMBER

Love

You will by now have realized that I have little in the way of wisdom to offer on the subject of romantic love, and I'm not sure that medieval sources are the place to look for enlightenment either. There is plenty of rape in medieval Irish literature and remarkably little in the way of mutual consent. Kings impregnate their slaves, igniting the jealousy of their wives, and the enslaved woman does not have the right to refuse his theft of her body. Wives are discarded when more advantageous alliances present themselves. Beautiful young women 'fall in love' with warriors they have never met, purely on the basis of their reputation for slaughter, and arrive in the warrior's kingdom, like groupies, with the sole object of sleeping with them. I've done something similar myself a few times in the past (musicians, not warriors) and I can assure you that it has little to do with love. Marriage among the aristocracy was arranged according to political strategy: daughters were among a king's most valuable resources and could be used to form and cement bonds between kingdoms. You can see why becoming a nun might be an attractive option.

The tenth-century story 'The Violent Death of Derbforgaill' illustrates the sheer strangeness of the saga narratives' approach to human relationships. It begins with Derbforgaill, a daughter of a Scandinavian king, falling in love with Cú Chulainn because of his fierce reputation. She transforms herself into a swan and flies to Ireland to find him, in the hope of sleeping with him.

Cú Chulainn is with his foster-son, Lugaid, who sees the swan-girl approaching and encourages Cú Chulainn to shoot her down. Cú Chulainn fires a stone from his sling and it enters between her ribs and embeds itself in her womb. She metamorphoses back into human form. Cú Chulainn sucks the stone from her body, and imbibes some of her blood in the process.

She tells him that she has come to find him, and why. He replies that he cannot sleep with her because he sucked the stone from her: scholars understand his statement as meaning that because he has consumed some of her blood, they now share a blood tie – consanguinity – which makes them, in a sense, related, and therefore any sexual relationship between them would be incestuous. She accepts this, saying, 'Give me to anyone you want.' (I mean, really?!) So Cú Chulainn gives her to his foster-son, Lugaid, and she bears him a child.

One day, in late winter, there is a heavy snowfall. The men create great pillars of snow. The women climb upon the pillars and urinate on them. Whoever can dissolve the most snow with their piss is the best of women. Insofar as scholars can see a logic in this, it is in the idea that the strength of a woman's bladder was linked to her fertility: a good child-bearing woman should have a strong urinary flow. (For the record, in an infamous event that my friends still bring up decades later, I once filled a pint glass with my piss in a pub in Cambridge: the incident was not taken as evidence of my femininity or wifely potential.)

The local women all urinate on the snow pillars, but their

urine is insufficient to melt all the snow. Derbforgaill is brought to the pillars and at first she doesn't even want to take part in the snow-pissing contest because, unlike the Irish women, and unlike me, 'she was not foolish'. In the end, she gets on the snow pillar and pisses it all the way down to the ground.

The Irish women are enraged at being out-pissed by an outsider. 'If the men discover this, none of us will be loved in comparison with this woman,' the Irish women say, so they decide to mutilate Derbforgaill to ensure that no man will ever consider her attractive. They gouge out her eyes, cut off her nose and her ears, shear her hair, and leave her in her house, bleeding and disfigured.

The men of Ulster are at an assembly on a hill near Navan Fort, and Cú Chulainn notices that snow is building up on the roof of Derbforgaill's house – her fire should be burning inside, to keep her warm, and its heat should be preventing the accumulation of snow on the thatch. He alerts Lugaid and the two men run towards the house, where Derbforgaill has barred the entrance and will not allow the men to enter. 'Lovely was the bloom under which we parted,' she says. She does not want either man to see her in her current state; she wants them to remember her as she was. The author then places a poem into her mouth. She looks back on her friendship with Cú Chulainn and her relationship with Lugaid and is thankful for the time she had with them – *Ní mad-génair cride crúaid*, she says, 'A hard heart is not happy.'

Cú Chulainn and Lugaid break down the door and enter the house, but it's too late: Derbforgaill is dead. Remember in January how Fergus and Derdriu faced their grief in such different ways? Fergus played out his grief with spectacular violence and devastation, whereas Derdriu turned hers inward and eventually took her own life. We see the same divergence between Lugaid and Cú Chulainn: Lugaid dies from grief (although the manner of his death is not stated in the story, another source says that he ran himself through with his own sword). Cú Chulainn, of course, goes off the deep end: he falls into a destabilized rage and slaughters one hundred and fifty of the women of Ulster in revenge. Cú Chulainn then offers up his own lament for his dead foster-son, Lugaid, and his dead friend, Derbforgaill, 'daughter of a noble king of Scandinavia'. He erects a gravestone for Lugaid and a gravestone for Derbforgaill and says 'between two graves, / my bloodied heart grieves'.

It's hard to know what to make of it all. The blood-sucking and snow-pissing all remind us how different the medieval thought-world was. The narrative is governed by ideas of anatomy and physiology quite different from our own. And yet the female jealousy, Derbforgaill's humiliation, Lugaid and Cú Chulainn's grief: these are threads of the tale that speak to us still. I think of the story whenever I hear of a woman being the victim of an acid attack: an attempt to erase a woman's facial identity through liquid as corrosive as envy. And Derbforgaill's outsider status is important. The story was written at a time when inter-ethnic marriages between Scandinavian settlers and the Gaelic-speaking population were becoming more common. Perhaps there is some xenophobia underlying the tale; a fear that Irish women might be less desirable to men than newly arrived immigrants. That's a story that never gets old, unfortunately.

I'm not lecturing this year, because of my research leave, but normally I would teach a first-year undergraduate course called 'Gender and Sexuality in the Celtic World'. Together, the students and I examine medieval Irish and Welsh law pertaining to family structures – marriage, divorce, paternity, inheritance – to sexual assault, to the social status of women. We look at religious texts that discuss pregnancy and abortion, masturbation and homosexuality. We read narratives that articulate ideals of masculinity and femininity, and ones in which those ideals are subverted.

Sometimes the material is very difficult, emotionally. We see legislation in which domestic abuse is delineated as acceptable, in which some types of women are denied all recourse to justice in the case of rape, in which the threat of public humiliation is used to coerce and control. It is important to read and confront these ideas in order to better understand the workings of a deeply hierarchical and unequal society.

Early Irish law, for example, legislated for disputes that might arise between a married couple if the husband thought that the wife was falsely claiming to be on her period and using it as a reason to deny him sex. It was the duty of the wife to satisfy a husband's sexual requirements and if he didn't believe her claim to be menstruating, to the extent that he wanted to take it to legal arbitration, a female observer would be sent in to examine the woman and confirm whether or not she was bleeding. Like the 'union of mockery', which forced vulnerable people to have sex for the entertainment of onlookers, we cannot be sure how frequently couples had recourse to this law, but the fact of its existence – the writing into law of a woman's obligation to provide sex on demand – is, at the very least, coercive: a threat that could be used against a woman who tried to make her period a form of refuge if she did not wish to have sex.

I burn with sexual desire but I want to act on it on my own terms. The rapes and sexual assaults I have experienced over the years have perhaps fractured me, rather than broken me. I try not to think about them. But sometimes, even mid-lecture, an image might flash fully formed in my mind: five fingerprint bruises on my inner thigh – four quite close together, the thumb further away, further up. A strong hand around my neck, pushing me against a wall. In none of these cases would I be entitled to compensation under early Irish law, because of my own apparent flaws. The punishment for rape could be serious, but it depended on both the social status and the perceived moral virtue of the woman who had been raped. There were categories of women who were denied compensation for rape: sex workers, adulterous wives, women who offer themselves to men 'frivolously'. If a woman is raped when there are other people in the vicinity and she does not cry out for help, she is denied compensation.

The law also differentiated between rape and what it calls *sleith*, which is defined as non-consensual sex with a woman who is in a drunken stupor, sleeping, or comatose for whatever reason. But if a woman falls asleep alone in a mead-house and is raped while unconscious, she forfeits her entitlement to compensation, because she should not have been alone in a mead-house in the first place. I once looked out on the lecture hall as I spoke about *sleith* and saw a young woman listening to me with tears rolling down her face.

Under early Irish law, if a marriage agreement was made between two families with the understanding that the girl being offered in marriage was a virgin, her family could be liable to pay compensation to the man for false advertising if that was not the case. An intact hymen was the marker of virginity, but the girl's family was not liable if they could prove that the hymen had been broken 'through innocence of stepping or climbing', that is, through physical exercise rather than sex.

In medieval Welsh law, if a man on his wedding night found that his wife was not a virgin – and again a broken hymen appears to be the proof here – he was required to leave the marriage bed and return to the wedding while he still had his erection, to show that he was immediately concerned about the lack of physical barrier to his penetration rather than continuing with the act through to climax. Medieval Welsh law texts are strangely performative: they have a literary quality which has led some scholars to characterize them as a form of 'political fiction', an imaginative exercise in jurisprudence creating forms of social theatre that worked to regulate behaviour through the threat of social humiliation, a loss of face within one's community. Hence the requirement for the man to emerge from the bedroom with an erect penis.

A similar kind of legal performativity requires in medieval Welsh law that if a woman accuses a man of rape she must place her right hand over a holy relic and her left hand on the accused man's penis while she testifies that her rape has caused shame to herself, her kin and her lord. It's hard to know if such a regulation is meant to humiliate the rapist or the rape victim or both. Or, it is perhaps a way of discouraging women from reporting rape. If a man admits to rape, he must pay compensation to the woman but also to her lord or king; one Welsh law text states that if he is unable to pay the fine, his punishment is castration. As with Irish law, rape provisions exclude sex workers: 'A whore has no status: though she be raped, she is not entitled to compensation.'

If a Welsh woman impugns her husband's manliness, or if she is found with another man through 'deception', he is entitled to a small payment of compensation from her, a *camlwrw*, because 'every woman's husband is her lord'. Or, if the husband prefers, he can beat his wife instead: 'three blows with a stick as long as a man's forearm and as thick as a man's finger'. He can beat her anywhere on her body except her head. If he chooses to beat his wife, he foregoes his right to monetary compensation because 'there is no right to compensation and vengeance for the same offence'.

Medieval Welsh law discouraged divorce, but a woman could seek a divorce if her husband was infertile. Again, the act of proving this demanded potentially humiliating public theatrics. A 'freshly laundered white sheet' is spread under the couple. They have sex and he has to pull out and ejaculate on to the sheet, which is then inspected. If the semen is visible on the sheet, 'she cannot separate from him for that cause'. If he is unable to cum on the sheet, she is entitled to the divorce.

Medieval Irish law does not possess this performative quality, but it had other ways of deploying shame as a legislative weapon. If a man rapes another man's slave and she becomes pregnant, he is obliged to replace her with a woman who will 'serve in her place' until the baby is born, and he is then liable for raising the child 'without hindrance to' the slave's owner. 'And if she dies giving birth, let him pay her value to her lord.' This kind of financial penalty was not designed with the protection of enslaved women in mind, but it did serve to discourage interfering with another man's 'property'.

One of my PhD students, who is researching early medieval Irish paternity law, is piecing together a fragmentary seventh-century law text which uses financial penalties – a medieval equivalent of child support payments – to discourage men from impregnating women other than their wives, and to discourage women from becoming pregnant outside of marriage. Within the messy and flawed dynamics of human relationships and desires, medieval law sought to legislate the nuclear family into existence through an entangled interplay of social and economic consequences to 'immorality'. Concerns for clear lines of inheritance and unambiguous parental liabilities combined with Christian morals to shape an idealized family unit, even though we know that life is always more complicated than that.

Looking beyond the law to literature: some themes

feature prominently, particularly an anxiety about serial het-
erosexual monogamy – men abandoning one wife to go off
with another woman. Other themes – homosexuality, bisex-
uality, masturbation – feature only obliquely. Normal facets
of many people's everyday life experiences – gay love, the
termination of pregnancies, the sheer mundanity of having a
wank – have to be teased out from a range of fleeting references in disparate sources in order for those stories to be
told.

Lesbian sex is the key to one medieval Irish story about
kingship and legal judgment: a woman appeals to the king
because she is pregnant but she swears that she has never had
sex with a man. The king asks whether she has had sex with
a woman and she confirms that she has. The king deduces
that that woman must have recently had sex with a man
(whether consensually or otherwise) and that his sperm
must have remained in her vagina and been transferred into
the other woman during lesbian intercourse, thereby causing her pregnancy. Apart from this story, references to
same-sex relationships are relatively rare in medieval Irish
and British sources.

When Ireland had its referendum on marriage equality in
2015, my first years sat their exam on the day that the results
came in. Normally, I would wait for exam papers to be
delivered to my office, but the news of the referendum result
made the day feel special and I wanted to see the students
coming out of the exam hall. So I went to collect the exam
papers myself and a group of students rushed up to me,
excitedly, wearing a variety of 'yes' badges and rainbow

scarves, rainbow T-shirts, rainbow earrings. They told me that they had all answered the question on marriage law, proud to demonstrate their historical knowledge of the changing institution of marriage on a day when in Ireland it had changed yet again.

I felt a glowing love for those students, as real and true as any other form of love. And even though I cannot remember their names now, and wouldn't recognize them if I saw them in the street, because so many other faces have passed through my doors in the years since that day, that feeling of love endures in the form of hope for the more tolerant, more open-minded future, which those students embodied.

With the referendum to repeal Ireland's constitutional ban on abortion, a lecture on changing attitudes in the Middle Ages towards the termination of pregnancies felt imbued with contemporary significance. We examined medieval canon law and penitentials – texts that ascribe particular penance for particular sins – which expressed varying opinions on the morality of abortion.

Nowadays – if my teenage experiences are still anything to go by – you get into the confessional, you unburden yourself of your sins and, pretty much no matter what you've done, the priest will give you ten Our Fathers and ten Hail Marys and send you on your way. But penance in the Middle Ages was hefty punishment and could include things such as a year on bread and water, for relatively minor sins. The evidence of the penitentials has the termination of a pregnancy sitting somewhere around masturbation and adultery in the sinfulness stakes. Some sources differentiate between a woman who terminates a pregnancy out of necessity and one who does so because she's a 'whore'.

In modern Ireland, the United States, Poland and El Salvador, abortion has become for many an unambiguous black and white issue, with none of the nuance we see in earlier forms of Christianity (and none of the nuance that passes through a pregnant person's mind when they decide whether or not to carry the cluster of cells inside them through to personhood). Medieval theologians debated when something called 'ensoulment' happened: when did a cluster of cells gain a soul and therefore become human? Opinions varied but while Christian thinkers were generally opposed to the principle of abortion at any stage of a pregnancy, they did not regard it as homicide if it happened before ensoulment. Some penitentials therefore differentiated between abortions in early pregnancy and those taking place later.

My happiest moments this month – when my heart is most full of love – are in the immediate aftermath of the US presidential elections. My youngest brother is still furloughed and I am master of my own time. We make our coffees, settle into armchairs side by side, and switch on CNN. We're fascinated by the glossiness of American news presenters; the unabashed partiality of their commentary; the ad breaks, which are selling some sort of pseudo-humanitarian globalized neoliberalism as much as they're selling footwear or holidays.

My brother has never even visited the States and yet within forty-eight hours we're debating the electoral minutiae of places we'd never previously heard of – like Maricopa County, which turns out to be pivotal to the result. For the most part we share the same political views, so there's no antagonism between us, just increasing contentment as our anxiety about the outcome abates and we lose whole days to watching another country's future unfold.

I certainly don't tell my brother that I love him during that time. I don't need to. In the early Middle Ages monastic brothers and sisters would greet each other with elaborate declarations of their love. Writing to an unnamed nun of English origin, the eighth-century Bishop Lull, originally from Wessex but eventually Archbishop of Mainz in Germany, declares *Crede mihi, quia te summo conplector amore* – 'Believe me, for I embrace you in the greatest love.' I could say this to my youngest brother, and mean it deeply. If I did, he would raise an eyebrow and reply 'twat', by which he means that he returns my love.

The irrational part of my brain can't help but take the US election result as a cause for optimism. As a historian, I know that utopian thinking is fruitless and illusory. As an atheist, I know that paradise will never come. As a rational person, I know that there is no linear progression towards justice and equality. And yet, and yet. History is full of incremental improvements and revolutionary convulsions – often these are followed by reactionary backlashes in which rights are revoked, inequalities re-established. And yet, and yet. Why would we carry on at all, unless we were hopeful that education, knowledge of history, hearing each other's voices, and love – above all, love – could change us all for the better?

One of my colleagues organizes an online poetry reading by the American poet Carolyn Forché. I open a bottle of wine and log into Zoom. Forché is beautiful and charismatic, and her poems are powerful and precise. She reads a poem called 'The Boatman', which makes my heart leap back to Ireland, where my Syrian 'little brother' is starting to make a new home with his pregnant partner. In the conversation afterwards Forché speaks of being 'in the lateness of the world', the title of the collection from which she has been reading. She expresses this 'lateness' in ecological terms – she talks about a sense that our ability to inhabit this biosphere might end within the next few generations. My mind flashes to Augustine's last age of the world and the eschatological condition of the Christianity of the Middle Ages – the continual idea that the end is imminent. Although ecological catastrophe is real – more real than belief in a divinely ordained apocalypse – the condition of lateness, the feeling of an imminent end, probably says more about our individual mortality than it does about this world, which will keep on turning long after we are all gone. We are always in the lateness of our own lives.

I can feel Forché's intelligence emanating from the screen and I scribble her words in my yellow notebook. She says that poetry can be 'an antidote to the decaying of public language', that poetry is 'abundantly necessary and probably useless'. I think history can be the same and is the same. But it will require love – of ourselves, of each other, of future generations – to steer ourselves away from ecological catastrophe and life-limiting social inequalities. I log out of Zoom and return to CNN's election coverage.

In the Old English Mary of Egypt story I told you about in May, long before Mary encountered the arrogant Zosimus in the desert, she lived a lust-driven life. She says that she was 'so inflamed with the fervour of sinful lust' that she wished that ever-greater numbers of lovers would rush to her 'so that I could satisfy the wicked desires of my fornications'.

I kind of see myself in that pre-conversion Mary. I know what it is to be driven by an all-consuming lust and to give my body freely. I'll spare you a Peter Abelard-style *History of My Calamities*, but suffice to say that this has not led to me finding a long-term life partner. In my twenties and early thirties I had a lack of solidarity with other women, which I now find troubling and nasty. My desire to sleep with men regardless of their marital status – and fewer of those men resisted than succumbed – led me to disregard the emotional consequences for their wives. I think I have improved in that one small but important regard. Whatever the truth may be about my own incapacity for commitment, I resolved some years ago to be open and honest, and not go about wrecking the lives of others any more than I already have.

In one medieval Irish poem, a monk states that he would rather be called to prayer by the bell ringing the canonical hours than be called to a tryst with a wanton woman. Perhaps he protests too much, or perhaps it is true: love of God can burn with as intense a passion as any sexual desire.

Religiosity, asexuality, commitment to celibacy are all genuine phenomena that may be at play when a poetic voice repudiates sexual temptation. Commitment to another person, enduring love, resisting fleeting temptation for the sake of a deeper, longer-lasting love are also things that I have witnessed amongst my friends and colleagues. And perhaps those things are on some ethical level better than multiple, overlapping sexual unions, throwing myself from relationship into affair and on to one-night stand. Perhaps they bring forms of contentment that I cannot know. I have loved many lovers, and that has brought its own happiness. But I always, always move on.

A sample. There was the guy who was thirty years older than me. He was, and still is, the cleverest and most interesting man I have been with. Eventually the age gap became an insurmountable obstacle. (My father didn't speak a single word to me for a whole year, when I first got together with someone far closer to his age than my own; and even after we reconciled, he refused to meet him.) The relationship crumbled, but we remain good friends. There was the guy with the most perfect body I have ever touched, who was twelve years younger than me and with whom I had little in common other than that we were both from Tallaght. It took me ten orgasmic months to grow tired of our lack of conversation. There was my ex-husband, of course; truly the best man I have known. And still I walked away. There was the drummer: tattooed and talented – that one lasted five years before I wrecked it with a bad one-night stand with a medical student who would have benefited from a few more anatomy lectures. There was the on-off affair that went in fits and spurts for more than a decade: the conversations more profound and intimate than the sex. There was the sound engineering student from one of the roughest parts of Glasgow, whose head I puked on one drunken night when he reached the sink before I did. There was the anxiety-ridden musician with the broken bed, who would get me to stand every night, post-coitally holding up the mattress, while he replaced the wooden slats beneath.

As for the one-night stands, there are so many of those that I cannot remember them all: mostly men, a few women. There is only one thing that I wholeheartedly regret: a relationship in which, over the course of nearly a year, I lost all sense of myself – I was coerced and controlled in ways that began subtly, but gradually came to undermine the very foundations of myself. He punched the doors, he punched the wall beside my head, he tore my glasses from my face; my fear grew as his fists moved ever closer to my body. He criticized my appearance, my career, my friends, my behaviour: I should have left sooner, but only truly realized what was happening when he turned on my daughter one afternoon. I immediately packed our bags, put ourselves into a taxi and got the hell out of there. I still kick myself: I should have seen what was happening, I should never have put her in that situation, I should never have been with him. But he is the only one: everyone else I have loved, I still love, in my own way.

There is a complicated ninth-century story called the 'Meeting of Líadain and Cuirithir'. The whole narrative centres on the verbal ambiguity of the Old Irish word *óentu*, 'union', which can have both an earthly and a godly meaning. Lovers can 'unite' in their lovemaking, but saints also 'unite' in spiritual union, and the story plays with this along the way. The main characters are Líadain, a female poet from Munster, and Cuirithir, a male poet from Connacht. Cuirithir is sexually attracted to Líadain, and suggests that they 'unite'; but she postpones their tryst and the story becomes an exercise in delayed gratification (a concept with which I am wholly unfamiliar). The pair have several intensely intimate moments, but it is deliberately left unclear until the end of the story as to whether they actually slept with each other at all or whether they resisted their physical urges for more spiritual ends.

By the end of the story, Cuirithir has fled his emotionally unavailable lover and Líadain, who has become a nun, devotes her life to prayer and ascends to heaven when she dies. But she never forgets Cuirithir: she sits on the stone on which he used to pray and laments her decision, and the stone becomes her gravestone after her death.

At one point in the story, when the pair of them are subjecting themselves to the trials of resisting temptation, they place themselves under the spiritual direction of St Cummíne. He gives them a choice: they can either see each other or hear each other, but not both. They choose the latter and so each in turn spends time as an *inclusus*, locked into a cell, and they talk to each other through the wall. I can relate: in my time, I have had lovers that I would choose to look at, and lovers I would choose to listen to.

The erotic high point (or low point, depending on your perspective) comes when the pair spend the night together, but chaperoned. Both Líadain and Cuirithir recite verses that are clever interplays of religious and erotic language: innuendo upon innuendo, which leave the reader none the wiser as to whether or not they will use their night together to have sex. Cuirithir says:

> If, you say, it is one night
> that I'll get to sleep with Líadain;
> a layman would think it important
> that the night not be wasted.

The verse clearly indicates that if Cuirithir were a layman he'd be getting his rocks off with Líadain, but he *isn't* a layman, because he has entered a semi-religious life under the direction of Cummíne. So will he or won't he? Líadain is similarly oblique:

> If, you say, it is one night
> that I'll get to sleep with Cuirithir;
> though we might give it a year
> we'd have something to remember.

The author is playing with his audience, and things could go either way. Cuirithir threatens the poor novice who is chaperoning the pair that he mustn't reveal what happens between them, but Cummíne threatens him that he must reveal everything.

Then, abruptly, Cummíne sends Cuirithir away: does that mean that the novice reveals that the couple did in fact sleep together? Or is Cuirithir simply sent away for having tried to silence the novice in opposition to Cummíne's authority? We only find out later that they did not, apparently, have sex with each other that night. Líadain tells us that the relationship remained unconsummated when she says:

> That Friday,
>> there was no camping in the sweet meadows,
>> on the tufts of my small white hide,
>> between the arms of Cuirithir.

Most of us have had intense relationships with people we haven't slept with. One of my bestest, oldest friends, to whom I've been unwaveringly close since our school days, is a very attractive guy and yet we've never had sex. That's not the same as Líadain and Cuirithir's situation, because we're not continually resisting a burning, passionate desire: we just didn't ever want to screw up our friendship with anything as messy as sex. I have a strong (mutual) attraction to a musician friend who is married but refuses to be unfaithful to his wife: that's something closer to what Líadain and Cuirithir were going through (I guess the musician's wife is God in this analogy).

Apart from these cases, generally I am impulsive and earthly and have never really tried to resist my urges. When I try to inhabit Líadain's mind I am not sure that it is a place that I would ever want to be. Her story ends with a poem of regret: Líadain repents her haste in taking the veil and wishes that she had taken her lover instead. It reminds me of Augustine's famous request to God: 'Lord, make me chaste – but not yet.' Like the rest of the story, Líadain's poem of lament plays with verbal ambiguity around unions, both sexual and spiritual, and that ambiguity is important. A decision can be both right and wrong at the same time. Or, at least, you can regret a decision even though it was ultimately the right one. Her opening stanza reveals little:

> Without bliss,
> the deed that I have done;
> he that I loved, I have offended.

As throughout the story, the poet cleverly plays with the audience: does she regret her relationship with Cuirithir because it offended God? No, we quickly realize that it is the opposite: she regrets not sleeping with Cuirithir.

> It was a moment of insanity
> not to satisfy him
> for fear of the king of heaven.

She eventually strips away all of the verbal play, all of the double entendres and is-it-this-or-is-it-that, and finally lays it out for us.

> I am Líadain,
> who loved Cuirithir.
> It's as true as they say.

She recalls her time with Cuirithir:

> The music of the forest
> would sing to me, with Cuirithir,
> with the speech of the savage sea.

And she ends her magnificent lament:

> A thunderbolt of pain
> has broken my heart;
> certainly, it will not survive without him.

Is it such a tragedy that Líadain regrets the loss of Cuirithir? If they had united, would he have annoyed her, limited her, bored her? Would he have made her give up writing poetry? She ends up going to heaven, and perhaps that's consolation enough.

I don't exactly know why I am unable to maintain relationships, why I smash them to pieces and walk away, but I don't regret as many of my decisions as perhaps I should. Líadain's regret overwhelms her enough to kill her. I carry on living.

Medieval scholars who entered religious life did so for manifold reasons, and each would have had a different experience of celibacy, whether they managed to stick to their vow, or succumbed to temptation, as many did; whether they made peace with their situation, or struggled with constant sexual torment. Or whether it was a relief not to think about it at all.

Many missed out on the experience of romantic love, but it is not clear to me that romantic love is all that it's cracked up to be. There were, and are, many other loves. For them, there was the love of God: not something I know myself, but it is something I have seen in others, and it brings deep joy to many. The love of brotherhood or sisterhood within a religious community. A parent's love of their child, even if the child was the product of a politically expedient marriage, a necessary heir. The love between a couple who do not feel passion for each other, but feel companionship and mutual support. A foster-child's love of his foster-siblings. A teacher's love of her pupils. An aunt's love of her nieces and nephews. A sister's love of her brothers. An adulteress's love of her lovers.

Strip back the body – the flesh, the joints, the sinews – from the word 'love', and contemplate its celestial fire. Bonds of love are as numerous as the stars, as the grains of sand on the shore. At least, that is what I tell myself as I move through the world, both alone and not alone: I love differently. Even though I cannot stay with you, my love endures.

DECEMBER

Memory

I have not told you many of the worst things. In part, this is because you are not my therapist: I am being paid to tell you a story, I am not paying you to heal my wounds. In part, it is because my publisher would like to avoid a lawsuit. ('How likely is X to sue you?' I'm not sure. Possibly pretty likely. 'Maybe you can find a way to write around it, then?') In part, it is out of consideration for the next generation of my family and how events, and the consequences of those events, affect them. Perhaps they will grow up to tell their own stories. If not, I trust a future historian to come looking for them.

At the beginning of the Old English 'Life of St Mary of Egypt' the author writes 'truly it is very harmful to reveal the secrets of one's kin'. It's so much easier to tell people's stories when they've been dead for a thousand years; the toes you're treading on have long decomposed to bare bone. They're no longer flesh and blood. They cannot hold a grudge. You may be able to form a reasonable inference as to why my nine-year-old self might have been so traumatized as to conjure a vision of the Virgin Mary. You may have a plausible supposition as to why my stepmother ended up raising quite so many children who were not her own. You may have noted who is present in my story and who is absent. But you cannot be sure, because the evidence I have given you is partial and fragmentary. You can think about what you know, and decide how to interpret it.

I have had to be a historian of my own life, on occasion.

And even after speaking to many different people, I still do not have any certainty about those first three years of my life: the testimonies are too contradictory to be reconciled. Memories are unreliable things, even for those with the best intentions. I sometimes think that the earliest writers of the Irish annals – the year-by-year accounts of key events – had the right idea. Sometimes all they have to say about an entire year is 'there was a solar eclipse' or 'Ciarán of Clonmacnoise died'. It can be absolutely maddening: all of the events that they chose to forget – all of the lives, the battles, the loves, the deaths, the births, the treacheries – gone, and all we are left with is something skeletal: 'Beginning of the mortality of children in the month of October' (in 683) or 'Sebdann daughter of Corc, abbess of Kildare, died' (in 732). You want to scream: *tell me more, please, tell me more!* And then, when you get the sources which do tell you more, they bring their own set of problems – memories are friable, witnesses are unreliable.

Maybe there's something more certain in the barest of stories. To what extent can you extract a well-evidenced narrative from the chaos of the imperfect minds of imperfect people? I have a box of court documents, affidavits and letters pertaining to my parents' divorce and the subsequent custody cases, up until my mother applied for, and was denied, custody of my older brother. This is official testimony, documentary evidence. Surely, this is more reliable than memory.

I can piece together an image of myself between my birth and my third birthday from the fragments of myself that I find in these documents.

'Elizabeth is wicked as always.'

'Elizabeth is wicked but adorable.'

... *'quiet'*, *'overshadowed'*, *'not settled'*, *'not eating'*, *'unemotional'* ...

'Her behaviour was ruining the holiday.'

'I don't think you will have any problems with her when you take her away from me.'

'Her "condition" has improved as has her disposition.'

'She thinks that you are in every aeroplane that passes over.'

Who is this little girl, with her short dark hair and big dark eyes? I do not remember her. I do not recognize her. At the age of three, I used to walk around carrying a copy of the Ladybird story of Rapunzel and ask people to read it to me.

'The children did not witness the assault.'

'Lashed out ... causing a fall.'

'Medical condition.'

'Deteriorated.'

'Had been out drinking.'

'Neurotic.'

'Inconsistencies.'

'Hope you don't end up in the Joy [Mountjoy Prison].'

Documentary evidence can raise more questions than it answers and be as insubstantial as memory. Sometimes there just have to be gaps in the narrative. Uncertainties.

When I took up my current post, there wasn't really much of a 'research culture' in my department. There were hardly any postgraduate students and no postdocs. The students were unfamiliar with the idea of voluntarily turning up to something extra-curricular just out of interest. Years later, we now have a thriving community of PhD students and researchers, and we regularly invite speakers from abroad or from other Irish universities to come and talk about their research. A huge crowd will turn out – we listen to our speakers, and afterwards students will mingle with professors, and we all talk with each other about ideas and problems and possibilities: these events are the highlight of my academic schedule.

A short while after I began my job, I organized a workshop where I invited some creative writers to come and talk about how they use medieval history imaginatively in their writing. The sparse audience was baffled at first by what I was trying to achieve, but they had turned up nevertheless. I was particularly excited that a Welsh novelist, Chris Meredith, had agreed to come and speak. I don't usually like historical fiction set in the Middle Ages: I spend the whole time noticing the mistakes and get too worked up to enjoy the book. But in 1991 Meredith had published a fantastic novel called *Griffri*, about a twelfth-century Welsh poet, and I had absolutely loved it; it was so beautifully written, an utterly compelling portrait of a medieval Welsh kingdom, and a good story. Despite having no idea who I was, and me contacting him completely out of the blue, he had accepted my invitation.

He spoke to this small, enraptured audience about being in an aeroplane, looking out of the window. Below is the cloud cover, but occasionally there are breaks in the cloud and you can briefly see the land below – fields, the contours of a river, a town – before it disappears beneath the cloud again. He said that those glimpses of the ground are the historical sources that survive from the Middle Ages, our records, our chronicles, our evidence. But, unlike the historian, who has to base their account on those glimpses alone, he, as a novelist, was free to invent what is under the clouds – using his imagination, he could connect the fragmentary fields and settlements to create a complete landscape.

I have thought about that analogy ever since. Those glimpses of the ground are memories. Humanity's collective historical memory. Much is obscured by the cloud cover, however, and innumerable stories are irrevocably lost.

History is, in some respects, an imaginative act, but it is one that has to be governed by evidence, by sources, by what has been remembered. If someone claims to be able to give you a complete and comprehensive picture of a period of history, the definitive account, 'the Truth', they are lying. There are gaps and uncertainties, and sometimes all we can do is make reasonable inferences. If we see, in a break in the clouds, a section of river and, a few moments later, another break, another section of river, it is reasonable to assert that they are different parts of the same river, and that if the cloud had parted we would see the section of river that connects these two parts. We can reasonably hypothesize the rest of the river. And sometimes the clouds can part unexpectedly – the discovery of a new manuscript, the translation of a newly uncovered document – and we can be astonished: instead of more river, there is a lake there, or a dam, or a waterfall, whose existence we hadn't suspected at all. All history is contingent, and it can be reframed and rewritten with new memories.

On my father's side I have just one surviving uncle now. My father's eldest brother. He's a northside Dublin jackeen if ever there were one. Unlike my father's accent, which softened somewhat during his decades in England, my uncle's voice is straight out of Marino. He was a fireman and a trade union activist, and his politics are slightly to the left of Che Guevara's. He is kind and good. He has the best laugh and a twinkly smile. A few years ago, a stroke caused large swathes of his long-term memory to disappear into the aether. He can remember his childhood, and he can remember more recent events, but great intervening segments of his life are just gone. Looking at photos of himself as a younger man, he knows that it is him but remembers nothing. Collective forgetting is a deliberate act, but individual forgetting is often beyond our control: a frustrating and confusing loss that destabilizes our sense of ourselves.

But what if we were unable to forget anything at all? Where would we be then? There was a seventh-century scholar, named Cenn Fáelad mac Aililla, who spent his career at the church of Derryloran in modern-day Co. Tyrone. He was a highly regarded thinker in his day and an aura of greatness accumulated around his reputation after his death. He becomes a symbol of the archetypal scholar. A couple of centuries after Cenn Fáelad's death, we start to see a legend about him appear in slightly different forms in various sources. The core of the legend is this: that Cenn Fáelad fought at the battle of Mag Rath (now Moira, in Co. Down) in the year 637. (The battle was a real one but the records from the time do not mention Cenn Fáelad's presence at it.) During this battle, so the later story goes, Cenn Fáelad sustained a major head injury. He was taken to Tuaim Drecain (Tromregan, in Co. Cavan) to recover. And either as a result of the injury or as a result of the cure (different versions of the story differ on this point), Cenn Fáelad lost his *inchinn dermait*, his 'brain of forgetting'. From then on, he remembered everything he heard. The story continues that Tuaim Drecain had three schools: one of Latin and ecclesiastical learning (*légend*), one of early Irish law (*fénechas*), and one of poetic scholarship (*filidecht*). Thanks to the loss of his brain of forgetting, Cenn Fáelad could absorb and remember all of the teachings of the three schools.

This is clearly an origin legend of sorts, perhaps designed to explain why medieval Irish scholars in one discipline should have knowledge of others: for example, the highest level of poetic scholar – the *ollam* – was also required to demonstrate a high level of ability in the fields of history and law. The story of Cenn Fáelad could be used to explain why interdisciplinarity was a core expectation of early medieval Irish scholars. And yet, although it is a legend concocted centuries after the real Cenn Fáelad's death – transforming him from a person into a pedagogical allegory – I can't help but sometimes try to imagine what it would be like to lose my brain of forgetting, to be condemned to remember everything. Everything. The act of forgetting makes life liveable.

In the story entitled 'The Lovesickness of Cú Chulainn', its author explores the emotional consequences of the abandonment of wives in favour of other women. The story is also concerned with how it can be necessary to forget in order to live with oneself and each other. A woman named Fand comes from the otherworld, where she has been abandoned by her divine husband Manannán. She laments the loss of her husband 'for being abandoned was shameful to her'; her experience has made her cynical about whether love can endure:

> . . . once I held him dear,
>
> but now my proud spirit does not love;
>
> love is a vain thing,
>
> that carries on foolishly, recklessly.

She sets her sights on Cú Chulainn as an alternative lover. She uses her supernatural powers to put him in a stupor and he agrees to abandon his wife, Emer, and go with Fand into the otherworld.

Emer's grief at the loss of her husband is a consequence of the often thoughtless behaviour of those inflamed by lust. Fand says that 'the senses of women are foolish', but Emer counters that stance with her wisdom and good sense. Emer speaks in favour of monogamy, of fidelity. She says to Cú Chulainn:

> . . . that which is red is beautiful, that which is new is
> bright, that which is tall is fair, that which is familiar is stale.
> The unknown is admired, the familiar neglected – until all

is known. Warrior, we lived together companionably once, and could do so again if only I still pleased you.

We are all attracted by what is new and exciting, and we often neglect our commitments to those who have stood faithfully with us for years. As Emer's character says, the unknown is admired 'until all is known'. Nothing stays fresh and new; everything grows old, grows familiar, gets taken for granted.

Fand decides to go to her husband and ask him to take her back. When she does so, Cú Chulainn loses his senses altogether and goes into the mountains without food or water. Ever-sensible, ever-patient Emer tells the king, Conchobar, what has happened and he sends poets and wizards to bring Cú Chulainn back. When Cú Chulainn is finally restored to sanity, he and Emer are left with the consequences of what has happened. Cú Chulainn is still thinking about Fand. Emer is still thinking about her faithless husband. They are facing a lifetime of regret and recrimination. So the wizards concoct a 'drink of forgetting', which Cú Chulainn drinks to forget his lust for another woman and which Emer drinks to forget her jealousy.

If only it could be that easy. If only we could drink potions of forgetfulness whenever things go awry. Cú Chulainn and Emer can have a 'happy ever after' in this story because all the bad things can simply be wiped away through magic.

Alcohol is my drink of forgetting to some extent. I kill off as many brain cells as I dare to. Take refuge in the peaceful buzz. I don't know how long my body will let me play that game, though. Books are a drink of forgetting for me too: when I am in their world, I do not have to remember mine. Other people's thoughts and words, hopes and disappointments, experiences and triumphs: I like to inhabit those in order to forget myself.

However, there are some traumas – collective and individual – that are impossible to forget, even if others try to brush them under the carpet. When I was in therapy, my therapist told me that the goal after trauma is to be able to remember the trauma without reliving it. This year, much of the public debate around race, colonialism and statues seems to be demanding that already marginalized people should somehow simultaneously relive and forget their trauma. Walk daily past monuments to Confederate soldiers who fought to enslave your ancestors, but at the same time 'get over' slavery: it was so long ago.

Certain segments of society – including various political and journalistic elites – refuse to do the difficult work of collective remembering which is required in order to repair, to heal, to move on together. Honest, introspective remembering, about prejudice and privilege, structures and systems.

In his final month in office, Donald Trump executes federal death row inmates in unprecedented numbers, because it is easier to erase a person than confront the causes of crime and the unequal application of what passes for justice.

The Ugandan president Yoweri Museveni cracks down on the election campaign of singer and opposition politician Bobi Wine. Police use tear gas to break up political rallies, and several of Wine's aides and supporters are shot.

In the Central African Republic, around eight hundred polling stations are closed during their December elections as a result of violence.

And in America, white supremacists are whipping up conspiracies of 'voter fraud' and 'electoral irregularities' as a barely disguised reaction to black and brown people exercising their right to vote. The world holds its breath in nervous expectation at what might happen in the United States. And also the world carries on as it always does, because life keeps going everywhere.

The negotiations between the UK and the European Union on their future economic relationship go down to the wire; there are disagreements about fisheries and customs borders. On Christmas Eve the Prime Minister makes a statement on the negotiations. He talks about the British people having 'voted to take back control of their money, their borders, their laws and their waters'. The rhetoric feels insular, small-minded and dangerous. A raising of the drawbridge. Retreating to ringforts and palisaded settlements.

In order to reflect, in order to repair, in order to be able to move on, remembering is a moral imperative. And we cannot remember in a triumphalist, flag-waving fit of national exceptionalism. Honest remembering is difficult: necessarily so, because all histories are difficult.

Sometimes cultures have catastrophic memory failures. Memory erasures. Disruptions. Ireland in the sixth century provides us with a good example of this. Something happened. Something huge. We can see it laid bare in the archaeology: a revolution. Fundamental shifts in the way that people lived, farmed, ate, organized themselves. People start to build ringforts and crannogs (settlements in the middle of lakes). Palisaded enclosures. But we don't really know what happened or why. Informed speculation allows us to propose various theories: perhaps it was to do with something cultural, like the process of conversion to Christianity; perhaps it was political, related to the emergence of the dynasty known as the Uí Néill, who would go on to dominate more than half of the island of Ireland for the following four centuries; perhaps it was something natural, like a catastrophic death toll from the Justinian Plague. Perhaps it was a combination of factors: did the effects of the Justinian Plague act as a catalyst for the establishment of the structures of the Church and also leave a power vacuum which the Uí Néill stepped in to fill? We don't know – perhaps there was some entirely different critical factor.

Our sparse records from that period refer vaguely to 'the first mortality' in 545, 'a great mortality' in 549, a 'pestilence' in 554, and another 'great mortality' in 556. They list battles, the deaths of kings, the foundations of churches. Beneath their laconic testimony the changes on the ground – visible in the archaeology but invisible in the textual record – show the radical transformation of communities. Why did no one write about what was happening? Why did no one record this change? Was it too gradual to be perceptible? Or did people want to forget what had happened before?

One historian, John V. Kelleher – a brilliant scholar with

a brilliant mind – once suggested that Ireland's sixth-century memory failure was deliberate. A manufactured forgetfulness orchestrated by twin forces of Church and State. Kelleher suggested that the Church of Armagh, encouraged by its Uí Néill patrons, set out to obfuscate the process by which Ireland became a collection of Christian kingdoms. He suggested that documents and records from the century either side of St Patrick's mission to Ireland were altered, falsified and destroyed in order to elevate the reputation of Patrick (and therefore of Armagh) and erase the missionary activities of innumerable humble, and now largely anonymous, preachers. In an essay published in the early 1960s Kelleher famously asserted that the Uí Néill 'emerge into history like a school of cuttlefish from a large ink-cloud of their own manufacture; and clouds and ink continue to be manufactured by them or for them throughout their long career'.

If the Uí Néill were newcomers to the political stage it made sense for them to obscure that fact too, and invent a pre-history and legitimacy better suited to their own interests. Although we have a great many words surviving from medieval Ireland, it can be easy to forget how few voices those words represent. Whether we accept Kelleher's theory or not, we are left with remarkably little information about one of the most transformational periods in Irish history. 'To secure a lie', writes Lewis Hyde in his *A Primer for Forgetting*, 'surround it with a moat of forgetfulness'.

The social changes of the sixth century are one of many reasons why it is highly unlikely that many – or any – practices or beliefs from pre-Christian Ireland survived intact into the Christian era. The drink of forgetfulness was too deliberate, too absolute, too potent. Our written sources surviving from medieval Ireland are the product of a very narrow intellectual elite, but it was an elite that was successful in its endeavour to reinvent Ireland and its prehistory. It's not so much that history is written by the victors, as the old saying goes, but the powerful do often have the capacity to make themselves heard and to erase the voices of others.

Oral cultures are notoriously changeable – their unstable traditions are always evolving and responding to current circumstances. Writing brings the possibility of fixity, of permanence. 'Writing damages forgetfulness', as Lewis Hyde put it. Only a highly educated, highly Christian, biblically and classically inflected literature survives from medieval Ireland, and it tells us the stories that its authors wanted us to hear. It presents the Ireland that its authors wanted Ireland to be.

We have to dig deep to find minority voices, marginalized voices, heretical voices, even simply to hear women's voices. Cú Chulainn and Fergus, Medb and Derdriu aren't timeless continuations of a pre-Christian mythology: they are conscious creations fashioned by their authors – Cú Chulainn's character created to be a type of King David and a type of Christ; Medb's character created to exemplify the dangers of permitting a woman to hold power.

The wish to make the characters ahistorical, to remove them from their precise contexts and romanticize them as an unbroken link to Ireland's deep past, is not only insulting to the authors who produced the sophisticated literature of medieval Ireland but it is also politically problematic as it feeds into a pernicious idea that Ireland didn't have real history until the English arrived. Once there are Anglo-Normans on the island of Ireland, historians start to take Ireland seriously. Before that, there's just some fuzzy notion of druids and Newgrange and Cú Chulainn and myths and 'Celtic' and everything packaged into a mush of non-history with an Enya soundtrack. But the inhabitants of Ireland – regardless of ethnicity – have always had their own agency, the ability to change, to fight each other, rule over each other, exploit each other, as well as to introduce new technologies, new ideologies, new ways of living.

The Neolithic period was not the same as the Bronze Age, which was not the same as the Iron Age, which was not the same as the early medieval. In the scheme of things, the introduction of the Celtic language family into Ireland during the Iron Age – and the subsequent development of Irish – is fairly recent. The people who built the impressive tomb at Newgrange thousands of years before spoke some other language altogether. We don't know what they were thinking about, or trying to achieve, when they built their Neolithic tombs and monuments, but it certainly wasn't anything to do with any of the heroes of Gaelic literature, because the Gaelic language didn't even exist yet, let alone the characters that populate its medieval literature.

It is a kind of forgetfulness that allows early medieval Ireland to be infantilized as a place of 'myth' and superstition, rather than the sophisticated set of interlocking kingdoms that it was – with all the political strife and intellectual achievement and economic upheaval that went along with that. It was a time of continual motion, continual change, and it deserves to be better remembered.

What the medieval Irish authors who wrote sagas about Cú Chulainn and Emer, Ailill and Medb were doing was writing historical fiction. They were looking from their perspective in the ninth, or tenth, or eleventh century, and when they looked back all they saw was clouds. The social disruption of the sixth century, along with the fact that the societies that had gone before that disruption were non-literate, meant that the cloud cover was thick, continuous and impenetrable. They wanted to write stories about characters living in a historic and heroic society, characters that could be the equals of Moses, David and Solomon on the one hand, and Aeneas, Achilles and Hector on the other – characters who rode around in chariots and performed violent feats, communed with gods and consulted prophetesses and sorcerers. So, they took the liberties of novelists and they imagined what was underneath the clouds. They created a storied landscape populated by gods and heroes.

However, these authors couldn't escape their circumstances: the weapons the heroes hold are ninth-century not Iron Age weapons; the legal principles that characters uphold or violate are medieval Christian laws, not Iron Age pagan ones; the healing that Dían Cécht offers is medieval medicine derived from North African sources, not some kind of ancient indigenous lore. Because these medieval Irish authors couldn't remember, and couldn't find enough gaps in the

cloud cover, they ended up creating brilliant works of literature instead of accurate accounts of history. And while it can
be hard to reconcile genius with anonymity, some of these
authors were geniuses; so we should not reduce their work
to one big indistinguishable myth, strip away their role, and
diminish their achievement, just because we do not know
their names.

The historical fiction the medieval Irish writers created
has been influential in ways beyond measure. Think of the
statue of the dying Cú Chulainn in the window of the GPO
on Dublin's main thoroughfare. The Republic of Ireland's
self-fashioning as a newly independent nation in the early
twentieth century drew heavily on its medieval literature:
the inconveniences of political fragmentation and regional
variation were ignored and scholars trumpeted ideas about
medieval Ireland's alleged 'cultural and linguistic unity', as if
that were ever a thing outside the heads of a few Uí Néill
propagandists looking to diminish the identities of their
rivals. And that literature was written by people who had
received their educations in ecclesiastical schools: a bilingual
education with the Bible at its heart.

Early medieval monks and nuns had to recite some of the
Psalms every day as part of the Divine Office. As the liturgical year cycled round, they would eventually have read
all the Psalms, over and over again. Students learning Latin
began with the Psalms. It is reasonable to assert that almost
every literate person in early medieval Ireland probably
knew the Psalms by heart.

If you have memorized the Psalms, why would you need a psalter, a book containing them? One Old Irish text notes that even if you know the Psalms by heart you should still read them from a book rather than reciting them from memory because the written word is itself a tool for concentration. 'There are three adversaries busy attacking me: *mo suil*, my eye; *mo tengae*, my tongue; and *mo menme*, my thoughts. The psalter restrains them all.' The book becomes a meditative object to control undisciplined thoughts, a distracted eye, a chattering tongue.

Máel Ruain, a holy man (and later saint) from my home turf of Tallaght, had no time for that. He objected that 'the thought is no less occupied with the meaning when one is reciting the Psalm by rote than it is when one is reading it with the psalter'. For Máel Ruain, concentration is concentration – whether or not you have a book in front of you to focus your eyes, your tongue, your thoughts. Memory, intellect and will: if you have them, you have all the tools you need for contemplation of the Divine. Or indeed for contemplation of anything you want to set your mind to, for that matter.

When St Patrick was anachronistically chatting with the warriors Oisín and Caílte in *Acallam na Senórach*, as I was discussing back in July, he asked whether it was God's will that he should hear their stories. Angels answered him:

. . . these old warriors will tell you no more than a third of their stories, because their memories are faulty. Have these stories written down on poets' tablets in refined language, so that the hearing of them will provide entertainment for the lords and commons of later times.

There is an anxiety about memory and forgetfulness here: about retaining memory in a time of change.

We can't be certain when and where *Acallam na Senórach* was written, but it is very likely that it was written in Roscommon during the reign of Cathal Crobderg, who died in 1224. This was a period of upheaval for much of the island of Ireland. The Anglo-Norman invasion had brought new groups of settlers to Ireland, new languages and cultures, and while some adapted to the changing situation many others resisted. Cathal supported the arrival of new religious orders from the Continent, and it is probable that *Acallam na Senórach* was written at a house of Augustinian canons. However, Cathal also held out against those who sought to usurp Gaelic political power and those who deployed Ireland's religious history as a weapon of colonization. John de Courcy, Cathal's Anglo-Norman contemporary, who was in the process of violently conquering large swathes of Ulster, commissioned a Life of St Patrick, a biography of another man who had come from Britain to Ireland, bringing a new world order with him. In some respects, *Acallam na Senórach* can be seen as a reaction to the appropriation of St Patrick's cult by these newly arrived French-speaking aristocrats from England and Wales.

Unlike the biography commissioned by de Courcy, which was written in Latin, *Acallam na Senórach* is written in Irish. St Patrick arrives with his priests and retinue and brings with him the promise of salvation, but – although their time may be over, their lifestyles a thing of the past – the warriors Oisín and Caílte possess deep knowledge of history and geography insofar as it pertains to the exploits of their leader, Finn mac Cumaill. They can explain the landscape of Ireland to Patrick through their stories.

Acallam na Senórach could be – and has been – read as a deeply conservative narrative: clinging on to past traditions in the face of change. It's more complicated than that, not least because no one can resist change: we are shaped by it. There is much about *Acallam na Senórach* that is deeply influenced by contemporary French and Latin literature, stories of King Arthur, crusading literature, and other things that were fashionable across twelfth- and thirteenth-century Europe. Even in seeking to write a story that asserts Gaelicness at every turn, the author did not reject the new literary trends that French religious orders and French-speaking invaders were bringing with them to Ireland. And perhaps the author did not want to: another way of reading *Acallam na Senórach*, rather than as reactionary and conservative, is as radical and disruptive, taking the best of the new literary trends and creating a Gaelic literary narrative that fuses Irish textual traditions with French and English ones and shows that Cathal Crobderg could be the patron of vibrant, international literary creativity just as much as de Courcy could.

Cathal and de Courcy both had long and complex careers – later in life, de Courcy fell foul of King John and lost most of his lands and status, while Cathal settled into a policy of peaceful coexistence with the English. In this uneasy state, then, when it was not yet clear whether Anglo-Norman domination of Ireland would be long-lasting and absolute, or localized and temporary, *Acallam na Senórach* was written, recounting a journey around the island of Ireland undertaken by a British saint and the remnants of a Gaelic war band, whose faulty memories would lead to the loss of their stories unless Patrick and his followers wrote them 'on poets' tablets in refined language' for the benefit of future generations.

The end of Cathal's reign and de Courcy's career brings me to the end of my period of expertise. In the thirteenth century new political structures emerge in Ireland, new economic and judicial systems; the new religious orders – the Cistercians and the Augustinians – begin to dominate the ecclesiastical landscape. Middle Irish starts to morph into Early Modern Irish, and French and English become important languages of Ireland in addition to the Irish, Latin and Old Norse that were already spoken on the island. In Wales, law and literature were changing in response to the Marcher Lords who conquered the borderlands that join Wales to England. In Scotland, Gaelic-speaking kings also became French-speaking kings and adopted aspects of Norman culture. In England, the French- and English-speaking Plantagenet kings and queens, who ruled large multicultural empires, would shape and dominate the country for several centuries, sometimes at war with their Scottish, Welsh and Irish neighbours, but frequently more concerned with their continental territories. In the Isle of Man, the Hebrides, the Orkneys and further north, the imperial ambitions of Norway would shape political and cultural life. I know a little about the centuries that lie beyond, but not enough: you will need a different guide to take you there.

How do we remember? Our Irish Latin poet said that remembering was an act of will; memory proceeded from will and intellect just as the Holy Spirit proceeded from the Father and the Son. In order to remember well, we need to think and we need to want to remember.

The end of the year means that the first anniversary of my father's death is approaching. Our first Christmas without him. Our first New Year's Eve. I remember him with happiness and love and a grief that has grown quieter now. My stepmum tells me 'no matter how awful our lives were, no matter the grimness – and sometimes things were really, really grim – we could always still have a laugh. Right to the end, we could always laugh.'

I sit in my dad's chair and watch my family playing mah-jongg. On my right hand is tattooed the white dragon tile from our mah-jongg set, slightly different from the white dragon tiles I have seen elsewhere. I look at my youngest brother: on his arm are tattooed three mah-jongg tiles – white dragon, green dragon, red dragon. Thousands of miles away in Thailand, my middle brother is with his wife and daughters: on his arm, the red dragon tile. We have branded our love, our loyalties on our skin. This is my chosen family. These are the people I will fight to protect. Those 'whom I bound tight with the chain of love within the inner chamber of my heart', as the Englishman Æthelwold wrote in Latin.

There's a line in Elaine Feeney's novel, *As You Were*: 'we should be valued in neither our successes nor our failures, but in our endurance'. This year, we have endured. We play games and eat pizza as the year draws to its end. My daughter and I drink champagne and hug each other at midnight.

In medieval Irish poetry, for a poem to be considered complete it needs to have a *dúnad*, a closing. This means that the poem should end with the word or words, or even the whole first line, with which it began. The end should mirror the start for the poem to be considered a good composition; the poem completes itself by coming full circle. So I, too, will end where I began, and leave you with the last words my father said to me: Happy New Year.

AFTERWORD

These essays have explored three interconnected temporalities. The first was the year 2020, as I experienced it. The second was the span of my life from my birth in August 1980 until the time of writing. The third was the period of history that I study: that is, roughly the fifth to the twelfth centuries of the Common Era, a period that is today designated as part of the 'Middle Ages' and described using the related term 'medieval'. The geography of these essays was also determined by my own life and by the places – Ireland, Wales, England, Scotland – I have lived in, and places I travelled to in 2020, which happen to overlap significantly with the places I study: predominantly Ireland, but also its neighbours on the islands of the North Atlantic archipelago (Britain, the Hebrides, the Isle of Man, Iceland, the Orkneys, and so on) and north-west continental Europe. Thus the Eurocentrism of these essays is a product of both my biography and my research area, but I hope through the course of these essays I have made clear that the study of the Middle Ages is far from a Eurocentric enterprise. There is a great deal of important literature – both academic and popular – on the medieval cultures of Africa, the Americas and Asia. But my focus was framed by both my lived experience and my area of expertise. The extent to which biographical considerations may or may not inform the way that I write history is something I have attempted, to some extent, to understand. I stumbled accidentally into the study of medieval Ireland, but I suspect that my approach, which is international and reads medieval Irish history as a history of interconnectedness and movement, may to some extent be a product of my own migrations and experiences as an immigrant.

The threefold timeframe was also an attempt to understand perspective: immediate, in the moment of experience (2020); slightly more medium-term, within the context of a lifetime, looking back from mid-life to what has gone before (1980–2020); and long-term, from the vantage point of a millennium or more removed from the people, stories and events under consideration (the Middle Ages). Do we see more clearly from further away? Or are we always hopelessly entangled in whatever we're looking at, no matter where we are?

Contrary to my usual academic style of writing, I decided not to include references or notes, so here I supply a guide to further reading, in the hope that readers previously unfamiliar with the Middle Ages might wish to find out more. All of the modern authors, poets and essayists that I have cited in these essays, all of the films, plays and albums that I have mentioned, are from works that I actually read, watched or listened to in 2020. All of the medieval texts that I have cited are from works that I have read over the course of my professional career. This juxtaposition is also an experiment in perspective, and, I hope, disrupts the orthodoxy that literature must be 'great' simply because it is ancient. Likewise, placing the cultural artefacts I read, watched or listened to in 2020 beside medieval literature attempts to question the idea that modern popular culture is more ephemeral, or less substantial, than the culture of Ireland's so-called 'age of saints and scholars' or of medieval Europe more broadly. I hope, as you indulged me in my attempt to make sense of my own life, that you discovered something new about early medieval history, since it is an attempt to make sense of that history which is my life's work.

If you want to read some really interesting, accessible, beautifully written books about the Middle Ages, three of my absolute favourites are Robert Bartlett, *The Hanged Man: A Story of Miracle, Memory, and Colonialism in the Middle Ages* (Princeton University Press, 2006); Seb Falk, *The Light Ages: A Medieval Journey of Discovery* (Penguin, 2020); and François-Xavier Fauvelle, *The Golden Rhinoceros: Histories of the African Middle Ages*, translated by Troy Tice (Princeton University Press, 2018). Enjoy!

All the translations of medieval sources in these essays are my own, unless otherwise indicated in the 'Acknowledgements and permissions' section. The most accessible translations of a selection of medieval Irish saga narratives is *Early Irish Myths and Sagas*, translated by Jeffrey Gantz (Penguin Classics, 1981), although the introduction and discussion of the tales are very outdated and should be disregarded. *Acallam na Senórach* was translated by Ann Dooley and Harry Roe as *Tales of the Elders of Ireland* (Oxford World's Classics, 1999). There are scholarly translations of the first two recensions of *Táin Bó Cúailnge* by Cecile O'Rahilly (Dublin Institute for Advanced Studies, 1976 (Recension 1) and 1967 (Book of Leinster version)). The two popular and accessible 'translations' of the *Táin*, by Thomas Kinsella and Ciaran Carson, are magnificent works of modern literature in their own right, but do not accurately reflect any actual version of the text. If you would like to read St Patrick's own words, as well as his earliest biographies, you can find them at http://confessio.ie, hosted by the Royal Irish Academy.

There are some anthologies of poetry that tend to privilege the modern translation as poetry, rather than literal renderings of the medieval texts themselves. These are still wonderful as poetry, although they need to be treated with caution as reflections of the medieval poetic 'voice'. A great example is the *Penguin Book of Irish Poetry*, edited by Patrick Crotty (Penguin, 2010), which has a few sections that offer modern English interpretations of medieval Irish poetry. Similarly for Old English, I highly recommend *The Word Exchange: Anglo-Saxon Poems in Translation*, edited by Greg Delanty and Michael Matto, with a foreword by Seamus Heaney (W. W. Norton & Co., 2011). My favourite anthology continues to be James Carney, *Medieval Irish Lyrics* (University of California Press, 1967). Thomas O. Clancy's, *The Triumph Tree: Scotland's Earliest Poetry AD 550–1350* (Canongate, 2008) is a wonderful collection of medieval poetry from five linguistic traditions (Latin, Gaelic, Old Norse, Welsh and Old English). Joseph P. Clancy's *Medieval Welsh Poems* (Four Courts Press, 2002) is hard to get hold of but worth finding.

The Early Medieval Archaeology Project (EMAP), led by Professor Aidan O'Sullivan at University College Dublin, has been a vital source for new archaeological information in recent years. If you want to read more about early medieval Irish homes and settlements, for example, you can read

Aidan O'Sullivan and others, 'Early Medieval Dwellings and Settlements in Ireland, AD 400–1100' (2010), which is available on the UCD research repository website: https:// researchrespository.ucd.ie/handle/10197/10187. Their findings are gathered together in what I have called 'the Bible of early medieval Irish archaeology': Aidan O'Sullivan, Finbar McCormick, Thomas Kerr and Lorcan Harney, *Early Medieval Ireland, 400–1100: The Evidence from Archaeological Excavations* (Royal Irish Academy, 2nd edition, 2021).

The study of race and racism in the European Middle Ages is a vibrant field, particularly in relation to later medieval England, and there are many important contributions. Geraldine Heng, *The Invention of Race in the European Middle Ages* (Cambridge University Press, 2018) is an influential study, and another significant voice is Cord J. Whitaker, *Black Metaphors: How Modern Racism Emerged from Medieval Race-Thinking* (University of Pennsylvania Press, 2019). For a differing approach, see Vanita Seth, 'The Origins of Racism: A Critique of the History of Ideas', *History and Theory* 59:3 (2020), 343–68. My discussion of the Irish slavery myth has been influenced by the excellent work of Liam Hogan. His blog is limerick1914.medium.com and you can follow him on Twitter @limerick1914. If you are interested in the Arabic-Carolingian-Irish 'Ballycotton Cross', you can see images of it at https://www.britishmuseum.org/collec tion/object/H_1875-1211-1.

My discussion of Old English literature and the history of early medieval England in these essays has been particularly shaped by Irina Dumitrescu, *The Experience of Education in*

Anglo-Saxon England (Cambridge University Press, 2018) and Emily Thornbury, *Becoming a Poet in Anglo-Saxon England* (Cambridge University Press, 2014). My discussion of medieval Irish medicine is informed by the work of Dr Deborah Hayden (Maynooth University). In particular, I draw from her 'Attribution and Authority in a Medieval Irish Medical Compendium', *Studia Hibernica* 45 (2019), 19–51, and her 'A Versified Cure for Headache and Some Lexicographical Notes', *Keltische Forschungen* 8 (2017), 7–22. The quotation by Donnchadh Ó Corráin is from his chapter 'Island of saints and scholars: myth or reality?', in *Irish Catholic Identities*, edited by Oliver Rafferty (Manchester University Press, 2013), p. 34. The quotation by John V. Kelleher is from his 'Early Irish History and Pseudo-History', *Studia Hibernica* 3 (1963), 113–27. Gregory Toner's analysis of *Pangur Bán* is '"*Messe ocus Pangur Bán*": Structure and Cosmology', *Cambrian Medieval Celtic Studies* 57 (2009), 1–22.

There are lots of excellent online resources for medieval studies that are freely available. The manuscript digitization project that I worked on as a postdoctoral researcher can be found at https://parker.stanford.edu/parker/, and a large number of medieval Irish manuscripts have been digitized by the 'Irish Script On Screen' project hosted by the Dublin Institute for Advanced Studies: https://www.isos.dias.ie/. The Celtic Studies Association of North America has a website which brings together a range of links to resources for the study of Irish, Welsh, Scottish, Manx, Breton and Cornish languages and cultures: https://celticstudies.org/resources/.

Increasingly, university research repositories are making PhD theses freely available online – these can be a fantastic resource for reading about the most recent research discoveries. For example, if you are interested in reading more about the poems of Blathmac, son of Cú Brettan (discussed in 'January: Grief'), I recommend the thesis of my colleague Dr Siobhán Barrett, 'A Study of the Lexicon of the Poems of Blathmac son of Cú Brettan' (Maynooth University, 2017), available here: http://mural.maynoothuniversity.ie/10042/. I try to make a selection of my own academic writings freely available on my website https://thecelticist.ie.

There is a huge amount of misinformation on the internet, so it is usually best to try to look for sites affiliated with universities or research institutes, or articles published in peer-reviewed journals, for more reliable information. There are also great and informative academic Twitter accounts, such as @ChronHib (historical linguistics) and @eDIL_Dictionary (history of the Irish language). Again, look for accounts where it is transparent who is behind the account. There are some well-meaning amateur accounts that unfortunately also spread a lot of misinformation. Try to find accounts linked to universities, research institutes or funded academic research projects. Trust experts!

Glossary and guide to pronunciation

Many of the names and some words in these essays are in Old and Middle Irish, Old and Middle Welsh or Old English. They are names and words which have fallen out of use or whose spelling and pronunciation have changed significantly over time. Some pointers may help the reader who wants to know how to pronounce them. In the glossary that follows I provide a phonetic approximation of the Irish, Welsh, English and some Latin words; when it comes to the small amount of Greek and Arabic, I'll leave you to do your own homework. I also give a brief explanation of each name or term, in case anyone is confused about who is who and what is what.

The Welsh 'll' is a distinctive sound that is hard to convey in English – if you place your tongue in the position you would for an 'l', and give it more force and breath you'll get the idea (you can search online to hear a Welsh-speaker pronouncing it).

In both Welsh and Irish names the 'g' is hard like 'glue', not 'gym'. The 'dd' in Old and Middle Welsh is pronounced a bit like English 'th' as it is pronounced at the beginning of the word 'them' (not softly as in 'bath'). Similarly, if I indicate a 'th' sound in the pronunciation of an Irish name, it is also a harder 'th' as in 'they' (not as in 'breath').

In Old and Middle Irish, and indeed in Middle Welsh, the sound 'ch' is quite a hard sound, like at the end of the Scottish word 'loch' or the name of the composer Bach. So, every 'ch' in the suggested pronunciations in the glossary should be pronounced in that way: it is never pronounced like English 'chips'.

In Irish names with more than one syllable, the stress is almost always on the first syllable.

Over the course of the Old Irish period (c.600–900 CE) the way that vowel sounds were pronounced changed, especially vowels at the end of words, which often fell together to become a kind of 'uh' sound: the same sound is at the end of Íte (*ee-duh*), Mac Con Glinne (*mac con glin-uh*) and Conaire (*con-air-uh*), but also Connlae (*con-luh*) and Fursa (*foor-suh*). The names Derdriu (*der-droo*) and Noisiu (*noy-shoo*) gradually, over the centuries, become *deer-druh* and *nee-shuh*.

Abbán, St (*ab-ahn*) – saint associated with two main sites (Killabban in modern-day Co. Laois and Moyarney in modern-day Co. Wexford). There may originally have been two separate saints with the same name who were merged into a single figure over time.

Acallam na Senórach (*ug-ull-uv na shen-ore-uch*) – thirteenth-century Irish narrative, written in prose and poetry, in which St Patrick encounters the last remaining warriors of the war band of Finn mac Cumaill, who recount their past exploits as they travel around Ireland. Violent, nostalgic, and influenced by contemporary British and continental literature.

Adomnán of Iona (*ad-uv-naan*) – an eighth-century abbot, scholar and diplomat, to whom an eleventh-century rant known as 'Adomnán's Second Vision', which complains about how terrible everything is and how much better things were in the old days, is falsely attributed.

Áed mac Diarmata (*eyeth mac yer-mud-a*) – a praise poem to this Leinster lord is preserved in the same manuscript as *Pangur Bán*.

Ailill (*al-ill*) – legendary King of Connacht, character in numerous medieval Irish sagas, married to Medb.

airchinnech (*ar-chin-uch*) – the manager in charge of the landholdings and tenants of a church or monastic community.

Alcuin (*alk-win*) – English scholar, teacher and writer who earned a significant international reputation during his lifetime and died in Tours in 804.

Al-Kindi – Abu Yūsuf Ya'qūb ibn 'Isḥāq aṣ-Ṣabbāḥ al-Kindī, a ninth-century scholar, philosopher, translator and mathematician, who was born, lived and worked within the Abbasid Caliphate. Amongst many other accomplishments, he translated Greek philosophical texts into Arabic around the same time that the Irish scholar Eriugena was translating Greek works into Latin.

Amairgen (*av-ur-gen*) – character in two related but different ninth- and tenth-century Irish stories, preserved in different contexts, in which he is portrayed as a developmentally challenged child who suddenly speaks about food in a highly poetic style of speech.

Armagh (*aar-maa*) – the most powerful church in medieval Ireland, primary cheerleaders and propagandists for St Patrick.

Augustín or **Augustinus Hibernicus**, 'the Irish Augustine' – author of a seventh-century Latin text, 'On the Miracles of Holy Scripture', which seeks to explain biblical miracles in a relatively rational, or materialist, way.

Augustine of Hippo – African theologian and writer, bishop of an area that is now north-east Algeria, who died in 430. One of the most influential and consequential thinkers in the history of Christianity. Once stole some pears and then wrote about it at great length.

Auraicept na nÉces (*aw-ra-gept na nay-gess*) – a complex Irish text (or related set of texts) on grammar, language and speech, the earliest parts of which date to the eighth century. Deeply indebted to the Latin grammarians of Late Antiquity. Much commented on and expanded by medieval scholars, and a core text in the medieval Irish curriculum.

Becán, King of Meath and Brega (*beg-awn*) – character in *Acallam na Senórach*.

Bede (*bead*) – Northumbrian monk, historian and scientist, who died in 735. His 'Ecclesiastical History of the English People' played an important role in the formation of English identity and is also a vital source of information about the medieval Irish-speaking people (who he liked) and medieval Welsh-speaking people (who he did not like).

Blathmac, son of Cú Brettan (*blath-vac, coo vrett-an*) – eighth-century Irish poet, who wrote a long poetic diptych to Mary, the first poem grieving with her on her son's Crucifixion, the second celebrating the news of his Resurrection. Notable for its anti-Semitic rhetoric, especially in the first poem, where the Jewish people are blamed at length and in abhorrent terms for Jesus' death.

Boniface (*bonny-fass*) – eighth-century English missionary who was part of a broader network of ecclesiastics attempting to convert the people of Frisia and Germania to Christianity. Frequent visitor to Rome and astute diplomat. Murdered by a group of armed robbers.

Book of Armagh – an early ninth-century manuscript containing, amongst other things, the earliest surviving copy of the writings of St Patrick, as well as the earliest surviving collection of stories about his life and career and the earliest biography of him.

Bran – central character in one of the earliest surviving narratives in Old Irish. 'The Voyage of Bran' is dated to the eighth century and is one of a cluster of early Irish voyage tales.

Brendan, St – the main protagonist in the medieval bestseller *Navigatio Sancti Brendani* ('The Voyage of St Brendan').

Brian Boru (*bree-an bo-roo*) – king from a Munster dynasty who gradually became the most powerful king in Ireland, ending the centuries-old Uí Néill domination of the kingship of Tara (a position which effectively recognized the most dominant king in Ireland at any given time). Fought against a combined Leinster and Hiberno-Scandinavian army at the Battle of Clontarf in 1014, where his army won, although Brian himself was killed.

Buí, the veiled woman of Beare (*bwee, bear-uh*) – see Caillech Bérri.

Cailb (*cal-uv*) – a female character in 'The Destruction of Da Derga's Hostel'.

Caillech Bérri (*cal-yuch vay-ruh*) – a poetic character, portrayed as a nun or penitent in a female religious community, in a ninth-century Irish poem in which she looks back on her lost youth and reflects on life and old age.

Caílte, son of Ronan (*kweel-cheh, roh-naan*) – central character in *Acallam na Senórach*, one of the last surviving members of Finn mac Cumail's war band.

camlwrw (*cam-loo-roo*) – fine paid under medieval Welsh law.

Cath Almaine (*cath al-vin-ya*) – fictional, ninth-century Irish dramatization of the historic Battle of Allen (722), in which the men of Leinster fight off a military assault by the Uí Néill. The fictionalized story is full of added supernatural elements and features Donn Bó and his mammy.

Cathal Crobderg (*ca-hal crov-der-ug*) – King of Connacht, who died in 1224. *Acallam na Senórach* was probably written in his kingdom during his reign. This guy deserves to have an entire biography written about him, but I am not offering to write it.

Cenn Fáelad mac Ailella (*ken vile-uth mac al-ill-a*) – seventh-century Irish scholar who later became a fictionalized character in various sources, including a story in which he loses his 'brain of forgetting'.

Chad – seventh-century abbot and bishop from Mercia who spent time studying in Ireland.

Christian Mac Carthaigh – member of a royal dynasty from Munster who ended up as the third abbot of the Irish Benedictine monastery of St James in Regensburg.

Ciarán, St (*keer-ahn*) – founder of Clonmacnoise who, according to a later miracle story, caused a lying man's head to fall off, but then took care of the headless man, who lived without his head for seven years.

Clonmacnoise – important medieval Irish multifunctional ecclesiastical site in modern-day Co. Offaly.

Colmán (*cole-maan*) – seventh-century Irish churchman who travelled from Iona to Northumbria, where he was Bishop of Lindisfarne; returned to Ireland and established the monastery of Maigh Eo na Sacsan.

Columba (Colm Cille), St – sixth-century Irish monastic founder, abbot and scholar.

Conaire (*con-air-uh*) – central character of 'The Destruction of Da Derga's Hostel'. Cast as a Saul-like character, he attains kingship through divine intervention, but falls from grace following an error of judgement and rapidly loses his grip on power.

Conall Cernach (*con-al ker-nach*) – Ulster warrior and exile in a range of medieval Irish saga narratives, also an inhabitant of hell in the 'Vision of Tnugdal'. Last seen with his arm hanging off at the end of 'The Destruction of Da Derga's Hostel'.

Conchobar (*con-cho-var*) – King of Ulster, central character in a range of medieval Irish saga texts. Had someone else's preserved brain embedded in his skull in a medieval Irish tale that I didn't have space to tell you about.

Confessio – St Patrick's own account of his life and experiences as a slave and later as a missionary. Important historical document, but Patrick comes across like someone you would not want to be stuck next to on a long journey.

Connacht – one of the medieval Irish provinces, in the western part of the island of Ireland.

Connlae (*con-luh*) – central character in one of the earliest extended narratives written in Irish, dated to the eighth century. The story tells how Connlae is led away from his father's royal court by an otherworldly woman, and is generally read as an allegory for choosing a religious over a secular career.

Cormac Mac Carthaigh – King of Munster, who died in 1138. Patron of Cormac's Chapel at Cashel, and brother of Christian Mac Carthaigh, Abbot of St James, Regensburg.

Cú Chulainn (*coo chul-un*) – central character of numerous medieval Irish sagas, a violent and volatile child soldier. Lives fast, dies young. Sometimes uncontrollable, to the detriment of all around him. Iron Man meets state-sponsored terrorist.

Cuirithir (*cur-ith-ir*) – sexually frustrated poet in poetic narrative about him and his would-be lover. Thwarted by St Cummíne and God.

Cummíne, St (*cum-een-a*) – saint whose tests of abstinence put a spanner in the works of the lust between Líadain and Cuirithir.

Cynddylan (*kin-thil-an*) – ruler of Powys in the seventh century, recreated as a literary character by a ninth-century Welsh poet who speaks in the voice of Cynddylan's sister, Heledd.

Cyngen ap Cadell (*kin-gen ap cahd-ell*; NB Welsh 'll' sound) – King of Powys, patron of the Pillar of Eliseg, died in Rome in 855.

Deirdre (*deer-druh*) – a modern version of Derdriu.

Derbforgaill (*der-vor-gill*) – main character in a tenth-century story, daughter of a king of Scandinavia, she comes to Ireland, wins a pissing contest, is horribly mutilated by jealous women, and dies.

Derdriu (*der-droo*) – central character in 'The Exile of the Sons of Uisliu'. Reared as a sexual plaything for Conchobar, she forces a warrior, Noisiu, to elope with her. When he is killed, she is devastated and eventually commits suicide.

'Destruction of Da Derga's Hostel' – a (probably) eleventh-century Irish story in its current form, though drawing on earlier sources. Tells of Conaire's rise to kingship and his fall from grace. The author seems to have had a thing about bodies.

Dían Cécht (*dee-an caycht*) – figure who appears in several medieval Irish mythological tales as a physician. Also functions as an authoritative figure in medieval Irish medical texts, in which international medical paradigms are repackaged as 'native' to Ireland.

Donn Bó (*don boe*) – much-loved son whose mother does not want him to go off and fight in the Battle of Allen in the tale 'Cath Almaine'. Beheaded in battle, his head is magically restored through the power of St Colm Cille. Good singer.

Drimnagh (*drim-naa*) – medieval Irish ecclesiastical site, now a suburb of Dublin.

Dubthach (*doov-thach*) – character in 'The Exile of the Sons of Uisliu'.

Eanflæd (*ay-un-fled*) – wife of Oswiu, King of Northumbria, she was still observing Lent when her husband celebrated Easter. After the death of her husband, she joined the abbey at Whitby and became its abbess in 680.

Elisedd ap Gwylog (*el-iss-eth ap gwi-log*) – King of Powys for whom his descendant, Cyngen, erected the stone cross known as the Pillar of Eliseg.

Emain Macha (*ev-an vach-a*) – Navan Fort, a high-status, pre-historic residential site, located close to Armagh, depicted in medieval Irish sources as the residence of Conchobar, King of Ulster.

Emer (*ev-er*; unlike the modern form of the name, there is no 'm' sound) – wife of Cú Chulainn in several medieval Irish sagas. Sensible, but tolerates a lot more crap than I would.

Emly – important medieval Irish ecclesiastical site in modern-day west Tipperary.

Éogan mac Durthacht (*ayo-gun mac door-thacht*) – king who Conchobar gets to kill Noisiu and his brother in *Longes mac nUislenn*.

Eriugena aka **Iohannes Scotus Eriugena** ('John the Gael born in Ireland') (*air-oo-gen-a*) – ninth-century Irish philosopher who made his reputation at the court of the Frankish emperor Charles the Bald. One of a group of Irish scholars at that time who were renowned for their linguistic abilities, he translated Greek works into Latin, as well as developing his own – heavily Neoplatonic – philosophical arguments about life, the universe and everything.

Étaín (*ay-dine*) – female character described in extremely erotic terms at the beginning of 'The Destruction of Da Derga's Hostel'; the description of her is later echoed in that of her descendant King Conaire.

Fand – inhabitant of the otherworld in 'The Lovesickness of Cú Chulainn'. Abandoned by her husband, she pursues Cú Chulainn, causing much hurt to Emer.

fénechas (*fay-nuh-chus*) – the study of the law in early medieval Ireland.

Fénius Farsaid (*fay-nee-uss far-sith*) – legendary scholar to whom the invention of the Irish language is attributed in numerous medieval Irish sources.

Fer Diad (*fur di-ath*) – foster-brother of Cú Chulainn and sacrificial lamb for Medb's relentless pursuit of the bull in *Táin Bó Cúailnge*.

Fergus mac Róich (*fur-guss mac roe-ich*) – central character of many medieval Irish saga texts, he is Derdriu's failed protector in *Longes mac nUislenn*, an exile with divided loyalties in *Táin Bó Cúailnge*, and suffering in hell with Conall in the 'Vision of Tnugdal'. Sold his honour for beer. Relatable.

Fíachu (*fee-a-choo*) – son of Fergus. Dies while trying to protect Noisiu.

fían (*fee-an*) – war band. Term most commonly used to denote the war band of Finn mac Cumaill.

filidecht (*fill-i-thecht*) – the scholarly study of poetry in early medieval Ireland.

Finn mac Cumaill (*fin mac kuv-ul*) – a literary character whose origins seem bound up with poetry and poetic learning, but who emerges in the central and later Middle Ages as a more 'heroic' character, the leader of a violent war band, whose exploits are most poetically expanded in the thirteenth-century *Acallam na Senórach*. Those earlier (eighth- and ninth-century) references to him may help to explain the nature and extent of the poetry found in the later texts.

Finnabair (*finn-a-var*) – daughter of Medb, her body is offered to male warriors for the sake of a bull in *Táin Bó Cúailnge*.

Fulartach (*fool-ar-tach*) – brother of Becán, a character in *Acallam na Senórach*.

Fursa (*foor-suh*) – guy from Ireland who founded a monastery in East Anglia and then headed off to Francia, where he died. Allegedly had a vision of heaven and hell which allegedly left him physically scarred. May, in fact, have been scarred by something other than the fires of hell.

Goídelc (*goy-del-ig*) – medieval Irish word for the Irish language.

Greth – the servant and/or student of a poet, Greth is the one who hears Amairgen utter his first banal but poetic words about food.

Hadrian – seventh-century North African scholar, teacher and abbot of monastery in Canterbury; best buddies with Theodore.

Heledd (*hel-eth*) – the poetic voice of a group of (probably) ninth-century Welsh poems, portrayed as the sister of Cynddylan, King of Powys.

Ibn Sīnā (sometimes known in Western Europe as 'Avicenna') – an early eleventh-century Persian philosopher, physician and scientist, he was one of the most important intellectuals of the pre-modern Islamic world. His influence spread widely and internationally, and his medical works formed the basis for the professional study of medicine across the Islamic, Jewish and Christian worlds up until the Early Modern era.

Ieuan ap Sulien (*yay-an ap see-lee-en*) – eleventh-century Welsh scribe, from a family of churchmen and intellectuals, based at Llanbadarn Fawr.

Ingcél (*ing-gale*) – a character in 'The Destruction of Da Derga's Hostel', he is the marauding leader of a war band from Britain. Has one giant eye in the middle of his head.

Iohannes Scotus Eriugena ('John the Gael born in Ireland') –
see Eriugena.

Ísucán (*ee-suh-gaan*) – a ninth-century poem on nursing the
infant Jesus. Possibly written by a woman poet, certainly written for a female audience.

Íte, St (*ee-duh*) – saint to whom the Ísucán poem was later
(falsely) attributed.

John de Courcy – Anglo-Norman invader, founded a lot of
churches, commissioned a Life of St Patrick, stole a lot of land,
lost a lot of land, died in 1219.

Leborcham (*lev-or-cham*) – female satirist, and Derdriu's companion during her upbringing.

Leinster – one of the Irish provinces, in the eastern part of the
island of Ireland.

Líadain (*lee-a-then*) – female poet in poem-cycle about her and
her frustrated lover, Cuirithir. Torn between God and sex.
Chooses God. Regrets it. A lesson for us all.

Llanbadarn Fawr (*llan-bad-arn vourr*; Welsh 'll' sound; *vourr*
like the second syllable of 'devour' but with a stronger 'r') –
the ecclesiastical community where Ieuan ap Sulien produced
the lovely manuscript Cambridge Corpus Christi College MS
199, a copy of a work by Augustine of Hippo.

Longes mac nUislenn (*long-uss mac nish-len*) – 'The Exile of the
Sons of Uisliu'. Story featuring Derdriu, Noisiu, Conchobar
and Fergus, on bad kingship and the dangers of excessive emotions, amongst other things.

Lugaid (*loog-ith*) – marries Derbforgaill, and dies from grief
after she is fatally mutilated by jealous women.

Lull, Bishop – eighth-century English churchman who became Archbishop of Mainz and was mates with Boniface.

Mac Cécht (*mac caycht*) – character in 'The Destruction of Da Derga's Hostel', a warrior, who fights to protect Conaire and then gives a drink of water to his decapitated head.

Mac Con Glinne (*mac con glin-uh*) – central character in the 'Vision of Mac Con Glinne'. A lazy, blasphemous and ingenious student-turned-poet, who escapes the bad-tempered Abbot of Cork and becomes wealthy and successful by recounting increasingly implausible versions of a vision which is largely about gravy and indigestion.

Máel Brigte (*mile vriy-juh*) – a common name in medieval Ireland. Máel Brigte aka Marianus Scotus was a scholar, traveller and *inclusus*; an eleventh-century poem to a Máel Brigte tries to convince him that scholarship is better than sex, which is patently untrue.

Máel Dúin (*mile doon*) – central character in a Middle Irish story about families and forgiveness and journeys of redemption.

Máel Ruain (*mile roo-an*) – eighth-century head of the ecclesiastical community of Tallaght. There are ninth-century Irish texts which claim to record some of his teachings and sayings.

Maigh Eo na Sacsan (*mag yo na sax-an*) – 'Mayo of the English', monastic community founded by Colmán of Lindisfarne.

Manannán (*man-an-aan*) – supernatural character in 'The Lovesickness of Cú Chulainn' who abandons his wife, Fand, leading her to attempt a rebound relationship with Cú Chulainn, who was married to Emer.

Marcus – twelfth-century Irish monk in Regensburg, author of the 'Vision of Tnugdal'.

Marianus Scotus (*marry-ahnus*) – see Máel Brigte and Muiredach mac Robartaig.

Martin Hiberniensis ('Martin the Irishman') – scholar and linguist who was active in ninth-century Francia.

Mary of Egypt – sex addict turned religious ascetic. Central character of the Old English 'Life of St Mary of Egypt'.

máthair (*mahth-ur*) – Irish word for 'mother'.

Mé Éba (*may ay-va*) – 'I am Eve', a medieval Irish poem written from the perspective of the biblical Eve. One of many examples of medieval poets adopting poetic personae or 'voices' which were not their own.

Medb (originally *meth-uv*; by eighth or ninth century *mev*) – central character in numerous texts in which she is depicted as Queen of Connacht, jointly ruling with her husband, Ailill. Portrayed across a range of sagas and tales as impulsive, foolish and unwilling to take advice. Has the world's heaviest period on the battlefield in *Táin Bó Cúailnge*, filling ditches with her menstrual blood. Dies from being hit by a block of cheese. Not a goddess.

Moling (Mo Ling), St – saint from Ferns, in modern-day Co. Wexford, and founder of Tech-Moling.

Mugrón (*mu-grown*) – medieval Irish poet who composed a 'lorica', or protective prayer.

Muiredach mac Robartaig (*mur-ed-ach mac rob-art-ig*) – eleventh-century founder of the Benedictine monastery of St James, Regensburg. Also known as Marianus Scotus.

Munster – one of the Irish provinces, in the southern part of the island of Ireland.

Ní ansa (*nee hawn-sa*) – common response to questions in medieval Irish educational texts, it means 'not difficult'. Used regardless of whether or not the answer is, in fact, 'not difficult'.

Níall Noígíallach (*nee-al noy-yee-al-ach*) – 'Níall of the nine hostages', ancestral figure of the Uí Néill, the dominant political dynasty in Ireland from the seventh to the eleventh centuries. In an eleventh-century origin story, Níall is depicted as the child of an Irish king and an enslaved English princess. After being abandoned as a baby, he is rescued and brought up by a poet and returns to free his mother and become his father's heir.

Noisiu (*noy-shoo*) – a central character in *Longes mac nUislenn*, he is shamed by Derdriu into seducing her, and is eventually killed through Conchobar's treachery.

óentu (*oyn-too*) – 'union', whether spiritual or physical, a term that is central in the poems about Líadain and Cuirithir.

Ogam (*ogg-um*; later pronounced *oh-am*) – Gaelic alphabet used from the Late Antique period onwards for writing in a range of contexts, including monuments, everyday artefacts and scholarly manuscripts. Only used for short inscriptions and texts – the Latin alphabet was used for sustained writing. Found mostly in the Gaelic-speaking world, but important examples survive in Wales and other parts of Britain.

Oisín (*osh-een*) – a central character in *Acallam na Senórach*, one of the last surviving members of Finn mac Cumaill's war band.

ollam (*oll-uv*) – the highest rank of poetic scholar in medieval Ireland.

Oswiu (*oz-we-u*) – Northumbrian king who ended up celebrating Easter when his wife, Eanflæd, was still observing Lent.

Pangur Bán (*pan-goor baan*) – a medieval Irish poem about a scholar and his cat which I really wish people would stop going on about, even though I have written about it here. Preserved in a manuscript which was the workbook of an Irish scholar studying grammar, literature and theology on the Continent.

Patrick, Bishop of Dublin – became Bishop of Dublin in 1074 and drowned a decade later in the Irish Sea. There is a bunch of lovely Latin poetry (and some less lovely Latin poetry) and a Latin theological tract attributed to him, although I am sceptical of whether he actually wrote any of it.

Patrick, St – fifth-century Briton who was enslaved by Irish raiders as a child, escaped, returned to Britain, had a religious experience, returned to Ireland, and converted some Irish people to Christianity. Comes across as a pain in the arse in his own writings, but is more positively portrayed by later writers who were keen to promote his reputation. Central character in *Acallam na Senórach*. Would have liked that there is a St Patrick's Day but hated the way it is celebrated.

Pillar of Eliseg (*ell-iss-egg*) – now a stump in a field, underwhelming to furniture removal guys (see 'June'), this was originally a large inscribed cross, erected under the patronage of Cyngen ap Cadell, in memory of his great-grandfather, a statement both of political power and religious devotion.

Priscian – a Latin grammarian from what is now Algeria. His *Institutes of Grammar* was hugely influential for how scholars in Ireland thought about language, not only in Latin but other languages including Irish.

Rath Melsigi (*rath mel-shi-guh*) – Clonmelsh in modern-day Co. Carlow, home to an early medieval English monastic community.

Rhigyfarch ap Sulien (*hrig-uh-varch ap see-lee-en*) – author of a Life of St David, brother of Ieuan.

'St Paul Codex' – the manuscript in which *Pangur Bán* is preserved, alongside a poem on Suibne Geilt and a praise poem to Áed mac Diarmata. The manuscript also contains learned grammatical and theological material.

Sebdann daughter of Corc (*sev-thann*) – abbess of Kildare, who died in 732.

Sedulius Scottus ('Sedulius the Gael') – ninth-century Irish scholar, teacher and poet, who made his career and reputation on the Continent, particularly at Liège. Wrote an instruction manual for kings aimed at the son of Emperor Lothar I.

Sigeberht (*see-ye-bert*) – King of the East Angles, gave land to Fursa to found his monastery.

Stafell Gynddylan (*stav-ell gin-thyl-an*; Welsh 'll' sound) – ninth-century poem, lamenting the ruined hall of Cynddylan, written in the voice of his sister, Heledd.

Suibne Geilt (*siv-nuh gelt*) – an obscure member of the royal family of the Dál nAiridi (in the north-east of Ireland) who became the subject of later literary traditions, with texts about him being composed from the ninth to the thirteenth centuries. Associated with St Moling. An early poem about him is preserved in the same manuscript as *Pangur Bán*.

Sulpicius Severus (*sul-pick-ee-uss sev-err-us*) – author of an account of the deeds of St Martin of Tours, amongst other works. Lived in the second half of the fourth century and first few decades of the fifth.

Táin Bó Cúailnge (*toin boe cool-nga*) 'The Cattle-Raid of Cooley' – a saga which survives in two major versions: the first, dating from the eleventh century but comprising sources as old as the eighth century, is structurally complex and portrays many of its characters in ambivalent terms. The second version, dating from the mid-twelfth century, is more 'polished' by modern narrative standards, has a different opening scene, and portrays Cú Chulainn in a more 'heroic' mode. In both versions, Medb and Ailill go after a bull in Ulster, Cú Chulainn tries to fight them off, the bull dies anyway (as do a lot of people along the way) and it's all pointless. Many more people have written about it than have actually read it.

Tairdelbach Ua Briain (*tare-dul-vach oo-a bree-an*) – eleventh-century King of Munster who rejected the approaches of Jewish emissaries in 1079.

Tallaght (*tall-a*) – important medieval Irish ecclesiastical centre, home of Máel Ruain, modern satellite town of Dublin, and most notably the place where I was born.

Tech-Moling (*tech mo-ling*) – monastery in modern-day Co. Carlow, associated with the seventh-century St Moling.

Teicht do Róim (*techt do roiv*) – poem on the pointlessness of going all the way to Rome to find Christ if you don't have Him in your heart to begin with.

Theodore – from Tarsus (modern-day Turkey), became Archbishop of Canterbury in the seventh century, bringing the latest scholarship and pedagogical methods to England. Best buddies with Hadrian.

Tnugdal (*tnooth-gal*) – protagonist of twelfth-century 'Vision of Tnugdal', a hair-raising account of the torments of hell, plus a tamer description of heaven, a place full of Irish VIPs.

Torna (*Tore-nah*) – poet who rescues the abandoned baby Níall Noígíallach, who grows up to free his enslaved mother and become his father's heir.

Tuaim Drecain (*too-am dre-gaan*) – place to which Cenn Fáelad was brought, after losing his 'brain of forgetting'.

Uí Néill (*ee nyale*) – the dominant political power on the island of Ireland from the seventh to the eleventh century, divided into two major parts, the Northern Uí Néill and the Southern Uí Néill, which each comprised various dynasties ruling their own smaller kingdoms. All claimed descent from Níall Noígíallach.

Uisliu, sons of (*ish-loo*) – Noísiu and his brothers, who are central to the tale *Longes mac nUislenn*.

Ulster – the kingdom of the characters of *Táin Bó Cúailnge* and related narratives. Envisaged as once being a large kingdom, spanning much of the territory of the modern-day province of Ulster, by the early Middle Ages (at the time these narratives were written) it had shrunk in political power and significance compared to its Uí Néill rivals.

Virgilius Maro Grammaticus – original and sophisticated seventh-century Latin grammarian, whose writings suggest that he was an Irish-speaker.

Willibrord – seventh-century English missionary active in Frisia, who became Bishop of Utrecht and founded the Abbey of Echternach, in modern-day Luxembourg, where he died and was buried. Alcuin wrote a biography of him.

Zosimus – arrogant monk in the Old English 'Life of St Mary of Egypt', who realizes that he can learn a thing or two from Mary.

Acknowledgements and permissions

This book exists because Patricia Deevy summoned it into being. I cannot even begin to express my gratitude to her for giving me this opportunity to attempt to make sense of myself and the history that I study. Colin Graham helped me to find my courage and voice, and he also enabled me to find my wonderful agent, Robert Caskie, who has offered incomparable guidance, encouragement and mentoring. The friends who were my first readers have given their time, expertise and energy in improving drafts of each chapter: heartfelt thanks and appreciation to Alex Ademokun, Liz Chapman, Fearghal Duffy and Máire Ní Mhaonaigh. The excellent Liam Hogan read a draft of a couple of chapters and helped me to articulate Ireland's history with and of slavery. I alone am responsible for any errors that may remain. Shân Morley Jones's copy-editing was brilliantly insightful, careful and sympathetic. I am grateful to everyone at Penguin Random House (in general) and Sandycove (in particular) for their faith in this project.

I am deeply indebted to all of my students (past and present) and colleagues in the Maynooth University Department of Early Irish, and to all those who taught me and learned with me at Glasgow and Cambridge. Particular thanks to Daniel Watson, Ellen Ganly, Seán Ó Hoireabhárd, Victoria

Krivoshchekova and Chelsey Collins, who have taught me
easily as much as – if not more than – I have taught them.
Thanks also to friends and colleagues across Maynooth University, who make it such a special community in which to
research and teach. This book was written while I was on
sabbatical leave from Maynooth, and I am grateful to everyone at the Centre for the Study of the Viking Age and the
School of English, University of Nottingham, for welcoming
me as an academic visitor for the 2020–21 academic year.

Extra special thanks go to Lindy Brady; Liam Breatnach;
Stafford Glover; Deborah Hayden; Andrew 'Baz' Jones; Fr
Conor McDonough OP; Terry O'Hagan; Barry Lewis;
Ruairí Ó hUiginn; Seán, Bindy and Jack Price; Anton
Reisenegger; Paul Russell; Paul Smith; David Stifter; Bettina
Talbot and Francesca Tinti. Kevin Sharp sent many late-night
Dropbox links and MP3s with 'drafts' of songs which often
formed the soundtrack to my next day's work: it was won-
drous to hear two albums being 'edited' in time with these
essays – thank you for the music and for so much more
besides.

To my family, for putting up with me and letting me write
about you: Antimo (especially, for everything); Robbie, Aof,
Cee and Leo; Dave, Steph, Francis and Ali; Becca; Siobhan;
Lucy; Taib, Natalia, Mohammed, Maha and Emily; Reg, Nina
and Sarah; Jacqueline, Patsy and Karen; Keith, Shona and
Felim, and many others. And – beyond all else – to Nora:
thank you for being you. Remembering, always, those who
are no longer here to tell their own tale. I am grateful to my
mother for granting permission for me to write about our

relationship. To others, I can only say that I have tried to write an even-handed truth, even though I know that it can only ever be my truth, my history, and your perceptions are different.

Oh, and Dad: I'm not sure you would have approved of everything in here (although you would have enjoyed it more than you'd have let on), but I thought of you so often as I was writing. See you again soon for pints and terrible life advice at the dream-pub!

The excerpt from the Old English poem 'The Ruin' is from a translation by Siân Echard and reproduced from her website with kind permission: https://sianechard.ca/web-pages/the-ruin/. The quotations from the poem to Máel Brigte on his coming of age are excerpted with permission from the translation by Liam Breatnach in *Ériu* 58 (2008), 1–35. The lines from *Na Reultan* ('The Stars') by Kevin Mac-Neil, from his *Love and Zen in the Outer Hebrides* ©1998, are reproduced with permission of Canongate Books Ltd.

'The Unfinished (I)', from *A Scattering* by Christopher Reid. Copyright © Christopher Reid. Reproduced by permission of the author c/o Rogers, Coleridge & White Ltd, 20 Powis Mews, London W11 1JN. The lines from 'The Tradition' by Jericho Brown, from his collection *The Tradition* (Pan Macmillan), are reproduced with permission of the Licensor through PLSClear. Molly McCully Brown, excerpt from 'Psalm', from *The Virginia State Colony for Epileptics and Feebleminded*. Copyright © 2017 by Molly McCully Brown. Reprinted by permission of Persea Books, Inc. (New York), www.perseabooks.com. All rights reserved.